No Bootstraps When You're Barefoot

WES HALL

No Bootstraps When You're Barefoot

My rise from a Jamaican plantation
shack to the boardrooms of Bay Street

RANDOM HOUSE CANADA

PUBLISHED BY RANDOM HOUSE CANADA

Copyright © 2022 KSS Holdco Inc.

www.penguinrandomhouse.ca

Library and Archives Canada Cataloguing in Publication

Title: No bootstraps when you're barefoot / Wes Hall.
Names: Hall, Wes, author.
Identifiers: Canadiana (print) 20220228507 | Canadiana (ebook) 20220228604 |
ISBN 9781039002371 (hardcover) | ISBN 9781039002388 (EPUB)
Subjects: LCSH: Hall, Wes. | LCSH: Businesspeople—Canada—Biography. |
CSH: Jamaican Canadians—Biography. | LCGFT: Autobiographies.
Classification: LCC HC112.5.H33 A3 2022 | DDC 338.092—dc23

Text design: Lisa Jager
Jacket design: Lisa Jager
Image credits: courtesy of the author
Back jacket image: KC Armstrong/CBC

Printed in the United States of America

2 4 6 8 9 7 5 3 1

To my grandmother, Julia Vassell, who raised me

Contents

Introduction 1

A Pot of Porridge 5

The Foundation of All Things 13

"Why Don't You Take One of the Girls?" 25

The Runaway and the Machete 35

"What You Burn the Rice For?" 41

Anywhere with a Roof 63

Going to Foreign 73

The Great White North 81

Police, Poultry and Private Security 95

Starting from the Bottom 109

Leap of Faith 125

"I'm Afraid for You" 149

VP or Bust 163

Being Black Is My Superpower 175

The End and the Beginning 193

The Founder 205

I've Been Working on the Railroad 221

The Running Back 243

BlackNorth 263

The BlackNorth CEO Pledge 279

Acknowledgements 285

Index 288

INTRODUCTION

I started with nothing. And it wasn't even the "dollar and a dream" kind of nothing, because, early on, I didn't have either of those. I was born in rural Jamaica—St. Thomas, the poorest parish on the island. I grew up in a plantation worker's shack with no electricity. Our only running water was the nearby river. I went to school barefoot because the only shoes I had were saved for church and special occasions, and I got made fun of for that, because I was the poor kid even in a place where everyone was poor. I didn't dream of the life I have today because I couldn't even imagine it. I expected to work long hours at a tough job for very little pay, like my grandmother did, and to never leave my hometown.

By most measures, today I am a successful man. After founding my first company, Kingsdale Advisors, in 2003, I professionalized the shareholder services industry in Canada, and I have since worked on many of the biggest deals in this country's history. I employy hundreds of people, live in a big house, drive a nice car and come home to a beautiful family—my wife, Christine, and our five children. In 2021, I joined the cast of *Dragons' Den*, a CBC reality show built on entrepreneurs' dreams of financial success. I am the first Black Dragon in the program's sixteen-year run.

This book is largely about how I got from my beginnings to where I am now. How I survived the disadvantages that came with being born into poverty in the "wrong" part of the world. How I escaped abuse and abandonment as a child. How I overcame all the obstacles faced by a newcomer to Canada. How I climbed to the top of the corporate ladder as a Black man, with missing rungs and everyone else taking the elevator. I hope anyone dealing with the same kinds of challenges and systemic barriers will read this and be inspired. I want to show you that just because the system is designed to hold you down, that doesn't mean it will succeed. And I want you to know that you are strong enough to drop your shoulder and run through the walls they put between you and your goals—for now, that may be the only way to reach them.

But I also want to make one thing clear: this is not an instruction manual. What I've accomplished should not have been possible. My aim in describing how I navigated a system created to limit Black achievement isn't to draw a map for those coming up after me; it's to prove that no one should ever have to make the same journey. In recent years, I have dedicated myself to that cause, going public with my own experiences and founding the BlackNorth Initiative, a project aimed at ending systemic anti-Black racism. BlackNorth's CEO Pledge, a detailed and benchmarked commitment to combat unconscious bias and racial discrimination, has been signed by the leaders of more than five hundred of Canada's biggest companies, but in the course of securing those commitments and others, I've heard the same thing again and again from some of the most powerful people in the country: "I just didn't know."

As a Black person, it can be hard not to roll your eyes at that excuse. Systemic racism is not exactly new. I've spent my entire career walking into boardrooms to find I am the only Black person there, and it's frustrating to think of top-level executives looking out over their organizations, seeing no Black faces and never wondering why that might be.

But it's hard to wrap your head around something you've never experienced, and white supremacy is both foundational in our institutions and sneaky. That's how it protects itself—it hides in processes and attitudes that can seem innocuous until you look at their results. And much of its impact is invisible unless you're the one taking the hit.

Our culture celebrates people who seem to have pulled themselves up by their bootstraps. But that phrase was originally meant to describe an impossible task. When I look back at my life so far, I am immensely proud of what I've accomplished. I was lucky, yes, but I also worked my butt off and found ways forward when it felt like the whole world was trying to beat me back. I think the story of how I did that is a good one, if you'll forgive the immodesty, but I'm not writing it here so it will be celebrated. Holding a story like mine up as proof that the obstacles society stacks against Black and Indigenous folks and people of colour *are* surmountable further entrenches those obstacles. It asks those impacted by racism to find ways to just deal with it, to succeed despite it. That is ridiculous. It's unfair. It's asking people to do something as impossible as pull yourself up by your bootstraps, and some of us don't even have boots—we start out barefoot.

I hope that my story makes all that clear. And I hope it inspires change.

1

A POT OF PORRIDGE

It was a gentleman passing by on a bicycle who heard us crying
and looked in to make sure everything was okay. My mother's
little shack only had one room, so he barely had to cross the
threshold to realize it wasn't okay. There were three of us inside:
me, my sister Joan and my brother Ian. Joan was the oldest, but
still just four. I was eighteen months. Ian was a baby. I'm not sure
how long we'd been on our own.

Our mother had gone while we were sleeping. Even as young
as we were, we may have put together that she wasn't coming
back. I would find out later in life that she'd abandoned us for
a man who didn't know she had kids; she was twenty-eight at
the time and had seven children, including us. She had left us
in Winchester, the tiny country town on Jamaica's eastern coast
where I'd been born, to move to May Pen, a small city on the
other side of Kingston, Jamaica's capital.

We'd woken up to find we were alone. There was a pot of porridge on the table, boiled cornmeal mixed with the sweetness of condensed milk, a last nod to her motherly responsibilities. We'd finished it, Joan helping Ian as best she could. When we got hungry again, Ian and I started crying. Eventually, the gentleman on the bicycle, a neighbour, heard us. Joan remembers the man asking her what was going on. She told him we'd eaten all the porridge our mother had left us and we were hungry. "Where is your mum?" he asked. When Joan said she didn't know, he got the idea. He knew our family—everyone knew everyone in the area—and he told us he would go find our grandmother, who was working on a nearby plantation. He headed off down the dirt road on his bicycle in the direction of the fields, and we were alone again.

I didn't know it at the time, but we were not the first children my mother had abandoned—three of my older siblings were already in my grandmother's care, and a fourth was with his father's family—but ours was the most dramatic separation. My mother, Dorothy Smith, was raised in extreme poverty in the workers' barracks of the plantation where my grandmother was employed. She had been a beautiful girl, and was now a beautiful woman, with a history of entanglements with men who were attracted only to her beauty. With each new encounter, she would convince herself that she had found the guy who planned to stick around, but none of them did. She had her first child at thirteen, and Joan, who was her fifth, by twenty-five. Me and my little brother were numbers six and seven.

But even though my mother was limited by the circumstances of her birth, her lack of education, and the responsibilities that came—or should have come—with all those kids, she was the most ambitious member of her family in many ways. She was the only one of her parents' four children to move away from Golden Grove, the town where she was born—first to neighbouring Winchester, a few miles inland, then to May Pen and later to Canada. And she was ever alert to any opportunity to improve her station and her situation, for better or for worse.

None of the kids my mother had brought into the world by the time she put that pot of porridge on the table shared a father with any of the others. But my dad was the one she pined for—in her way—for many years after their relationship ended. Leonard Hall was the *man* in Winchester, and a celebrity across the entire parish of St. Thomas. His father, an ice cream maker and entrepreneur with some standing in the community, doted on him. Leonard wanted for nothing growing up, and his family would've been considered rich by most in the neighbourhood. They would have been considered uppity, too—proud and a little puffed up.

In those days, many businesses across Jamaica fielded professional cricket teams. My father had a job on the assembly line at the Goodyear tire factory in Morant Bay, the capital of St. Thomas, but he'd really been hired to be the star fast bowler on the factory's cricket team. A bowler is a lot like a pitcher in baseball, and as is the case with pitchers, there are different types. Some rely on precise placement of the ball to retire a batsman, or on varying their speed between deliveries. Fast bowlers like my dad opt for the direct method: they take a long running approach to build momentum and then hurl the ball as hard as they possibly can. When a fast bowler is both tall and skilled, as my dad was, he is about the scariest thing a batsman can face. He dominates his opponents, retiring them by overpowering them.

When my parents first met, my dad was a handsome man in his early twenties, fit and athletic. His position as a fast bowler showcased that athleticism and commanded attention. In the centre of the pitch, with the ball in his hand and all eyes on him, he would begin his approach. His graceful strides built like a long-jumper's approaching the fault line, and then he would kick his front leg up like a dancer and deliver, his arm arcing high over his head as he let the ball loose with all his strength. That tall young man, running the sixty-yard dash and throwing the ball as hard as he could, was truly something to behold, and he was also playing in the heyday of cricket in Jamaica, when people cared less about track and field or soccer and lived and died with the fortunes of the West Indies cricket team. My father's Goodyear team travelled all over the country for games and weekend tournaments, and the towns they visited would shut down as everyone went to the pitch to watch. Everybody loves a fast bowler, especially the ladies, it seemed, and Leonard Hall took full advantage of that.

My mother was always jealous when it came to my dad. If another woman so much as looked at him when he was in my mother's company, she made it abundantly clear that she was having none of it. But I don't think the two of them ever really had a relationship, at least not in the boyfriend-girlfriend sense. My mother was somebody my dad fooled around with—one among many. He was a young sports celebrity who had been told by his father and all those cricket fans that he was God's gift to humanity, and he behaved that way, sowing his wild oats all over the place. So much so that I have two sisters on my dad's side who are exactly the same age, born in the same month to two different women. Sure, he was happy to spend his time with my mother here and there, drawn to her beauty—she looked like a young Mary J. Blige. But she was older than him by a number of years and, as much as she wanted to, she never truly possessed his heart.

When I was born on May 8, 1969, my dad's family refused to acknowledge me. Upholding the double standard of the time, they viewed my mother as a promiscuous woman who already had five kids and was trying to trap a promising young man with a wealthy father. To them, I was what's known in Jamaican patois as a "jacket"—someone else's child that his mother was trying to foist on a man who isn't the biological father. For the whole time I lived in St. Thomas, whenever I encountered my paternal grandfather in town, he behaved like he didn't see me. Still, my dad claimed me without hesitation and named me after his hero, the famous West Indies fast bowler Wes Hall, a man who shared my father's last name but was no relation. Yet that recognition didn't mean he was ready to play a meaningful part in my life— at least not back then, and not for a long while.

When I was a year old, my dad emigrated to Canada. His girlfriend at the time, the woman he was truly in love with, had moved to England with her parents, even though she was pregnant with their first child. Determined to make a better life for her and the family they would have, he could have followed her to England, but he felt the opportunities were better for him in Canada. So, he moved to the Toronto area, leaving me and his other daughter behind in Jamaica. His girlfriend joined him shortly after he got there, and they married and got on with building their lives.

I didn't even know what my father looked like until he came back to St. Thomas for a visit when I was eight or nine years old and someone pointed him out to me in town. When I went up to him and introduced myself, I remember him calling me "buddy"—a term exclusively used by foreigners. The only impression I have of him from that first meeting is because of that word. *This is a foreign man*, I remember thinking.

My mother must have mourned the loss of him, but she did so in her own way. She'd already had Ian by the time he left—another man's child—and it only took her six more months to hook up with the man in May Pen and arrange a departure of her own. It was thoughtless and cruel of her to abandon us. But when I look back, I see it as the greatest gift my mother ever gave me, because it led to a childhood spent with my maternal grandmother, Julia Vassell.

After the man on the bicycle found her on the plantation, my grandmother left work and came for us, rounding up my older sister Barbara, who was already living with her, and a trolley to help carry us back. The walk from Golden Grove to Winchester was a few miles. Though I can't remember what happened when she got there that day, over the next decade I would see her coming back from the fields so many times I can picture it: her men's work shirt with the sleeves rolled up above her wrists; her baggy work pants tucked into a pair of rubber boots; the strength that emanated from this tiny woman, as though nothing in the world was heavy enough to break her; the calm set of her face; the love and kindness in her eyes.

With the addition of me, Ian and Joan, she now had six of my mother's seven children in her care. (The seventh, another girl, was being raised by her paternal grandmother.) Mama, as I would soon come to call her, had at least three of my cousins living with her full-time as well, along with her daughter Daphne, who was born with special needs and required constant care. Ten dependants on a plantation worker's wages, living with her in a two-room, zinc-roofed shack. And that number was often nearly doubled because all my cousins who didn't live with her, strictly speaking, still spent much of their time at her house and ate all their meals there.

It would've been hard to blame Mama if she'd felt resentful or put-upon, burdened by the poor judgment of her children and their refusal to face the consequences of their actions. But my grandmother was not a bitter person. On the day the man turned up on a bicycle to tell her that three of her grandbabies were alone, hungry and crying in a shack a few miles away, she didn't turn to God to ask why He demanded so much of her. She knew there was no one else to step up and care for us, so she went and collected us and then figured out how to make it work. She entered my life as a model of hard work, dignity and selflessness—of how to live the right way. She would continue to embody those qualities for as long as she lived, and it is no exaggeration to say that her example, along with the love and support she gave me at a crucial time, ultimately saved my life.

2

THE FOUNDATION
OF ALL THINGS

When I tell Jamaicans that I'm from the parish of St. Thomas, they tell me I'm lying. They don't believe a person as successful as I am could come from a place like that. St. Thomas is the most impoverished parish on the entire island of Jamaica. If you were to drive east from Kingston, you would see and feel the roads change as soon as you crossed the parish border. The people of St. Thomas are so poor, with so little economic and political power, that the government spends zero dollars on them. The roads are completely neglected—potholes forever—as are every other social support and piece of public infrastructure. It's as true today as it was when I was growing up there in the 1970s.

If you had to spend your childhood in St. Thomas, though, Golden Grove wasn't a bad place to be. It was a local hub, the site of a bustling weekly market immortalized by the Jamaican poet and screenwriter Evan Jones in his poem "The Song of the Banana Man." When the buses passed through, heading to Morant Bay or Port Antonio or Kingston or wherever, they would all stop in Golden Grove. It was not much more than a town square, but it had a gas station and a convenience store, a general store, a police station and a soccer field. And kids bussed and walked in from all over the area to attend primary school there.

My grandmother lived in workers' housing that served the plantations that surrounded Golden Grove. The neighbourhood was the poorest in St. Thomas and was known simply as "The Barracks." To be from The Barracks carried a stigma. You were looked down on for the extremity of the poverty you lived in, and "You're from The Barracks" was a put-down. But people were also proud to say they came from there: it was a signal that they were tough, because you had to be tough to survive in such a place. There was no indoor plumbing, no electricity, no running water—except the river—and next to no money. Everyone in The Barracks worked in the fields. After my older siblings finished primary school, they went straight to work on the plantation.

It was a place that people were born into and never escaped, but my grandmother had ended up there by choice, and for love. Julia Vassell was originally from St. Elizabeth, a parish in south-western Jamaica with a lot of German and Cuban immigrants and other white folks who'd come to cash in on the area's bauxite trade. That influx of foreigners resulted in a lot of interracial relationships, which led to a lot of light-skinned kids. Light-skinned Jamaicans are often assumed to be from St. Elizabeth, just as dark-skinned Jamaicans, like myself, are assumed to be from St. Thomas. Such assumptions aren't innocuous; they are shot through with the colourism that exists in Jamaican culture as it does everywhere else in the world. The lighter-skinned St. Elizabethans are expected to be wealthier, better educated and of a higher social standing than darker folks. They are also often discouraged from entering relationships with anyone darker skinned, despite the fact that they owe their own existence to such relationships.

Mama was one of those light-skinned Jamaicans. She met my grandfather David Smith in St. Elizabeth and soon fell in love with this really dark-skinned man. I don't know anything about the family she came from—what they did or their standing in the community—only that they disapproved of her relationship and forbade her to be with my grandfather. In response, she and my grandfather moved to The Barracks. Her brother, Winston, came with them as well, the only member of her birth family she had any contact with for the rest of her life. When she died, no one from her family, except Winston, came to her funeral.

By the time my siblings and I went to live with Mama, she and my grandfather had separated. That wasn't something I understood at the time, though, because he was always around. He was an alcoholic, and his drinking had driven them apart. She was constantly after him about it, telling him the drink would be the death of him. She also wouldn't let him come around us grandkids when he was drunk. But she continued to care for him at a bit of a distance, feeding him and letting him stay the night, though always in the other room with all of us kids. She never took another companion—I don't remember anyone else making even a brief appearance, no "Hey, this is Horace or Delroy." I still marvel at the strength it would've taken for her to stand up for herself in that time and place. She decided she wasn't going to tolerate drunkenness from a man, and she stuck to her decision. She told him, "You're not going to be a part of my life unless you fix yourself up," and she didn't bend or twist. For a woman in rural Jamaica in the early 1970s—an utterly male-dominated environment—to stick to her guns that way is amazing.

My grandpa David could never leave off drinking long enough to find his way back into her heart, but us kids just loved the man to death. Papa, as we called him, was tall and slender, a calm, kind man and very laid back—nothing ever seemed to bother him. Even when Mama got after him about his drinking, he would quietly let her anger run its course. He had his own place, way up in the hills in a town called Cheswick, but he hung out with us almost every day. He took us on adventures into the bush to tend the gardens he and my grandmother had there— plots they'd cleared on unclaimed land—or up into the hills or to neighbouring villages to pay visits to his friends. He'd come walking down the road with all us little kids running around his legs, holding on to his hands and playing games. The friends he was bringing us to call on always had gifts or treats for us, often something small and sweet to eat.

I remember that the zinc roof on Mama's house made a wonderful racket every time it rained and that her wooden walls were covered in a thin coat of white paint, peeling away in places to expose the raw wood. The only decorations were sheets of newspaper she'd pasted up to seal any cracks where a draft had snuck in—not particular photos or articles, just any piece of newspaper she'd had at hand. The shack had just two rooms: her bedroom, which she shared with my aunt Daphne, and ours. The beds were small and metal-framed with old-fashioned springs and thin straw mattresses. She had a bed of her own, but in our room, there were a few beds here and there that we all piled onto at night. When she allowed Papa to stay over, he slept with us, and I remember how safe and loved I felt lying next to him.

The story of my grandfather's passing is one of the first of my life that I know is my own—not passed on to me from someone older. I was very young, just four years old at the time, but the intensity of the experience made it stick in my mind.

There had been a huge rainstorm and significant flooding. Papa was drunk and got caught in it, becoming soaked and chilled as he tried to get home. A few days later, he came to play with us and stayed the night. He must have been sick, because he died in his sleep.

I had been tucked in on the other side of him, up against the wall. When Mama woke us, I remember how serious she sounded as she said, "You got to get up. Papa is dead." I had to crawl over him to get out of the bed. I didn't know what death was or what it meant—that was my first experience with it—but I will never forget the strange, unsettling juxtaposition of my grandmother's urgency and our movement against the stillness of his body and his hand frozen in death, fist clenched.

My grandmother wasn't one to cry or show her pain in any obvious way, but I could see her sadness as she grieved for him. After some local men had taken him away and prepared his body for burial, they brought the casket back so she could look at him.

She was kneading dumplings when they brought the casket to the front of the house; she pulled her hands out of the dough and went to it. She looked at his body, just a quick look, and said, "I told you this is how you were going to die. I told you." I had never seen her so angry, but I knew it was anger not so much at him as at the loss of him, along with disappointment and sadness that she had never been able to help him with the problem that stranded him outside overnight in the rain, and likely led to his death. She was saying, *Why didn't you listen? Why didn't you stop drinking?*

She took just that one look. She didn't say anything to the men holding the casket. When she was done looking, she turned and went back to her dumplings.

I never knew my grandmother to dwell on the fact that she was poor or to despair over the things she didn't have. She woke up in the morning with everything she had to do that day lined up in her head, and sometimes she spoke the list out loud as she prepared our breakfast. Then she got to work. Most of her time was spent on her job at the plantation. When it was coconut season, she worked coconut; when it was banana, she worked banana; and when it was sugar cane, she worked sugar cane—the same cycle, the same rotation of crops, year after year.

When we were still too young to mind ourselves or weren't in school, she brought us along to help. With coconut, workers would scale the trunks of the tall palms and knock the fruit down with a machete or by kicking at it. Our first job was to stack the coconuts knocked down, all over the ground, into piles, then tractors would drive up and we'd throw the coconuts into the back. With the sugar harvest, the fields of ripe cane were burned first and then workers were sent into them with machetes. They cut the cane in sections from the top down, chopping it into lengths of about five feet. We arranged those pieces into piles, and then a tractor came with a loader on the back, picked up the piles and dumped them onto big trucks that carried them to the refinery where they were boiled into sugar. Whether it was coconut or sugar cane, you were in for back-breaking labour in the fields.

In banana season, Mama worked on an assembly line that prepared the fruit for export. There was a large vat of water at one end of the line into which huge bunches of bananas were dropped. My grandmother's job was to reach into the water and pull out a bunch, then cut hands of green banana off it with a curved knife and pack them into shipping boxes. Our job was to put the boxes together. When you cut green banana, the stalk oozes sticky sap. Mama, chatting with her friends on the line as she worked, wore an apron and gloves to protect her skin and clothes, but still the sap would cover her.

Mama was about sixty when my siblings and I came to live with her, so she would have been four or five years older in my earliest memories of her at work. She was still so physically strong that she could put in a full day in the field or on the line and then walk home in her work clothes and rubber boots, balancing a basket of coconuts or bananas on her head while both her hands were full of more fruit and vegetables. She worked that way from the time she ran away with Papa until she died—six days on, one day off. And even on that one free day, I never once remember her sitting around, saying, "Man, isn't it nice to be off today?" She always had that list running through her head.

There was her garden in the bush miles from the house that needed tending, an endless cycle of tilling, planting, weeding and harvesting. There was feeding and minding all of us kids, which was a full-time job on its own. Then there was all our laundry, done by hand. And there was everything she had to prepare to sell on market day, a crucial way to bring in extra cash.

The Golden Grove Market took place in the main square, usually on Saturdays. It was the liveliest thing that happened in the town on any given week, with people coming in from all over the area to shop and barter. Farmers sold their crops, other vendors offered prepared food, and Mama set up alongside them, right in the middle of the action, selling fruit and vegetables from her garden to people from The Barracks who, after long days working on the plantation, didn't have the energy to clear a plot in the bush and grow their own. She was like a one-woman market research firm in her knowledge of what would sell best when and to whom. For instance, she knew which people were stopping at the market to load up on produce they intended to sell in Kingston, and gave them wholesale prices for buying in bulk. She also sold homemade sweets and baked goods. Her puddings, in particular, were locally famous, attracting lineups and always selling out. One of my happiest childhood memories is lingering at her hip on a Saturday morning as she made them.

Mama did all her cooking—all our meals and everything she prepared for the market—over an open fire in an outdoor kitchen with a dirt floor. It was our job to get the wood for the fire, which meant walking out past the plantations that stretched for miles around The Barracks into the bush, gathering wood, tying it up in bundles and carrying it back on our heads. We were also responsible for grating the coconut, yam and cassava for the puddings, running even the smallest pieces back and forth across the grater with the tips of our fingers to make sure we got every single bit. Many times we would grate our fingers too in our hurry to get the job done so we could head out to play. Since Mama didn't have an oven, she had to make do without one. She would build up her cooking fire until she had a good bed of coals and then set the pudding tins on a grate over them. Next, she would cover the tins with sheets of zinc and pile coals on top to bake the puddings, creating a delicious crust.

When the puddings were done, she'd take them out of their tins and then give the tins, which had remnants of crust all around the sides, to us. We'd take our spoons, scrape all the crust out and eat every bit. We would literally fight over those tins, though sometimes a few of us would all end up working at the same big tin—a bunch of famished kids just going to town with our spoons. Each bite was pure joy, 100 percent gold.

I feel that there are ways to express love without saying you love somebody. My grandmother never said, "I love you," to any of us kids, but she made her love plain by the way she treated us. I could see it in her eyes.

My dad used to send church clothes for me from Canada. He always sent shoes a few sizes too big so they would last. My grandmother would stuff the toes with newspaper to make them fit, taking it out a bit at a time as I grew. Every now and then, she made sure to get a picture taken to send back as an update for my dad. He kept them all and later gave them to me. In those pictures you can see the look of pride on Mama's face. She has put her care into dressing me and into raising me, and she is proud of the result. On my face, you can see the confidence of someone who knows he is loved unconditionally, who doesn't need anyone to tell him that in words because the truth of it is so evident. I cherish these pictures.

Mama was too busy trying to make a living to read to us or tuck us in at night and kiss our heads. When it got dark, she would simply announce, "Okay, everybody, it's bedtime," and we all knew what we were supposed to do. We'd go down to the river to bathe and clean our teeth, we'd dry off and get dressed, and then we'd come back to the house and put ourselves to bed. Sometimes before she headed to her own bed, she would tell us folktales, like the adventures of Brother Anansi, a genius spider who was always coming up with inventive ways to solve people's problems. When she left us, we usually had the last of the day's energy running through us and found it hard to settle down, so we would talk and joke. Occasionally, we would get a bit too rowdy, rushing around and wrestling and making noise, rousing Mama. At the sound of her footsteps, we would scatter, diving for our beds as she burst through the door, whirling her belt above her head like a tornado. She meant it as a playful gesture, but the message was serious: *I need my rest. Go to bed so I can get it.* We would calm down after that, piled up on those straw mattresses, and fall asleep dreaming of coconut and cassava puddings.

————

The confidence my grandmother's love instilled in me served me well back then, and still does. I always went to school with a clean uniform, but I never wore shoes. To me, that made perfect sense: Shoes were for special occasions. You wore them to go to church or a funeral or something like that. You didn't wear shoes to school because that would be a waste of shoes. But most of my classmates weren't as poor as we were, so kids made fun of me for being from The Barracks and being unable to afford shoes.

School is one of the first places where kids learn to compare themselves to other people. They see the brand names on their classmates' clothes, for example, and quickly pick up on the signifiers of wealth, comfort and status. It's natural that they start to want those things too. Though we all wore the same uniform, when you're one of the only kids without shoes or a lunch, your relative economic position is pretty clear. I remember seeing a candy lying in the sand and gravel in the schoolyard one afternoon, a drop made of coconut and brown sugar. I was hungry, so I picked it up intending to eat it. A kid saw me and started yelling, "Eww, you picked it up! You're going to eat it!" And I didn't eat it because he saw me.

In that moment, I felt like a lesser person than he was, like a dirty person, but I soon learned that what separated us wasn't a matter of right and wrong or good and bad. When I was laughed at in school, it was always by kids looking to put me down and belittle me for something I couldn't control. They were laughing at me for being poor, pointing out my poverty as though they were the first ones to discover it. But I knew I was poor simply by the fact of where we lived, and so did everyone else. It wasn't news and it wasn't remarkable. It was written into the soles of my feet, callused by every inch of ground they'd had to cover. What was I supposed to do about it? Was I supposed to pretend that my bare feet had shoes on them? Was I supposed to pretend that I wasn't hungry?

Pretending I wasn't poor seemed far more ridiculous to me than accepting that I was, so I accepted it. I grew a thick skin. When kids mocked me, I made it clear that what they thought was worthy of ridicule was no big deal. *You're laughing because I'm too poor to afford shoes? Go ahead. It doesn't bother me.* I moved on, and it didn't take long for them to do the same.

My grandmother's example helped me grow that thick skin. Maybe she was the biggest reason I was able to do it. I saw how hard she worked for us. I saw the dignity with which she lived, and the honest effort she applied to everything she could control in her life. How could I ever be embarrassed by the life she worked so hard to give me?

As I've grown older, I've always tried to carry myself the way she did. What embarrasses me aren't the things I can't control, only the things I can. Poverty, sickness, hunger, having a crappy job or only being able to afford a small apartment or shabby house—these things aren't failures. Failure is having the power to affect positive change for yourself or others and not acting on it. That's when I have a problem—when I myself can be better, do better, and I don't. Because I know better. I was taught better.

3

"WHY DON'T YOU TAKE ONE OF THE GIRLS?"

Apart from church clothes and those spoonsful of Mama's pudding, the only other luxury I experienced growing up was television. School brought me into contact with people who made fun of me, sure, but it also connected me with friends whose families had done well enough to afford electricity in their homes. And if you had electricity in Jamaica in the mid-1970s, chances were you also had a TV. Now and then, one of us kids would be invited over to watch TV, and a small group of us would always tag along.

At that time, Jamaica only had one channel, the Jamaica Broadcasting Corporation (JBC). After a walk that was usually at least a few miles long, we'd all sit down and watch whatever JBC put on. I remember a lot of westerns, which sometimes led to the viewing party breaking out into imaginary gunfights. The shows themselves didn't have a lasting impact on me, but the walks home afterward sure did.

There were no streetlights in our part of the island, so when it got dark, it got *really* dark. People would stay outside until the early evening, standing around and chatting, but once the sun started to go down, they'd wrap it up and go home. It just wasn't safe to be out too late because we lived by the main road leading to Kingston and cars would drive that narrow stretch as if they were being chased by Lewis Hamilton. We didn't have an indoor toilet at my grandmother's house, but no one used the outhouse after dark. Many nights you couldn't see your hand in front of your face.

Those TV days, though, always seemed to be the exception to that rule, at least when I was a little bit older, say nine or ten. We would come back in the dark, making the miles-long trip with only the moon to light our way. It was a *tough* walk, even in a group. Most people from St. Thomas are superstitious. They believe in ghosts and other supernatural occurrences. Walking those gravel roads at night, a bit out of breath from the adrenalin coursing through us as we moved faster than normal in the dark, we would tell the ghost stories we'd heard from adults and other older kids. We'd get good and worked up, and then, as we passed by the plantation fields, the moon would cast light through the banana palms and a breeze would move the branches. The shadows would look like the long fingers of a witch or a ghost reaching for us, and we'd get so scared we'd run like thieves. We wouldn't stop until we got back to Mama's, sweaty and panting.

Those TV days were an exception in another way, too. We usually didn't have our entertainment provided to us by JBC or anyone else. Since we couldn't afford toys or games, we had to be creative and make them ourselves. We built two kinds of toys, again and again. Because I know you'll want to try them out for yourself at home, here's what you need for the first: a car tire, two sticks, a tin can or plastic bottle and some breadfruit so ripe that it's fallen off the tree. We would smush the breadfruit and then rub it all around the inside of the tire, as a kind of grease or lubricant. Next, we'd put the tin can or bottle through the centre of the tire like a little axle and put a stick in each end. Two of us would stand on either side of the tire, grab hold of a stick and then run around, pushing the tire as if driving a car. We'd race other kids with their tires to establish who had the fastest one in The Barracks (actually, the fastest boys with the most stamina). In all of St. Thomas. In Jamaica. In the world.

The second toy was also a type of imaginary race car, though a slightly more complicated one. We'd get a length of broomstick and a couple of smaller pieces of wood and stick them together to make a shape like a capital *I*. On either end of one of the smaller crosspieces, we'd attach something like a shoe polish tin to be our wheels. Then we'd run string from the upper crosspiece down to the one with the tins to create a steering system. It would be the same racing game from there on, driving our stick cars around the neighbourhood.

It didn't weigh on us at the time because it was a simple fact of life. But as I look back on it now, one of the saddest things about growing up in The Barracks was living in poverty and hunger while being surrounded by abundance. The banana, coconut and sugar cane plantations that my grandmother worked on stretched for miles around our neighbourhood. We were dirt poor, so absolutely poor that I didn't have a lunch to bring to school. Yet if my grandmother had walked onto the plantation and taken a hand of bananas or a coconut to make us a pudding, she would've been arrested. To me, that juxtaposition shows, in the simplest terms, how unfair society has always been to the poor. It reminds me that, now that I have means, I have to be different.

Back then I had no choice but to be subject to the system, but it's also self-evident that you can't raise a child next to sugar cane, coconut and banana fields and not expect him to take a piece now and again. I'd be hanging out with my buddies and someone would throw out the suggestion, "Hey man, I'm hungry. Let's go get some cane." We knew it was a dangerous thing to do—the plantations were all patrolled by armed guards, men we knew from the neighbourhood—but that was all it took to get us on board because we were all hungry.

As far as we were concerned, the sugar cane that grew at the edges of the fields, along the roads and paths, wasn't the good stuff. To get the best of the best, cane that was worth the risk, you had to get out into the middle of the fields. We never took much, just a small piece each, enough to chew on and forget our hunger for a portion of the afternoon. Still, the day we got caught, the size of the pieces we'd stolen didn't matter.

We weren't doing anything we hadn't done and gotten away with many times before. It was just bad luck. A group of us had snuck into the field for cane, and when we were coming back out, the ranger happened to be walking by, his rifle slung on a strap across his chest. He yelled at us, and everyone dropped their cane—so there would be no hard evidence of the crime if he caught us—and ran. We scattered in all directions. I was the one he chose to pursue.

It was about a mile back to my grandmother's house. Since the ranger lived in The Barracks, he knew who we all were when he busted us. But he still chased me the whole way. I was fast enough to put distance between us, but it was terrifying to be chased by a grown man with a gun, even one I knew. When I got back to the house, I ran straight into Mama's room and hid under her bed, the safest place I could think of. I was shaking like a leaf.

I'd been under the bed for a minute or two when I heard him out front. Fortunately, Mama was home, and she met him there. Blocking the doorway, she asked him what his business was. He told her he'd caught me stealing. He said he knew I was inside and demanded that she bring me out, and Mama told him he was out of his mind. "What's wrong with you?" she yelled at him. "What are you doing chasing my grandson?" When she told him to back off, go away and leave me alone, he had no choice but to heed her because I wasn't the only one who looked at Mama and saw something more formidable than any gun. He left with a weak parting shot: "Tell him not to go back to the plantation again—or else." Mama gave him the cut-eye before turning back to her business.

While we were living at Mama's house, my mother would turn up for flying visits a few times a year, never staying long. Maybe I'd see her for an hour at most before she disappeared again, and she wouldn't really give me her attention for any of that time. She would appear unannounced, hand my grandmother a little money or some other small offering, argue with her for a while and then she'd be gone.

To me, she was like a celebrity, and the way she breezed in and out of our lives added to that impression. I felt like she was a different kind of person, one our world couldn't contain for very long. She was a slim five-ten or so, still beautiful. She showed no sign of having carried seven children, as though she'd shrugged off any physical traces of her kids when she left us behind. She wore her long hair relaxed and styled in loose curls and was always dressed impeccably—I never saw her in the same outfit twice. She was glamorous, someone the dirt and dust of The Barracks couldn't stick to.

Her visits always upset my grandmother. Her daughter Dorothy was one of the few people who could get under Mama's skin. It was the way she treated us that bothered my grandmother—her near-total disregard for her abandoned children—and Mama wasn't shy about saying as much. She would tell my mother that she needed to spend time with her kids, that the way she treated us was shameful. My mother seemed unaffected by it all at the time, but now I suspect she didn't like hearing the truth and avoiding it was part of the reason she stayed away.

Then one day when I was eleven years old, my mother showed up and announced that she was taking me to live with her. Though I had heard my grandmother speak out against her treatment of us dozens of times, none of those lectures changed the way I thought of my mother or how good it felt to be the only one she chose. If anything, it seemed to me that my mother was finally doing what Mama had always asked her to: stepping up to look after at least one of her kids.

The news was delivered with zero fanfare. She just showed up and said, "I'm taking Wes. He's coming back with me." That was it. There were no fireworks or balloons, but still I felt joyful. This beautiful woman, my mother, picked *me*, and not any of my sisters or brothers. It had to mean there was something special about me, right?

That seemed to be confirmed when everyone—my grandmother, my aunts, even some neighbours who'd turned up to see what the commotion was all about—started in on her and she held her ground. "Why are you taking the boy?" they asked her. "The boy's going to take care of himself. The girls are going to get pregnant. Why don't you take one of the girls?" All my mother said in return was "I'm taking Wes."

I have amazing memories of life with my grandmother. In her house, I felt cared for and knew I was loved every second of every day. Mama's love came with no conditions and gave me the confidence to survive and even thrive in a place like The Barracks. She didn't expect to get anything out of the work she put into raising me other than the satisfaction of watching me grow up right. She was one of the most loving and selfless people I have ever met in my life.

But since I had nothing to compare to life in my grandmother's house, I had no reason to suspect that I wouldn't feel similarly loved and protected with my mother. I had never been out of Golden Grove. I didn't know how good I had it, so I took my circumstances for granted. When my mother said, "I'm taking Wes," I was excited to go.

I packed a small bag of clothes but had nothing else to bring. I don't remember the particulars of my grandmother's goodbye. I wish I did, but I was so young and so thrilled to be going somewhere new that leaving my grandmother didn't really register. I followed my mother to the square where we caught a bus to Morant Bay, the capital of St. Thomas. I'm not sure I'd ever seen a traffic light before then, and a big city to me would have been any place with more than two hundred people. But if Morant Bay was overwhelming, it paled in comparison to our next stop. To get to my mother's house in May Pen, we had to change buses one more time, in the Half Way Tree neighbourhood of Kingston.

Half Way Tree, in the capital, is the centre of everything in Jamaica. I had never seen so many people in one place. The depot we arrived at had buses coming and going to every part of the island. Moving through a bus station in Jamaica, you not only have to contend with the crowds, but the bus conductors. Every bus has a driver as well as a conductor. The driver's only job is to drive the bus, and the conductor is responsible for everything else: loading the luggage, collecting fares and, most importantly to the bus company, making sure the bus is full.

In Half Way Tree, the conductors usually subcontracted out that last duty to entrepreneurial young men who then prowled the station hunting for passengers. To get the job done, those men had to be ruthless. If they saw someone looking around for a bus, they rushed up, asked where the person was going and grabbed the luggage before hearing the answer. Those men would put you on the bus they were filling, no matter where you were trying to go. If you were the first passenger on a bus, you had to sit there for maybe an hour and a half, because the bus wouldn't leave until it was absolutely packed.

To avoid those problems, seasoned travellers guarded their bags and shopped for the bus they wanted. They walked around the station looking for one that was almost full and headed in the right direction. That was the bus they chose. My mother was a seasoned traveller, and so we walked around looking for the perfect bus. When a bus filler grabbed her luggage at one point, she raised her fist and yelled at him, "Let go of my @#$%& bag!"

Everything was so new to me and there was so much to take in it added to the feeling that something special was happening. The trip proved to me that my mother really did belong to another, bigger world, and the way she guided me through the chaos all around us with such confidence felt like magic. So, when we got to her house in May Pen and went inside, it took me a little while to recognize the feeling in my stomach. It wasn't more nervous excitement over the incredible new life I'd been pulled into; it was the creeping suspicion that something wasn't right, that this new opportunity might not be so special after all.

4

THE RUNAWAY
AND THE MACHETE

Before I get into the story of the years I lived with my mother in May Pen, I need to offer a warning: I'm about to describe a time in my life when I was subjected to brutal physical and emotional abuse. As a survivor, I know what reading or hearing descriptions of abuse can do, how quickly it can send you back to your own experiences. I know how unwelcome that trip can feel. If you too have experienced something like this, please take care and be kind to yourself when reading this chapter and the next. To make sense of my life, I need to share what happened to me as a child, but you might need to skip ahead.

My mother lived in a small house not far from May Pen's main square. In the time since she'd abandoned me, she'd also abandoned the name her mother gave her, which was Dorothy, and started going by Yvonne, and she had married a man named Lenford Gordon. I'd known about her marriage to Len—I remember finding it odd how close the name *Lenford* was to *Leonard*, my dad's name—but she hadn't warned me that there was anyone else living with them. It turned out they already had four kids under their roof: Hillary and Carlton, who were Len's from a previous relationship and both a little older than me; and two they'd had together, Natalie and Michael, who were still babies. My mother hadn't told Len that she had seven kids until well after they were married, and Len had only recently discovered that I existed.

I'd thought my mother chose me because I was special. I'd even expected that she would tell me what it was that set me apart once we got to May Pen. At the bare minimum, I thought, she'd come all that way to fetch me because she actually wanted to spend time with me, to live with me. But it was soon clear that my mother couldn't stand me.

She beat me for the first time within days of my arrival. Physical punishment was common in Jamaica at the time. I'm sure my grandmother spanked me a couple of times over the years, and I have already mentioned the way she would come in waving the belt when we were horsing around before bed. But there was no anger in my grandmother's actions. The whole point was to let us know how annoying we were, not to punish us.

My mother didn't wave a belt—she used the buckle end to beat me. She used a broomstick. My grandmother had spanked us only when we'd done something wrong, but my mother didn't need a reason. She beat me out of anger, and she hurt me and scarred me. She beat me every day. She beat me just for existing.

My mother and Len didn't have a lot of money and they already had four other kids to care for. Why they'd decided to take on another mouth to feed didn't make any sense to me, and after the beatings started, I figured the whole thing had to be a mistake. My mother didn't want me around and her house was not a place where I wanted to be. So, I did the logical thing: I ran away.

I knew no one in May Pen, so when I ran, I went to the only place I could: Mama's. That meant making the bus trip I'd done with my mother in reverse with no money. I don't know how I did it. No clue. It doesn't seem possible to me now. But it's funny how, when you're young and determined, you can get things done that no one would expect you to be capable of. Clearly, I must have walked into town and asked people which bus was headed to Kingston—"Which one ah dem bus yah ah go Half Way Tree?" Also, somebody must've given me money for the fare. When I got to Kingston, I would've done the same thing, asking how to get to Morant Bay or St. Thomas and hoping for the fare. Again, people must have taken pity on an eleven-year-old travelling alone.

I had no way to let my grandmother know I was coming. I couldn't call because she had no phone. So, I got off the bus in Golden Grove with the same bag I'd packed when I'd left her, and just showed up at her door. I remember the surprise on her face when she saw me. "Wes," she said, "what are you doing here?" I told her I'd come back because I wanted to live with her again.

"Wes, you can't run away like that. Your mother's going to be upset."

I explained to her about the beatings, and about my mother not actually wanting me there with her in May Pen. Mama kept quiet and let me speak, listening with a look of concern on her face. When I was done, she told me I could stay until my mother turned up to get me. I was overjoyed. To my mind, there was no way my mother would ever come for me, because it was obvious she didn't want me. But it took only a day or two to prove my assumption wrong.

My mom arrived in Golden Grove like a whirlwind hitting the town. Word got to me before she did. I'd told people what she'd done to me, how awful it was to live with her, and most were sympathetic. They even agreed to hide me from her. But when she got to my grandmother's house and realized I wasn't there, she put it together that neighbours must be helping me and—I have no other words for it—she just went nuts.

I could hear her screaming as she went from shack to shack through The Barracks, trying to figure out whose bed I was hiding under. Eventually, she stopped looking and just stood in the street with a crowd gathering around her as she cursed and threatened them all. *You better bring him here. If you don't, this and that is going to happen.*

At some point, I crept out of my hiding spot and found a place where I could watch her from a safe distance. In Jamaica, swearing in public is a criminal offence. You can be charged with indecency and taken to jail. After my mother had been screaming some of the most offensive language you can imagine for a while, drawing a growing crowd, a policeman on his rounds stopped to see what all the fuss was about. As he approached, he started asking some of the people what was going on. Then he caught sight of my mother and heard what she was saying, and decided he had to intervene.

A neighbour named Carl was standing nearest to my mother. He'd been on his way home from working in the bush when he saw all the commotion and wandered over to check it out. He had his machete with him. When the policeman tried to arrest my mother, she grabbed the machete and swung it at him. The policeman jumped out of the way in time. To this day, I don't know whether she was trying to kill him or just scare him off, but she certainly escalated the situation. He jogged back to his car and headed for the police station to get reinforcements.

As soon as he was gone, someone came to tell me that it was serious now. I had to go with my mother before the police came back and took her to jail. It may seem odd that a group of adults, who had been told that she beat me regularly, turned me over to her after witnessing her attack a police officer. I genuinely don't think they were worried about her doing anything worse to me. People beat their kids all the time in Jamaica. It was something other people kept out of—you don't tell someone how to raise their child. They'd been willing to protect me when my situation looked like a bit of entertaining family drama, but when it escalated so far beyond what anyone expected, they figured that someone was either going to die or go to jail. It was time for the fun to end and the boy to go back to his mother.

I didn't fight it. When I realized she was in real trouble, I felt guilty because I was the one who'd caused it and I went willingly.

When she saw me, my mother didn't have an extreme reaction; she didn't hit me or even shout at me. She just said, in a cold monotone, "We've got to go." Our friends and neighbours had helped me hide from her, and now they helped both of us hide from the police. It was dusk when she'd swung at the officer and getting darker by the minute. We were led to a spot in the middle of one of the cane fields and told to duck down and stay still. When the police returned, we could see their flashlights shining all over my grandmother's house from our hiding spot. We watched the lights move through The Barracks, swarming over each of our neighbours' houses. When they started searching the cane fields, we moved from one to another, keeping ahead of the darting and sweeping beams. After an hour or more, the police got back in their cars and left. My mother knew the police would be waiting at the bus stop for her, so we headed instead for the train. Though it went to May Pen, no one I knew ever rode it in those days, possibly because it was more expensive.

For months after our return, my mother lived in fear. She was sure the police would come and find her, even all the way to May Pen, so she refused to leave the house. She wouldn't go into town or even into the front yard. Though her paranoia eventually faded, she refused to go back to St. Thomas for years. It was only when she heard that the police officer she'd attacked had been transferred to a different parish that she was willing to risk it.

5

"WHAT YOU BURN THE RICE FOR?"

After everything that had come from my running back to Golden Grove, I expected to face serious consequences. But when we returned to May Pen, my mother treated me well for a while. There was no big "you did this and this and that" lecture—she didn't seem to blame me for her altercation with the police. She even stopped the daily beatings. It was as if the whole experience had changed her view of me—not enough to spark kindness, but enough that she let me be.

I suspect now that she was in shock. Maybe experiencing the extremes to which her anger could drive her had scared her. More likely, she'd been frightened by how close she'd come to being caught and having to face criminal consequences. Whatever the reason for her calm, it soon passed. She started to hit me again.

She threw things at me, screamed at and berated me on sight. I woke up every morning knowing that something bad was going to happen to me that day and feeling powerless to stop it. If I brought home a poor mark from school, she would tell me how stupid I was while she beat me—which is ironic because my mother is illiterate. If I was asked to do a chore around the house and made a mistake, she would tell me how useless I was while beating me. If I made it through a day and by some grace hadn't made a single misstep in her eyes, she would beat me for that too.

My stepsister, Hillary, received the same treatment as I did for reasons I still cannot understand. At the same time, my mother treated her and Len's two little children like royalty, like they were her crowning achievements and, as a result, untouchable. This I also cannot explain. My mother would set Hillary and me impossible tasks, chores practically designed to spark a beating. We were each made to do the cooking from time to time, for example, but my mother didn't offer any instruction or give us a recipe. She would tell me to cook some chicken or rice and peas and then just walk out of the room, leaving me to figure it out. I was eleven years old. There was no internet, no way to look anything up, no cookbooks in the house, no one else to ask. I had watched my grandmother cook, and my mother too, so I had a general idea of how it was done, but that wasn't enough. I'd be cooking with my hands shaking, like I was preparing a meal for Gordon Ramsay and knew I was going to miss an ingredient or guess the cooking time wrong. And if it wasn't good when my mother tasted it, I was going to pay.

I don't know how I managed to learn under those conditions or succeed at making anything edible. But the reality is I figured out how to cook through an extremely painful process of trial and error because I had no other choice. To make rice and peas, a staple dish in Jamaica, I knew that the beans had to be cooked first—the "peas" being red kidney beans—and that they went in the pot with coconut cream and some other stuff. I took more than a few licks before I figured out that the other stuff was scallions and thyme. With all those ingredients in the pot, you boiled the beans for a long time. Then you took out one of them and pressed it between your thumb and forefinger to make sure it was soft. You needed to check because if the beans were too hard, there was going to be a problem. You also had to press a few of them, not just one, to make sure they hadn't cooked unevenly. When the beans were good, you added the rice and some water. You couldn't put in too much water though, or it would turn out soggy, so you just barely covered the rice. The heat couldn't be too high, just enough to keep the rice and beans simmering, or the dish would burn on the bottom. And you needed to taste it throughout to make sure it was okay, and so you'd have a better chance of figuring out where it went wrong if it wasn't.

Every way it could go wrong, it did. And every time it went wrong—"What you burn the rice for?"—I got a beating.

After the first few months under my mother's roof, I was sure that I was going to die there—that she was going to beat me to death. It was the only future I could imagine, the only outcome that made any sense. She attacked me with such cruelty it scared my stepfather, and he was not a man who shied away from violence. I remember a particularly nasty fight where she was out in the road in front of the house screaming at him as I watched from the doorway. There was a broken fence post tipped over at the side of the road. My stepfather took it up and started to hit her with it, breaking her leg right there in the middle of the street.

I felt so powerless watching that. I wished I was big enough to protect her, but I wasn't and couldn't. I felt bad for her every time she was abused, even though she would take that pain and pass it along to me and Hillary as soon as she could.

One of the few times in my young life that I was tended to by someone in the medical profession, I had been caught by her when she was in the wrong mood. I don't even know what I'd done to earn her attention, but she was so upset with me that she took my face in her palm and shoved my head backwards as hard as she could. Houses in Jamaica are typically built with concrete block, and when she shoved me, the back of my head hit the concrete and split open. I was knocked unconscious and fell to the floor, blood pouring from the deep gash in my scalp, soaking my shirt and pooling around me. When my mother saw the blood, she panicked and rushed me to a clinic across the street from her house. I regained consciousness there as a nurse tended to me, careful to hide me from the doctor as she stitched me up. At one point, I heard her tell my mother, "If the doctor sees this, you're going to jail." The doctor never did, and though the wound got infected and didn't heal for months, I wasn't allowed to go back to the clinic.

On another occasion, she was in the kitchen, cooking on the cast-iron stove. The stove was oval-shaped and stood about three feet high, with a compartment in the middle that you filled with hot coals. When I said something she didn't like, she took up the stove and threw it at me. It missed, but the shock of it flying near me and the deafening noise as it crashed to the floor and spilled hot coals everywhere was terrifying. My stepfather came into the kitchen to see what was going on. When he saw the mess of the stove and the look in my mother's eyes, he told me, "Wes, you have to go to the police station."

I was scared of my mother getting into trouble with the police, but I was more scared of my stepfather, so I took his advice and went to report her. The walk to the station wasn't long. When I got there, I froze in front of the building and started crying because I didn't want to go in. A police officer who knew my stepfather saw me and came over. "Wes, what's happening?" he asked. When I told him, he brought me back home, where he sat my mother down and gave her a talking-to. He told her she couldn't keep beating me like she was. In an echo of our trip to the medical clinic, he also told her that if his sergeant caught word of what she'd done, she would be going to jail and he wouldn't be able to do anything to help her. My mother sat quietly and let him finish his lecture. He left, and she beat me again the next day.

As brutal as the physical abuse was, it was the verbal abuse that hurt me the most—and she knew it. The specifics are deeply painful to recall. She would say things to me that no mother should ever say to her child. "You're black and ugly, and you're not mine," she would tell me. Out in public or meeting friends, she would introduce my half-siblings as her children, but not me. My appearance, particularly the colour of my skin—I was darker than her—was also a constant target.

"I don't like your face."

"You're good for nothing."

"I don't like the way you look."

"Stay away from me."

I internalized the verbal abuse—particularly the idea that my Blackness made me undesirable and somehow lesser—in a way I never did with the physical abuse. I knew a beating was coming to me every day and could have existed in a constant state of anxiety waiting for the first blow. But I learned not to let the sword hanging over my head have too big an effect on how I approached my day and what I did. I also found that I could bounce back from a beating and shake it off, something that was far more difficult to do with the thoughts my mother put in my head. Hillary and I would talk about what we were both going through, taking whatever small solace we could in our shared experience. I remember telling her, "I wish she would just hit me, punch me in the face, instead of saying what she just said."

It's really hard to overcome the knowledge that your own mother hates you. How do you rationalize that or explain it away? If the one person on earth who is supposed to love you unconditionally doesn't, how can you not take it as a sign that something might be wrong with you, that you might not be worthy of love? My mother went beyond simply not loving me. She actively and vocally hated me. She tracked me down and fought off the police only to bring me home and tell me how ugly and worthless I was. The absurdity of that tortured me, along with my inability to understand why she treated me that way. *You could have just left me in Mama's house. I want to be there. I tried to get back there and you came and fetched me. Why? For what?*

At the time, the only answer I could come up with was that she took some kind of satisfaction from hurting and humiliating me. There was no shortage of evidence that that was the case. When she finished washing my infant brother's and sister's soiled diapers, she would take the dirty water, full of all kinds of shit and urine, and throw it in my face. There is no reality in which that makes sense as anything other than a violent attempt to dehumanize. And it was being done by the person who gave birth to me.

She also took pains to shame me in front of other people. Many mornings before school, she would get after me, telling me I was dirty. Her anger would build in volume and intensity until she was yelling about how I was embarrassing her by going out in public looking the way I did. She would then take me into the front yard and strip me naked as my classmates walked by on their way to school. She would go back into the house and come out again with a basin of cold water and a stiff bristle brush for scrubbing clothes, and she would scrub me with it in full view of everyone passing on the street. The brush hurt, its stiff bristles and the frigid water combining to set my skin on fire. As she scrubbed, she would loudly berate me: "You don't bathe. You're nasty. I'm going to show you how to clean yourself." When she was finally done, I would have to dry myself, get dressed and go to school, where I would see all the kids who had walked past. Again, that is not discipline; it's torture.

The first school I went to in May Pen was a primary school similar to the one I'd attended in Golden Grove, only bigger because it was serving a more populous area. No matter how many times my mother told me I was stupid, I was always a decent student. When my teacher had to step out of the class, I was the one he left in charge, getting me to continue the lesson until he returned. I picked things up quickly and my work was often singled out for praise. (I still recall a teacher's feedback on an essay I wrote about forgiveness. "You must have gone to church before writing this," he said, "because this is amazing.") But my mind worked in ways that didn't always fit the confines of a traditional education. I thrived in environments where I was allowed to find my own path to a solution as opposed to having to follow a prescribed one. Schools didn't tend to celebrate, or even appreciate, that kind of intelligence, favouring memorization and the ability to follow instructions. I could do that, but not as reliably, and I was particularly terrible at taking tests.

Before a test, I was able to spit out all the answers. My classmates would actually come to me for last-minute advice and instruction, asking me how to solve a particular type of equation or to walk them through some plot point or thematic element in a story we'd read. But when the test papers were passed out and the room fell quiet, I would fall apart. The people I'd tutored at the last minute would do well and I wouldn't. I can't explain it, really. It wasn't that I felt overly nervous, at least not consciously. But there's something about the process of writing an examination— being required to think and do things in exactly the intended way—that creates problems for some people, and I am definitely one of them.

After a year or so at that school, it was time to write the national high-school entrance exam. It was a big deal. Every twelve-year-old in the country wrote it on the same day. You picked the high school you wanted to go to in advance. If you didn't pass the exam, you wouldn't be admitted to that school, and you'd have to go to what was called an "all-age school." Everybody would write you off as dumb for the rest of your life. It was a lot of pressure to put on a kid.

Ridiculously, not getting admitted to your school of choice didn't even mean you'd failed the exam. Because admission for every school was capped, it was ultimately determined through a lottery system. You could earn a mark good enough for a placement and still be denied if your name wasn't drawn from the hat, which was what happened to me. When my stepbrother, Carlton, got in, he was treated like a king. I didn't get in, which gave my mother fresh ammunition.

I kept trying to find ways to negotiate the minefield that was living with my mother. From the time I was a small child, I've been good at building relationships. I am interested in most people I meet and want to know about their lives, and so I enjoy chatting with them. Even as a little boy, I could sit with an adult and hold a conversation. Once they sensed that my interest was genuine, I was usually able to engage them in such a way that they'd forget they were talking to a kid.

Trying to find ways to be out of the house, I would accompany my mother while she ran errands—she might still say nasty things to me, but she was far less likely to beat me in public. Ideally, I'd try to get out on my own. My mother was strict about what I got up to before and after school. If I played with classmates and she heard about it, I was almost guaranteed to catch a beating for running around instead of doing the cooking and cleaning or watching after Natalie and Michael. It was far safer to spend time with *her* friends, to tag along with someone she knew and respected from town. They were almost exclusively adults, and I would chat with them pretty much the whole time I was with them. She almost always gave me permission to go if it was one of her friends asking for me.

For instance, there was a fairly large industrial bakery, with around a hundred employees, almost in our backyard. United Bakery mostly produced bread that it shipped all over Clarendon Parish. Hillary and I would slip over there on a regular basis because we'd often be given something good to eat—part of a loaf that had come out of the oven a bit burnt or damaged, along with some salted butter, which they always seemed to have a lot of. The rich creaminess of the butter with its hint of salt spread on freshly baked bread was a real treat.

Hillary and I would talk, joke and laugh with the people who worked there. I especially liked the head baker, a kind older man who always made sure we were fed. He had a special aura about him because he seemed to be the only one who knew the secret recipes for United Bakery's hard dough bread and spiced buns. I got to know and befriend many of the staff, including one of the delivery drivers, a Chinese-Jamaican man named T.Y. Chung.

T.Y. was a friend of my mother's. If I ran into him at the loading dock, he would sometimes invite me to come along on his route to lend a hand. I would sprint home, find my mother and say, "T.Y. want me to come with him." If she said, "Okay, go with T.Y.," I would run back and jump up on the bench seat between him and his son, who worked as his conductor on the route, loading and unloading the bread.

I was never picky about an opportunity to escape my mother's house for a few hours, and while most of the outings were fairly benign, like riding along with the Chungs, I also ended up in a few genuinely dangerous situations. My move to May Pen coincided with the run-up to the 1980 general election—the bloodiest in Jamaica's history. So intense was the violence that many people fled the country if they had the means. Neighbourhoods were divided between the incumbent People's National Party (PNP), led by Prime Minister Michael Manley, and Edward Seaga's Jamaica Labour Party (JLP), both of which hired local enforcers who were armed to the teeth. Like in a gang turf war, you could be killed for wearing the wrong colours in a neighbourhood. Flashing the wrong sign—the raised freedom fist of the PNP or the two-finger peace sign of the JLP—could get you killed. There were bodies dropping all over the place, and as a kid you had to learn to navigate through all of that. If you visited a friend in a PNP neighbourhood, you better not do anything to suggest you were anything other than a PNP supporter. If you did, you could be beaten or killed for your perceived political allegiance, despite being too young to vote. That's how ridiculous it was.

We lived in a JLP neighbourhood. Occasionally, men my mother knew who were associated with the party would turn up to fetch me and Carlton to help them put up posters and make deliveries. She may not have had any real say in whether we went, since she always agreed to it. Though I usually tried to avoid members of either party, I went along happily with these men because they treated Carlton and me well and got me away from my mother for a time. They would hoist us up on their shoulders to put up the party's posters as high as possible, so PNP supporters wouldn't find it easy to rip them down. On one occasion, we had just finished putting up posters in front of a police station in a strip mall when a car came tearing up and a bunch of PNP guys jumped out waving guns at us. The apparent leader of that group levelled an ultimatum: "Take those posters down or we're going to shoot all of you."

I knew our guys were armed too—they made no effort to hide that fact. While the tension built, both sides ready to open fire at the slightest provocation, I was sitting on the shoulders of a man right in the middle of the standoff. I remember being curious about what was going to happen, but not scared. Maybe I was in shock. Maybe I was thinking there was no point in worrying about something I couldn't control. Maybe I'd used up all my fear on my mother.

The police station sat totally silent and still as death threats were yelled back and forth. Not a single officer came out to deal with the situation. Eventually, our leader was the one who backed down, calling out, "Okay, take them down." We ripped down the posters and got out of there.

Another time, we were making a delivery to a fairly remote place at night. The driver turned onto a dead-end street and followed it as far as it went, stopping by some bushes. We had been sitting there in the dark for a short while when an armed man appeared at the driver's window, visibly annoyed. "Why didn't you give the signal?" he asked. "We don't allow just anyone to drive up here. I was going to fill this vehicle with bullets."

Most of our deliveries were done at night. Carlton and I would be put in the back of the truck with the cargo, a bunch of large, plain bags. We were forbidden to look in the bags, and for a long time, we didn't know what was in them. Then one night, while we were driving between towns, Carlton and I stole a peek: the bags were full of guns. It turned out that the reason we were along for the ride was so that if police stopped the truck, the men could claim the bags were ours. Given that we were minors, the charges wouldn't be as severe. I guess their rationale was that a year or two in juvenile detention wouldn't be all that bad for a couple of boys like us.

Tagging along with T.Y. in the bakery van was a lot less dangerous, of course, but it could still prove dramatic. He had a bad gambling habit and would sometimes lose all the money he'd collected on the job playing mah-jong. He ran up some huge debts with the bakery, but somehow managed to stay employed. Still, it caused him a lot of stress. He was always giving little speeches about how he was going to win back all he owed.

The usual division of responsibilities on a truck was that the driver took inventory, collected the money and wrote the receipts, and the conductor handled all the labour, unloading the fresh bread and retrieving any stale inventory the store was returning. T.Y. ran a looser ship, often letting his son handle the money transaction with the shopkeeper while he unloaded. His son would often take extra bread out of the truck, sell that in a side deal and pocket the money. Anytime he noticed me watching him, he would tell me to keep my mouth shut about it or else. I always kept my lips sealed. They were both so brazen, I figured the bakery had to have at least some idea of what they were doing. It wasn't my place to hold them to account.

Whether I went with the Chungs or the JLP guys, the point of tagging along was to get away from my mother and have a little fun driving around Clarendon. But there was another blessing in disguise: spending all that time with adults helped me to mature quicker and to think like an adult. At eleven and twelve, I already understood that life meant paying bills, juggling responsibilities and looking out for yourself. When you're a kid, you usually don't have to worry about where the next meal is coming from or how you're going to pay the rent, but I saw first-hand what it took to put food on the table and keep a roof over your head. On the bread truck, I learned what it was like to be a person who took in cash and had to be accountable for it, and I also saw what it looked like to mess all that up—to fail in an adult responsibility. As much as I liked T.Y., I was shocked by his addiction and the way it made him jeopardize his position. I knew I would never be so careless. I just didn't know I would have to call on these skills so soon.

Of the three of us older kids, Carlton was the only one my mother didn't regularly abuse. I don't know why, but he did spy for her, keeping tabs on what everyone else in the house was up to while she was out, for instance, which usually provided her with an excuse to punish me or Hillary or both of us. Eventually, Carlton stopped acting as just the middleman and started beating me himself. When I was coming home from school, he would stick his hand out the window of the house and show me the belt. The message: *When you come inside, this is what you're going to get.*

He wasn't much older than me and wasn't any bigger, really. But I had no confidence in myself and no belief in my right to *not* get hit. My mom had set the example for how I was to be treated, and just as Carlton picked up on it and went along with it, so did I. Carlton and I have reconnected as adults and we get along well now that we're free of my mother's influence, but there were months in my childhood when he beat me with a belt regularly and I barely protested. It was only when I got a little bigger than him that I finally realized I could fight back and eventually got him to stop.

While Carlton's motives and influences were clear, my mother's remained impossible to grasp. Hillary and I often talked about what we were going through, and our connection made things easier to bear. Together we struggled with the same question: Why? Initially, we came to the same conclusion: my mother somehow enjoyed hurting and humiliating us. But that conclusion only led us to more questions: Why was she like that? Where did that evil come from?

My grandmother was the most loving person I've ever known, and none of her other children had a shred of Dorothy's malice and vengefulness. (Though I do recall a time my mother travelled to St. Lucia, leaving us in the care of her sister Winnifred, and my aunt beat me so hard with a stick from a guava tree that it left a permanent scar on my left foot.) Even when I was a child, I knew my mother was not passing down violence she'd experienced in her childhood home. Later, when I had learned more about her and about my own origins, I assembled, if not explanations for her behaviour, at least some contributing factors.

My mother started having kids when she was thirteen years old. She was born into extreme poverty just like everyone else in my family, and then spent her teenage years having more kids and not going to school. Her lack of education—she didn't read, and when I lived with her, she often got me to write letters for her—stripped her of what few opportunities may have come her way in life. Still, as I wrote in the opening pages of this book, she was an ambitious person. With nowhere else to put that ambition, she placed her hopes in the men she took up with. She seemed to believe that each of them was going to sweep her off her feet and carry her to a better life. All of them swept her off her feet but only managed to carry her as far as the bed. When she got pregnant, which seemed to happen easily, they all ran off eventually. Many of them, including Len, also abused her. That may have been enough to sour her on the world and every person in it, including her own children.

I eventually found out that the only reason she came to get me from Mama's was because my father had called her from Canada to check on me, and he had told her to do it. Understandably given his own experience, he believed that a child was better off with his mother. For my mother, my dad was the one who got away—the handsome, athletic man who'd treated her well before going abroad to make the kind of life she dreamed of. She held out hope that he would come back to her, so she went and got me as he asked. But she also resented the fact that he'd left, and likely hated me for being what she'd ended up with instead of him. Not only was I unwanted by her, I was a reminder of the person she couldn't have.

Of course, this explanation is only my best guess, and it fails to explain why she was equally awful to Hillary. My stepsister has spent her adult life trying to find some more conclusive rationale.

She has taken criminal psychology courses in both the United States and the United Kingdom to help her figure out my mother. I understand all that effort. Without a concrete answer to why your abuser acted as she did, you are left with the possibility that there was something about you, the victim of abuse, that invited the violence, that in some way you "deserved" it. It is an easy idea to pick up on—just look at me and Carlton—and a very difficult one to shake. Where Hillary loses me is in her belief that anyone can find a satisfying answer.

There was no sense to the abuse my mother inflicted on us. She was torturing children. I don't need to look for a more complicated explanation, because when we were kids, my sister and I identified the only one that still rings true to me: There are people in the world who are inherently good, and there are people who are the opposite. My mother was the opposite.

My mother and stepfather only rented the house near the town square in May Pen where I first lived with them. A little more than a year after my mother brought me there, they bought a place of their own in the Paisley Housing Scheme, a new sub-division on the outskirts of town. It was a single-storey concrete box with a living room, kitchen and bathroom grouped together and three bedrooms off a single hallway at the back. It had a backyard of less than half an acre with a small veranda out the front and was identical to every other house in the scheme. But it was theirs to do with as they pleased. Neighbours soon added additional floors, expanding to six or seven bedrooms in some cases. My stepfather eventually built a wall around the front yard and a chicken coop out back, and we planted tropical flowers around the property to make it look nice.

In the weeks leading up to the move, my mother regularly told me that she was going to leave me behind. I wasn't worth bringing, she said, taking obvious pleasure in the idea of abandoning me again—or at least in the reaction her threat inspired. On one level, getting away from her was all I wanted, but her words still scared me. After living in May Pen for eighteen months, going to school and making all new friends, I felt my life was there. If she decided not to take me with them, I didn't know where I would live or how I would eat. I'd moved on from Golden Grove, and going back there didn't seem like an option. As loving as Mama was, there was no hope for a better life in The Barracks. At least in May Pen there were some opportunities. The uncertainty terrified me more than the nightmare I faced by staying with her—a sign of how broken I was. She ultimately brought me along to the new house, but she left me to agonize right up until the final day of the move.

She took me with her, but the new setting didn't inspire any significant changes in my mother. She remained violent and aggressive, beating and berating me every day. I did feel a fundamental shift of my own, though: I gradually stopped being afraid of her. Looking back, I think that was less to do with the change of scenery and more to do with the period of anxiety she put me through before the move. I had spent weeks with my stomach in knots at the thought of being left behind. When that didn't happen, and the reality of being stuck in a house with my mother's hatred sank in all over again, something inside me turned off. I stopped caring what happened to me. *So, she's going to punch you in the face. Why cry? You can't do anything to stop her anyway. Just take it and move on.*

In a way, my attitude was the ultimate expression of my mother's power. She'd broken me—stripped me down to the point that everything she did felt so inevitable it wasn't worth resisting at all. But when I stopped reacting to the abuse, she lost her power over me. As much as her motivation for treating me the way she did seemed senseless to me, she delivered every insult and blow with a goal in mind: to create a visible reaction. She seemed to feed off witnessing the evidence of my pain. Now when she beat me with a broomstick, I didn't cry. And so the beating became pointless. It didn't "accomplish" anything. It was just exercise.

She felt the truth of that immediately, and it made her angrier than I'd ever seen her. She was beating me in the backyard—over what, I can't remember. After she'd hit me four or five times and I hadn't cowered, cried out or shed a tear, she stopped, her arm frozen above her, ready for the next blow, as the realization played out on her face. She gave me a look of pure hatred, turned and walked into the house. She came out less than a minute later with a straw bag she'd stuffed with some of my clothes.

"So, you're a man now? Okay, you can be on your own like a man," she said. She threw the bag toward me and it landed in the dirt. "You can be out of here." Then she went back into the house and slammed the door.

She had brandished the threat of kicking me out like a weapon many times. I had been so afraid of that weapon, but when she finally used it, all I felt was joy. I was thirteen. I didn't know where I was going to sleep that night or what I was going to eat.

But as I walked out of the yard, I was grinning, practically whistling down the road. I thought, *Okay, life starts here.* I might have even said it out loud.

I am a naturally happy person, but no matter how sunny your disposition, living through the kind of abuse my mother put me through is supposed to leave marks. I should, by rights, have a dark side, or at least a deep well of pain waiting for me to slip and fall into. I don't. I have painful memories—including many I have shared here—but I made a conscious choice from the moment I started walking down the white gravel road away from my mother's house not to be defined by them. I looked at the person I seemed destined to be, the person my mother was trying to torture me into becoming, and I decided to do everything possible to be the opposite.

I was destined to be an abuser. My mother was an abuser; my stepfather was an abuser.

I was destined to be an alcoholic. My grandfather was an alcoholic; my stepfather was an alcoholic; my great-uncle was an alcoholic; my brother is an alcoholic.

I was destined to be a womanizer. My father was promiscuous and so was my mother.

I thought about all these things I was destined to be and, walking down that road at thirteen, I looked back through my life for someone who wasn't any of them. I looked for a role model. I found one.

My grandmother was the only and obvious choice. She was selfless; she'd cared for my grandfather and her disabled daughter and all those kids. She was community minded and had strong, lasting friendships. She was hard-working and entrepreneurial.

She didn't let things worry her and wasn't resentful when the world didn't go her way. She was the person I wanted to be like, and I'd had eleven years with her—more than with anybody else.

In my grandmother and the childhood she'd given me, I had a centre. There was the proof that the world is not evil; only people are—and not everyone. I could return to that centre and find a model to live by that would allow me to be happy and to make the people I love happy. I could rediscover hope.

My time with my mother had been awful, devastating, but she'd only had me for two years. Two years wasn't enough to turn me into a bad person, to make me forget my grandmother and all that she'd taught me.

As I walked away from my mother's house, I felt that I was heading for a life that I controlled. I could decide what type of person I wanted to be, and I vowed that whatever I did with myself, I was going to do it right. I would work hard, roll with the punches, be kind and worship God. I now faced all the problems I'd just spent weeks and months worrying about—*Where was I going to sleep? What was I going to eat?*—but they no longer seemed so heavy.

I wasn't worried; I was motivated. I felt like myself again.

6

ANYWHERE WITH A ROOF

It was a long walk into town from where we lived in the Paisley Housing Scheme, but that was okay. I needed some time to come up with a plan. My mother had kicked me out with no money and only the clothes on my back and what she'd stuffed into the straw bag she'd thrown at me. I'd had no advance warning, but that was a blessing. You might think, *If she'd given you some notice, you would have been able to talk to people and make arrangements.* Yes, I might have. But I can tell you for a fact that, instead, I would've spent that time worrying about what was going to happen to me, falling into the same pattern of anxious thoughts that had plagued me when she threatened to leave me behind in the move. When you get thrown into a situation and you have to find a solution on the fly, there's no time to wring your hands. Today, in my professional life, I'm constantly presented with challenges that require me to problem-solve in real time. My childhood provided excellent training for them.

After leaving my mother's, I remember passing by all the identical-looking houses on the street, just walking and thinking, walking and thinking. First, I had to figure out where I was going to sleep that night. I started running scenarios in my mind. I knew I had to ask a friend to take me in, but who should I try first? What was I going to say to them when I arrived? How long would they let me stay? If they said no, where would I head next? This was 1982. I couldn't call anyone; we had no cellphones. I would have to walk all the way to the first house and present myself and my case. Since each rejection would eat up precious time, both for the conversation itself and the walk to the next place, I had to plan my list of candidates wisely, putting the most likely to say yes at the top. I could only try so many before it got too late to be knocking on people's doors. If they all said no, I had no idea what I would do.

Sleeping on the street is heavily stigmatized in Jamaica. People think you have to be out of your mind to do it, and mental health challenges are even more profoundly stigmatized than homelessness. I had to get indoors because there was no other option. If I slept outside even for one night, word would get around—*Did you hear Wes slept on the street?*—and it would plague me. I would have an even harder time convincing someone to take me in the next day, and it would get harder still every day that followed. No one would want to help me because I'd be seen as already beyond help. It felt to me like my future was on the line.

I quickly ruled out most of my school-age friends, except as last resorts. None of them would be able to take me in without their parents' permission. Persuading those parents would be almost impossible. They lived in packed houses and most of them were poor; they didn't have extra beds and couldn't afford another mouth to feed. My best options were the friends of my mother's I'd been friendly with, I decided, and of them, the best bet would be adult men who lived alone. They had space, even if it wasn't much, and they could make a unilateral decision— I only had to win over one person to achieve my goal.

When we lived near the centre of May Pen, one of the men from the neighbourhood was a devout Rastafarian guy named Oscar. He used to talk to my mother if we ran into him while we were out and about, and he and I would hang out a bit from time to time and chat. He was friendly, he lived alone, and he didn't seem to have a care in the world. His house was the first place I visited. I knocked on the door, and when he answered, I quickly explained my situation and asked if I could stay with him for a while. "I don't care if I have to sleep on the floor," I said. "I just want to be indoors." Amazingly, he said yes.

It's hard to overstate how out of the ordinary it was for Oscar to take me in—people just didn't do things like that in Jamaica. My grandmother loved me and my siblings and slaved and sacrificed for us, but when she made the trek from Golden Grove to Winchester to rescue us, she did it because no one else would. People had problems of their own to deal with, and they didn't volunteer to take on anyone else's. But here was this full-grown, weed-smoking Rastafarian agreeing to help a thirteen-year-old he didn't even know all that well. Oscar's was a special act of kindness.

Right from the beginning, though, he made it clear that he was only willing to help me to a point. The morning after he took me in, Oscar sat me down and explained that my new living situation was a temporary thing. I had to find some other arrangement, and soon. He was happy to help me, he said, but only so long as I was helping myself. In the end it was a few months before Oscar finally said, "Wes, I'm sorry, bro. You've got to find someplace else." I'm still so grateful.

Over the next couple of years, I lived with anyone who was willing to have me. I don't remember how long I spent in any one place—sometimes it would be days, sometimes weeks—but that first stretch with Oscar was the longest I spent in any one home until I was fifteen. After I left his house, a neighbour put me up for a little while, but then I was back out on my own, and I had to jump around, juggle and get creative.

Given the upheaval of being out on my own, I had every excuse to stop going to school. After not getting into the high school I had chosen, I had endured months of my mother telling me I was dumb and destined to fail at everything in life. I often didn't know where I would be sleeping in a few nights' time, which meant that not only were there always things on my mind more pressing than homework, but also that the most basic elements of attendance—getting to school, cleaning my uniform—were significant barriers. Also, all-age schools like the one I was going to only went to grade eleven, and most of the people who ended up in them stopped going after grade nine, the end of which was only months away.

But my grandmother always valued education. She'd worked hard to make sure we stayed in school and got what we needed to have a chance at success. I had resolved to live the right way and there was no doubt in my mind which path was the right one. I may not have been good at test-taking, but I was always a hard-working student who earned my teachers' respect. I was determined to stick with school as long as I could and do my best to learn whatever it had to teach me.

The school I'd been assigned to was in a neighbouring town called Osborne Store, which I had to take a bus to reach. No matter where I was staying in May Pen, I had to get up early in order to make it to class on time, not only because it was a long ride, but also because it was hard to find a bus that would take me. Kids' fares were cheaper than adults', so no driver wanted to pick up kids. It was even harder to catch a ride in the afternoon, when all us kids would stream out of the schoolhouse at once and there were more adults out and about needing to take a bus. My friends and I could be stuck forever waiting for a ride.

Most days, we would just start walking, trying to create distance between us and the other kids while keeping an eye out for buses. If some adults got off a bus between the school and whatever corner we'd reached, maybe there'd be room for us. We avoided the bigger buses if we could help it, favouring the mini-vans. They were faster and played nice music, but their capacity was limited, so it was tougher to get them to stop for you. The large buses, on the other hand, had their own attractions. They would often be so full that the only way to board—if you could board at all—was on the outside. You could ride on the ladder that ran up the side to the luggage rack on the roof, or on the steps at the front and back. We loved riding on the steps. We'd hang off the side, one leg on the bus and the other in the air, the scenery whipping past that dangling foot. Bus drivers in Jamaica drive like they're trying to win a rally race; when they took corners, we'd be hanging on for dear life. After hours spent cooped up in a school designed to hold you for a few years until you graduated to some form of low-paying manual labour, riding on the outside of a bus was the most fun part of the day by a mile.

Back in May Pen, I'd get off the bus, go to wherever I was staying and get changed, and then head to the United Bakery, where T.Y. had become the conduit to my "job." The bakery sent out ten to fifteen delivery vans every day of the week to stores all over Clarendon Parish. Each driver would give a list of the inventory he needed for his route to a supervisor, who worked with the conductor to get everything out to the van. The conductor would then load the cube van based on the route, making sure that the items needed early on were easily accessible and that the items needed toward the end of the route were tucked in at the back, just behind the cab.

My job was never official—it was just me hustling. If I hadn't been doing it there, I would've found someplace else. No one at the bakery minded me trying to make myself useful and earn a bit of money, so that's where I went. When I got there after school, I would check in with each of the conductors to see whether they wanted to subcontract the loading of their truck out to me. Some days I'd get a quick, "We don't need you, kid. Get out of here." But usually I'd get at least one taker. I would load a truck for two Jamaican dollars (1.6 Canadian cents today). If a truck needed washing, I'd offer to do that too.

I didn't have to pay for rent or groceries—whoever was putting me up would feed me enough to get by—and so my meagre wages were mine to do with as I pleased. Usually, when Friday came around, I would go to a restaurant and eat my entire week's earnings in a single meal. Not a fancy restaurant, just a hole-in-the-wall that served typical Jamaican fare—curry goat, curry chicken, rice and peas and stuff like that. The music would be turned up loud and I'd be just about the only one eating in the place.

After eating up my week's wages, I would go back to wherever I was staying. And that was how I lived: I went to school, I went to the bakery and I went back to wherever I was staying, which was a new place every week or two until I finally landed a more stable roof over my head.

The new steady arrangement came together as though it was fated. As I'd grown older, people were becoming less willing to put me up. At thirteen, I was still close enough to being a little kid that it was relatively easy to attract sympathy, but when I turned fifteen, I'd finally run out of places, favours and people's patience. One day I told a school buddy who lived with a foster family in May Pen that I didn't know what I was going to do when my latest host told me to move on, and he said he might have a solution. He was about to move out of his foster family's house and offered to put in a good word for me with them.

When I look back on it, the Grahams had no reason to take me in. They had more means than the average family, sure, given that Mr. Graham had a good-paying job. But they had seven kids of their own, Mrs. Graham's sister also lived with them and Mrs. Graham didn't bring in any money, since she needed to stay home to care for the children and the house. They didn't need another mouth to feed. But thanks to the persuasiveness of their eldest son, Dave, they begrudgingly agreed to take me in.

Dave Graham and my buddy from school had been friends since they were younger. When my buddy had needed a place to stay, it was Dave who'd talked his parents into taking him in. Dave ultimately argued on my behalf as well. I can only guess as to why he stuck up for me. It could've been nothing more than another favour to our mutual buddy, but I think for him it was a matter of principle. Dave was only a little older than me, but he had a gravity to his words and actions. He was smart, never without a book in his hand, and he stood up for what he believed to be right. There were times when the family sat down to dinner and Mrs. Graham said, "Listen, we don't have enough food here. Wes is not going to eat tonight." Without the least hesitation, Dave would say, "If he doesn't eat, I'm not eating," and what they had would be shared with me.

Dave secured a roof over my head and did everything he could to ensure I didn't go hungry, but he couldn't protect me from the negative energy my presence provoked. I was a kid who'd appeared out of nowhere, a friend of a friend of Dave's. His parents didn't really want me living there. They were never cruel to me—I am grateful to this day for everything they did for me—but it could be a difficult dynamic to navigate. And it was made much trickier by my mother.

May Pen was the biggest town I'd ever lived in, but it wasn't big enough to disappear into. After she kicked me out, I still ran into my mother regularly. Every time she saw me, she'd stop me and interrogate me for a minute or two about where I was staying and what I was getting up to. In all the time I'd been bouncing around town, struggling to find the next person to take me in, she hadn't shown any interest beyond the bare facts of my situation. But something about me living with the Grahams set her off. She resented them for helping me. Any time she saw Mrs. Graham, my mother would scream and cuss her out, claiming that she and her husband were a corrupting influence on me. Mr. Graham loved horse racing, and he occasionally asked me to walk to the off-track betting site and place his bets for him. My mother saw me there once or twice and flew into a rage. When I explained what I was doing, her anger shifted to the Grahams, and she accused them of trying to turn her son into a gambler. Mrs. Graham would come home from the encounters understandably upset and wonder aloud why they kept me around. Dave would have to step in and soothe her while gently pleading my case.

In short, I had to tread lightly at the Grahams' house and try to do as much as possible to help out and win over the household. I had to make peace with the idea that they could change their minds and ask me to leave at any time—which wasn't particularly difficult given the way I'd been living. I had to accept that people I actually respected didn't want me in their lives, and I couldn't let myself be hurt by that, because a moping, resentful attitude would threaten my relationship with the family and my place in the house.

That was fine, because I genuinely wasn't hurt. To my mind, the situation was similar to the one I'd experienced at my first school, where the kids had made fun of me for being barefoot. The Grahams didn't want me around for reasons I couldn't control: the poverty I'd come from, my lack of a safety net or support structure, my rage-filled, violent mother. Since none of those factors had anything to do with who I was as a person, why be offended? They were a pain for me as well.

My presence in their house demanded much more of the Grahams than it did of me, something I was acutely aware of. They gave me their food, their shelter, their company and a remarkable degree of kindness. How could I be anything but grateful to them? When I left their home a year later, it wasn't because they'd decided they'd had enough of me. It was because my father had sent for me. I was going to foreign.

7

GOING TO FOREIGN

I'd always been told that my father left Jamaica in pursuit of a better life. He had ambitions the country couldn't hold, and he wanted to make enough of himself to support his family and set his kids up for the kind of lives most Jamaicans of that time only glimpsed in movies and magazines.

But there was another part to the story, one I didn't learn about until I was older. Yes, he had been chasing the dream of a big house, a big car and a big spread on the dinner table every night. But he had also been chasing the love of his life, a woman he couldn't bear to lose, whom everyone in Winchester knew as Little Girl.

Her given name was Bernice, and when my father met her, she was living with her parents and sister. They were the ones who had given her the nickname, but it spread quickly around town because everyone saw Little Girl as a shining example of virtue, youth and innocence, a young woman they could all agree had been raised right. Bernice was pursued by many men, but she turned them all down until she met Leonard Hall.

At the time, Bernice's parents had gone ahead to England to prepare the way for the family to move there, leaving her and her sister with their aunt. True to form, my dad soon got her pregnant. Then her parents sent for her and she had to go. It didn't take long after she arrived for her predicament to be discovered, and it's not hard to guess how the situation looked to her parents: *We take our eyes off our sweet, innocent Little Girl for the first time—only for a short while and only to make a better life for her—and some hotshot fast bowler climbs into her bed, knocks her up and then sends her off to England.* Those would not have been Bernice's most comfortable months.

But the feelings she and my dad had for one another were not simple infatuation, and they both knew it. As soon as she left Jamaica, my dad started planning his own departure. A year after I was born, he emigrated to Toronto. Shortly afterward, he brought Little Girl from England to join him, leaving their three-year-old daughter, Marcia, in the care of Little Girl's parents and sister. They married and had four more kids together, finally sending for Marcia when she was ten. And their love did last: they celebrated their fiftieth wedding anniversary in 2021.

Throughout his whirlwind early years in Canada, my dad stayed in touch with my mother so he could keep track of what was happening with me. He sent clothes and money for my care to my grandmother and to my mother. He also advocated for what he believed were my best interests, which is how I'd ended up at my mother's house in May Pen. (On that count, all I can say is he meant well.) When I was living with her, my mother would get me to read his letters to her, and I would print out her responses in block letters as she dictated. From those letters, I got my first real sense of him, and of the concern he had for me. I was his reason for writing. Since it was clear he cared about me, I wanted to speak to him directly, without my mother as a go-between. I copied down his address and, after my mother kicked me out, wrote him a letter of my own.

I didn't say much in that first letter. I just told him that I'd gotten his address from my mother and wanted to say hello for myself. When his answer came, in beautiful, flowing cursive, he included his phone number and told me to call whenever I wanted. I took him up on that and began reaching out regularly.

I'd already been on my own for a while when we began to speak. I knew I could take care of myself and was determined to make my own way in the world, but of course there were times when things got a bit hard. I never wanted to burden Mama when I was struggling, because it was important to me that she believed I was in a good place, and the upshot was I didn't have much contact with her. I think I first called my dad during one of those really hard times. I wasn't aware of my motivation then, but I think I sought him out because I needed to talk about what I was going through with someone who cared. His letters to my mother had shown me that he genuinely wanted to know about my life. After we started communicating back and forth, I felt I could tell him what was actually going on with me. So I did.

Though my situation was obviously extreme, my dad didn't immediately run out to the visa office and go buy me a plane ticket. He'd brought over one of his other kids from Jamaica—my sister Antonella—and it had ended badly. After Antonella arrived, her mother claimed she hadn't known it was a permanent move and took legal action to bring her back. Antonella was a minor at the time and my dad had been forced to send her back to her mom. He'd sworn then that he wouldn't bring any of his other kids to Canada until they turned eighteen.

He couldn't help taking me on as a project, though. I would call him collect from a pay phone, and if he wasn't available, I would sit down and write to him. When I did get him on the phone, he would always comment on the spelling and grammar of my last letter, correcting the mistakes and critiquing my handwriting. "You misspelled this and this and this," he'd say, highlighting several different words. "I wonder whether or not you're going to school, because if you were going to school, you would know how to write things properly."

I *was* going to school, just not a very good one. The more we communicated, the more concerned he became for my education. He was someone who believed deeply in the power of education to create a bridge to a better life. He had not had a chance to go to university himself, but he paid for any of his kids who gained acceptance. He also took pains to educate himself, keeping up on the news and reading widely. I remember him once asking me what I wanted to be when I grew up. "I want to be a mechanical engineer," I told him. I didn't know what a mechanical engineer actually was—I just thought it sounded good—but he took me seriously. "To be that, you have to be very smart," he said, before listing the degrees and qualifications I would need. Then he got on me about my spelling again.

My dad insisted that I write every letter to him in cursive to improve my penmanship. I suppose all his corrections and directions could have seemed like a means of scolding me, but it never felt that way to me. In fact, the corrections made me feel good; they were further proof that he cared, that he saw enough value in me to try to help me be a better person. I took pride in that. I also took his instruction seriously. I still remember how long I would spend on a letter, working to make my chicken-scratch cursive legible. (I should add that I still write like a doctor, so those lessons didn't stick.) I would also look up any words in his letters that I didn't know and try to use them in my own writing.

Looking back now, I think those letters back and forth were an effort to prepare me for life in Canada, without telling me he was preparing me for life in Canada. He saw from my letters that my language was quite simple—this was not a kid who was schooled; this was a kid who was actually kind of ghetto. He was taking steps to ease my transition into the Canadian education system, if I came. He may have also been gauging whether I could take instruction and learn and grow, or whether I was a lost cause.

As I've mentioned, I've always been interested in other people. If I have a chance to engage with someone, and hear their thoughts and their story, I usually take it. It's amazing how many good things my interest in other people has brought into my life. In the case of my dad's family, it felt only natural to try to get to know them as well. He never answered the phone himself, so when I called, it was always my stepmother or one of my siblings who picked up. Instead of immediately asking for my dad, I would chat with them for a while. I was a polite kid, because my grandmother had raised me that way, and that, along with my clear interest and the care and respect I showed in conversation, made an impression on my stepmother. We built a relationship, and she started to say positive things about me to my dad. He heard the same from his sister Edna, with whom he was very close, and who would pay me visits whenever she was back in Jamaica from her home in New York. I'd also taken it upon myself to start writing letters to his other children, and he liked that. He took all of it together as a sign that I would fit nicely into the family if he brought me to Canada, so he decided to break his rule. One day about a year after I'd first reached out to him, he said to me in the middle of one of our usual conversations, "Wes, I'm going to try to get you to come to Canada to live with me. I'm sending all the paperwork to your mother."

It was nice to hear, but I didn't take it seriously. It wasn't so much that I didn't believe him as that I didn't believe something so incredible could happen to me. It felt like I'd dreamed the conversation.

It became real the next time I ran into my mother. "Your dad sent me the paperwork," she told me. "I'm going to Kingston to the immigration office to file them and I need a couple of things from you."

I was sixteen and had lived on my own for three years at that point, but she was still my legal guardian. There was no way for me to get out of Jamaica without her sign-off, but that wasn't the only reason my dad sent all the paperwork to her instead of asking my aunt to handle it or sending it directly to me. He knew my mother was someone who could get things done. She was loud, aggressive and intimidating, and nobody crossed her if they could help it. When she set her mind to a task, people got out of her way.

Hearing from my mother that my dad wanted me to live with him in Canada made it real, but with her involved, I felt like something was going to stop me from going—the most obvious something being my mother herself. That feeling was amplified when she immediately put conditions on giving her consent. She told me I couldn't tell anyone that I was leaving, that I couldn't even hint that there was a possibility I might leave. In particular, she demanded that I not tell Mrs. Graham, whom she hated. If I let word get out, she warned me, "I'm going to burn every single paper, including your passport, and you'll never leave this island."

Now, I'm not sure how she would have found out if I had told anyone—especially Mrs. Graham, who ran the other way whenever she saw my mother coming down the road—but I wasn't willing to take any chances. The possibility of going to Canada gave me something precious to lose for the first time in my life. As much as I expected it to fall through, I knew I would be crushed by disappointment if it did. Like everyone else I knew in Jamaica, I'd seen pictures, heard stories and daydreamed of life abroad. When a friend would say, "You hear so-and-so gone to foreign?" it always sounded like the person who left had won the lottery. "Foreign" was anywhere outside of Jamaica—the United States and the United Kingdom most often, but Canada was on the radar screen too—and it was where we all wanted to be. If you got there, we thought, you'd be set for life.

Going to foreign was regarded as such a transformative event that it would strip you of your Jamaican identity. On the island, people who move away and then come back to visit are called "foreigners." (Those who are born abroad are called "tourists.") Even if you still speak like a Jamaican, traces of a British or American or Canadian accent creep in and everyone hears them. You dress differently, out of touch with the island's style and influenced by the rest of the world's, and people notice that too and treat you differently. When you go into a store, for example, they charge you extra because you're not from Jamaica anymore. It's that big a deal. So, I kept my mouth shut.

Despite the fact that I was following her terms, I still expected my mother to sabotage me. I thought she'd do it out of spite and cruelty alone, just to watch me suffer. But as the weeks passed, my paperwork was filed, my application was approved, arrangements were made and a flight was booked. One of the big regrets of my life was that I didn't let the Grahams know that I would be leaving for Canada because I believed that my mother would carry through on her threat. I only told them on the morning of my flight, when I thanked them for taking me in.

On the ride to the airport, I was still waiting for the trip to fall apart, but my ticket turned out to be real, and I made it through security and onto the plane. When it finally took off, I could breathe easily for the first time in weeks. You couldn't have taken that smile off my face if you had hit me with a shovel.

It was September 27, 1985, and I was going to Canada.

8

THE GREAT WHITE NORTH

I remember nothing about the plane ride, not the peanuts, the drinks, the in-flight movie, the landing, the questions at customs and immigration—nothing. When I think back on my life, I can still pull up the fine details of driving a tire around Golden Grove—the slickness of the crushed breadfruit, its sweet smell mixing with the sharper odour of the rubber—but I can't remember anything about the single most important trip of my life. I don't even know how I got to the airport in Kingston. My memory kicks back in at the moment I walked out of the arrivals area and saw my dad, my stepmother and their five kids waiting for me. It kicks back in as I thought, in utter disbelief, *Wow, I'm actually here.*

Before I left Jamaica, my dad had sent me a View-Master with a cardboard disc that had photos of Canada on it. There were seven views, all nature scenes. You pulled a lever on the side to advance the disc, and there was a satisfying swish and click as it shifted from one photo to the next. All I focused on in the pictures was the snow and cold. To get an idea of the culture shock waiting for me as soon as we left Toronto Pearson International Airport, all you need to know is that my entire image of Canada came from that one cardboard disc.

My dad had never sent me any pictures of his family, so when I arrived at the airport, it was my first time seeing everyone. It was the first time I'd seen *him* apart from the one chance encounter in Golden Grove when I was a kid. In the six months that led up to that moment, I'd corresponded with most of my siblings and spoken to everyone on the phone, so they weren't total strangers, but it's a different thing to meet someone in the flesh for the first time. It felt like the fresh start I'd been dreaming of, like I was beginning a new life.

Getting all eight of us back to my dad's house was only possible for two reasons: First, they'd correctly guessed that I would have almost no luggage. And second, the family car, Betsy, was an older brown Chevrolet that went on for miles and had a trunk as big as all outside. My dad and stepmom sat up front, and all us kids piled into the back, and we set off toward my new home. I remember leaving the airport complex and merging onto the 401, a major, eight-lane highway, and instead of the beautiful snowy scenes of the View-Master slides, I saw more cars than I ever could have imagined on one road. To get to Malvern, the neighbourhood in Scarborough where they lived, we took the highway right across the top of Toronto for about half an hour. I saw that it wasn't just cars that existed here in unbelievable numbers, but also buildings, homes, roads, lights, concrete, people—you name it.

Like an echo of the last time I'd lived with one of my parents, my dad's house was in a subdivision that was only just being built. There were a handful of finished houses on his street, Hupfield Trail, all surrounded by construction. It was a sea of dirt and plywood—mud and plywood when it rained. None of the houses had lawns yet, and there were planks laid down to get you from the driveway to my dad's front door. But I had no frame of reference for what a Canadian house or neighbourhood looked like, so none of that dented my wonder at the place. A big car had come to pick me up like a limousine. A big family had come along with it, everyone looking happy and healthy and clean. A big house was waiting for us at the other end—brand new, with a second storey and four bedrooms and a laundry room. And at the centre of it all was my dad. I was impressed. I thought he was clearly a successful man.

I would realize later that my father *was* very successful, though not in the way I imagined when I first arrived. Barely into his forties when he took me in, he was working himself to the bone in a glue factory to provide for his family. He was out the door every morning before we woke up, and not back until late—he worked overtime to cover the mortgage and to put his kids through college. He had the kind of stamina and work ethic I'd only ever witnessed in my grandmother, and he took his job very seriously. I can still hear the warning he would level at us kids: "If you get into trouble at school, and the principal calls *my* work and interrupts *my* day because of what *you* did, you're going to pay for it when I get home." He would say this with his pointer finger extended, wagging it to emphasize certain words. "*Never, ever* let me get a call that interrupts my work and risks me getting fired."

I remember he once had an accident on the job and half of his face was burned quite badly. He went to the hospital and got patched up and was back at work two days later, with bandages on him like the Phantom of the Opera. In twenty-nine years at that factory, those are the only two days I'm aware he missed.

I shared a room with my brother Michael, who was a little younger than me. Space had been made for my things and I had my own single bed. It felt like everyone in the household had been made to adjust a bit in anticipation of my arrival. That bed seemed to have been sitting there for days, maybe weeks, and all my siblings had been told, "When Wes comes, that's where he's going to sleep." They were prepared, is what I'm saying, but there's a difference between being told someone's coming and having them there in the flesh. I don't think they could've known in advance how my presence was going to make them feel—it was just something they had to experience.

Injecting me into the household changed the dynamic. My youngest sister, the baby of the family, is named Chanel. Why Chanel? Because the famous perfume is No. 5, and she was the fifth born. Their routines and hierarchies were completely established, and then my dad decided to add me. For all my efforts to get to know everyone before I came, I was still a stranger. I was the oddball, too. I'd grown up with very little and knew even less about life in Canada. I'd never heard of my siblings' favourite TV shows, restaurants, stores, toys or clothing brands. Even in my blood I was the exception. They were full brothers and sisters, and I was just their dad's kid from Jamaica who talked funny.

I was used to being the extra wheel. I'd spent a year being a far more extreme version of that when I'd lived with the Grahams.

I hadn't really *fit* in any of the places I'd stayed since I'd left Golden Grove. To their credit, my dad's family treated me very well and worked to include me and make me comfortable. Some of that was certainly due to my dad not giving them much of a choice in the matter. His word was law in that house, so if he told them to treat me like a brother, they did. Thankfully, it wasn't all down to coercion. My stepmother was incredible to me. I never once felt that she treated me differently from my siblings, that she didn't see me as her child. From the moment she hugged me at the airport, I felt the warmth of a mother, and that never changed. And eventually, all my relationships with these siblings got to that level too—the genuine bond of brothers and sisters.

But in the first days after I landed, there was still a lot to be navigated, a lot of adjustments to make—and that was just in the home. The outside world of Canada presented an even more daunting challenge.

I landed in Toronto on a Friday and started school the following Monday. My dad ran a tight ship and expected his kids to approach life with the same kind of discipline he did. He'd registered me at Lester B. Pearson Collegiate Institute—the high school that Marcia already attended, a fifteen-minute walk from our house. There would be no resting and relaxing as I acclimatized to my new life. My father wasn't interested in that kind of idleness.

You have to understand that I was pretty much finishing up with school in Jamaica when my dad asked me to come live with him. I was already working in the bakery and I had intended to graduate and continue on there—that was all I'd really imagined for my future. The thought of coming to Canada had opened up new worlds in my mind, but none of them had necessarily involved staying in school. I wanted to work, earn money and start building an independent life. The first hurdle I faced upon entering the Canadian education system was shaking off that thinking and getting my focus back on my studies.

The second hurdle was my accent. I thought I spoke English when I came to Canada, but the people I tried conversing with quickly showed me that I didn't—at least not a version they could comprehend. They would look at me sideways and, speaking slowly in that loud voice North Americans use on anyone foreign, ask me to repeat myself. In school, if the teacher asked a question and I put up my hand, everyone would start laughing when I answered. One of my classmates would raise their hand right away to ask, "What did he say?" That would prompt even more laughter. Despite me putting on my best English, I had such a heavy accent that no one understood what I was saying. Keep in mind that I grew up in the bush of Jamaica and even other Jamaicans have a hard time understanding people from St. Thomas.

My siblings made fun of me constantly for it, but in a good-natured way that probably brought us closer together. Michael always cracked up at the way I said *photography*, with next to no differentiation of the syllables. He would sing the one-line jingle of the photo chain Black's—"Black's is photography"—pronouncing *photography* like a Jamaican: "phuhtugrrphy." He thought that was just hilarious.

For my part, I didn't understand why they singled out half of the stuff they did. They'd mock me for how I said a certain word, but to me it sounded like we were saying the same thing. I only understood when I started to record myself on Michael's tape deck—no, I wasn't saying words the same way. So, I practised in the mirror, contorting my lips and tongue to generate Canadian pronunciations and recording my progress. I eventually managed to train my Jamaican accent away almost completely, though it still jumps out every now and then.

Meanwhile, I still had to contend with the challenge of making myself understood. At school, they quickly shifted me into some ESL classes, which was a shock—I hadn't imagined that my introduction to the Canadian education system would involve them trying to teach me a language I already spoke. I was soon moved back out of them but into the general level, the simpler of the two academic streams offered by Ontario high schools. I think all of this could have done a number on my self-confidence if I hadn't had faith in my own intelligence and my abilities as a student. I knew I wasn't dumb, and I knew I was willing to put in the work necessary to catch up.

I eventually earned my way into some advanced classes, which was an overwhelming experience because they were so far beyond anything that had been on the curriculum in my all-age school. The idea that Canada let you choose which advanced classes to take was exciting and empowering. In Jamaica, everyone had been taught the same curriculum. I felt like I was declaring that I could be a professor or doctor or lawyer—any of those white-collar professions that had been so out of reach in Jamaica because of my lack of access to a proper education. But at first, I struggled in that higher stream. The territory was so unfamiliar to me. It was designed for kids like my siblings, who had been in the system their whole lives, had been conditioned to exist in that environment and had been building toward those specific lessons. I remember my sister getting exasperated as she tried to help me with my homework, saying, "I can't believe you don't get this stuff." I could only tell her, "I'm trying, but this is a little higher level than I'm used to."

I was motivated to fit in academically, because I didn't want my siblings or classmates to think I wasn't bright or that I didn't belong. So, I responded to the challenge those classes presented by buckling down. I was never an academic superstar, but I didn't need to be one to either fit in or clear the bar my dad set for his four boys. He was always much more concerned with my sisters' academic performance. In his eyes, even if his boys got poor grades, as long as they graduated, they could get decent-paying jobs in the trades or at a factory like he had. But he was determined that his two girls would never have a man call the shots in their lives, and in his view, that meant they had to be educated.

For an old-school Jamaican man of my dad's generation, wanting his daughters to call all their own shots was a remarkably progressive attitude. My stepmom worked outside the house just as hard as him, but when he got home, he expected her to have his dinner on the table and to look after him. He was very traditional in his own household and relationship. And yet he didn't want that for his daughters. If either of my sisters came home with a B grade, they had a problem on their hands. Me, I could come home with my Bs and Cs and the occasional D and get nothing worse than him saying, "That's terrible."

Though he was easier on us boys academically, my dad clamped down on us in other ways. When he came to Canada, he joined a West Indian cricket club in the neighbourhood that competed all over Ontario. This group of Jamaican immigrant fathers would get together and share stories about what was going on with their kids. Malvern was a rough neighbourhood, and many of those other kids would get in trouble, and even end up in jail after getting caught up with drugs and gangs. The stories scared my father. He saw the possibilities for us to cross a line and head down that criminal path everywhere in our lives. Imagining one of us in jail or worse hurt him on two levels: he worried about what it would do to us and he worried about it bringing shame to the Hall name. He would get home from a game and repeat all the stories his friends had told him, wagging his finger at us, saying, "That will *never* happen in this house."

His fear caused him to take what he saw as precautionary measures. He demanded that I get home from school by a certain time every day, worried about what I might get into if I dallied. He told me who I could be friends with and where I could hang out with those friends. Looking back, I see where it all came from and know he meant well, but at the time his demands felt like shackles to me.

When I came to Canada to live with my dad, I knew that there would be rules and expectations I'd have to deal with, but I didn't anticipate him trying to parent me like the rest of his kids. In my view, it was too late for him to step into my life to try to change who I was. He'd left me in Jamaica for sixteen years, and when I moved in with him in Scarborough, we still didn't really know each other. He hadn't been around enough to suddenly start playing the dad card. As good as he'd been to me, he hadn't earned that yet. Also, it was too late for me to be parented by anyone. I wasn't a kid anymore. My childhood ended at eleven, when I moved in with my mother, and a version of adulthood started for me at thirteen, when she kicked me out. He treated me like a kid just like the other five, but I had been through so much more than they had. I had been on my own and calling the shots for three years, right up until the day I got on that plane. My dad hadn't been there telling me when to go to bed, what to eat or who to see, and I'd managed just fine. To have him treat me like the other kids felt like he was trying to erase what I'd been through and what I'd accomplished on my own. It felt like he was trying to turn me back into a kid, like he was forcing me to move backwards when all I could think about was my next steps in the other direction.

It's not like I was going out drinking or smoking weed or hanging around with the wrong crowd. I was a good kid. I hadn't gotten into trouble in Jamaica, and I had no intention of getting into trouble in Canada. The fact that I was behaving and he *still* didn't trust me was an added frustration. I pushed back, trying to persuade him that I didn't need all the rules he was laying on me, but sometimes I just got frustrated and argued with him: "I don't care what's going on with your friends' kids. That's just not me. I'm not going to do those things."

My dad knew only one way to run his household, though. It wasn't in him to set different rules for me than for my siblings, and he certainly wasn't going to stand for backtalk in his own home. On a few occasions when I pushed against the structure he was trying to impose, he administered physical punishment. His licks were not like the ones my mother had given me, if only because he clearly took no pleasure in them and they always had a clear cause and purpose, even if I disagreed with the logic behind both. But they were awful reminders of the absolute worst moments of my life, forcing me to relive the trauma that my mother had inflicted.

The incident that still stands out to me happened when I was a few months shy of my eighteenth birthday. My dad had a weapon that Jamaicans call a "buss mi cock." It's a strip of rubber about a foot long, cut from a car tire, and yes, it really is called a buss mi cock. Essentially, if you think you're a man, the buss mi cock will show you you're mistaken. Feel free to take the time you need to get over the name.

I can't remember what I did to incite him, but I do remember him telling me to go get the buss mi cock. I think that only Jamaican parents send you to fetch the weapon they're going to beat you with. I'm sure I wasn't the first Jamaican kid to wonder to myself, *Why didn't I destroy that thing one day when he was out at work?*

This time, instead of doing as I was told and getting him the weapon, I ran. He was after me, buss mi cock in hand, faster than could be believed, and he started swiping at me with it, connecting on some swings and missing on others. When he missed and hit the house's white walls instead, the buss mi cock left a black mark on the paint. I eventually dodged past him and sprinted for the front door, but it was locked and I couldn't make it out of the house before he caught up to me. I was finished there, and after he was done beating me, he said, "You need to get soap and water and clean the walls."

The humiliation of having to clean up hurt more than the actual blows. It forced me to come face to face with the evidence of my own cowardice scattered all over the house. If I hadn't run, if I'd taken the beating like a man like I was supposed to, those marks wouldn't have been there.

Escaping my mother's house at thirteen was one of the best feelings of my life. Walking down that white gravel road, the smile on my face was as big as the one I'd worn on the plane to Canada. That happiness had a simple root: I was free, and I never had to go back. But when my dad hit me, I *did* have to go back; it turned me into that thirteen-year-old who was so badly abused. I don't think my dad ever understood the impact his physical punishment had on me, because I don't believe he ever fully understood what had happened to me in my mother's house. When he hit me, it turned a difficult situation—struggling to fit in with the structure imposed by school and parents—into an impossible one. It was the straw that broke the camel's back.

While I was a minor, I had to play by the rules and take my licks. I was only able to stay in Canada because my dad had sponsored me. Until I turned eighteen, he could pull that sponsorship at any time and I would be sent back to Jamaica. I felt I had nothing to go back to there, so I played by his rules until the day I turned eighteen. That night I packed my bags and moved out of his house.

I didn't tell my dad or my stepmom that I was leaving, only my siblings, and I asked them to keep it a secret. Marcia later told me how the morning after my departure played out. It was a Sunday and all the kids were already at the breakfast table when my father came downstairs. When he saw everyone but me, he said, "Someone go get Wes for breakfast." Instead of jumping up to follow his order, they all started looking around at one another, waiting for someone to take the lead. My dad picked up on this instantly and asked, "What's going on? Go get him."

"He's not here anymore," someone finally admitted.

"What do you mean he's not here?"

"He moved out last night."

My father took in that information, said, "Okay, let's have breakfast," and sat down at the table. He ate in silence. When he was done, he issued a decree: "None of you are allowed to talk to him again," he said. "Ever. He's a bad influence. He's not going to influence this house anymore. He's not going to ruin this family."

My dad viewed my departure as a betrayal. He had done so much for me, offering me sanctuary and opening a brighter future than I ever could've had in Jamaica, and this was how I repaid him? If I wanted to prove I was a grown, independent man, that was fine; he wasn't going to try to stop me or persuade me to come home. But if I was out, I was all the way out—I would get no support of any kind from him or his family. He saw my leaving as my first step toward bringing shame to the Hall name, and when I slipped—as he believed I would—he wanted nothing to do with the fall.

With hindsight, I learned to appreciate my dad, both for what he did for me and for the example he set with his work ethic and his dedication to family. I would realize the honour there was in waking up early and putting in long hours to make sure the people he loved were cared for, and I would respect the loyalty he showed to the company that employed him. I would also eventually recognize how witnessing his effort and sacrifice helped shaped my life—how his example echoed that of my grandmother.

But in the moment, I wasn't able to see any of that. At eighteen I couldn't grasp how much he had helped me—how he'd started preparing me for school in Canada when he corrected my letters, for example—or what it was like for him to work at the glue factory. That perspective was obscured by my frustration with the rules he set and the ways he enforced them.

When my dad told my siblings to stop talking to me, everyone obeyed except for Marcia. She continued to meet with me in secret, and she was someone I could confide in—a gift I was grateful for. She kept me updated on the family and she worked on me, too, trying to convince me to make things right with our dad by continuing to call him even though he would not speak with me. But apart from that one point of contact, I was completely cut off.

That isolation could have been scary. I was still a newcomer to Canada, and there was so much I didn't know about life here, which became painfully clear to me as soon as I moved out. But I felt no fear or apprehension. I had been on my own before and had figured things out, and that had been when my earning potential maxed out at around two Jamaican dollars a day. In this country, where my dad had arrived with nothing and made so much of himself, I knew I was going to be okay. I just didn't know what okay was going to look like.

9

POLICE, POULTRY AND
PRIVATE SECURITY

It didn't take long for me to regret my decision to move out. I hadn't thought to line up a place to stay, so I had to figure everything out on the fly. But I did already have a job, working as a dishwasher at a place called Hurley's Restaurant, which was next to a Travelodge and connected to the hotel's restaurant. I was familiar with the Travelodge, so I got a room there for the first few nights while I looked for something more permanent. The first place I found was a rooming house run by a Caribbean woman who was even more strict than my dad. "You're not allowed to bring anybody here," she told me when I handed over the money for the first month. "You're not allowed to bring your friends here, and certainly no girls. You're renting a room. That's it. You come in and go upstairs to your room."

I bounced around four or five places like that in the first six or seven months of being on my own in Canada before I finally found a basement apartment with a separate entrance in North York. Despite the meagreness of the accommodations, the rent wasn't cheap. I remember paying something like ten thousand dollars that first year. I'd thrown away a free roof over my head with my meals included so that I wouldn't have to put up with someone telling me what to do, but the effort and the scrimping and saving it took to cover my expenses meant that I wasn't able to do anything but work and go to school anyway. I'd be in the kitchen at Hurley's with cold water up to my ankles and scorching hot water up to my elbows, thinking, *This is my life. This is it. And I didn't have to live this way. I didn't have to worry about paying rent. What's wrong with me?*

Without my father's knowledge, my stepmom had even come to see me at one of my jobs a couple of days after I left to appeal to me to come home, offering to smooth things over with him on my behalf. But that was still early enough in my adventure that reality hadn't yet set in. I thought I would find a nice apartment and be riding high, and so I refused: "No, I'm not going back in that house." She shook her head and said, "Okay, fine, I tried. Don't come crying to me about it later."

She stuck to her guns on that too. Years later, shortly before I got married, I knew I had to save some money for the wedding. My dad and I had reconnected by that point, and I went to him to ask whether I could move home for six months to a year in order to save some money. He was open to the idea, but my stepmom was having none of it. "You remember when I came to get you and you said no?" she asked me. "That was it. No, you can't

come back here for a year to save some money. You're out, man."
I had to kick myself all over again.

I stayed at Hurley's only as long as it took me to find a better opportunity. Whatever I happened to be doing to earn a paycheque—all the way up until I founded my company, Kingsdale Advisors, in 2003—I was always open to other work. In the two years since I'd come to Canada, I'd had a paper route delivering the *Toronto Star*, got a job cleaning offices, worked as a stock boy at a discount department store called Bargain Harolds and finally moved into the kitchen at Hurley's. Each of these jobs had been a step up of some kind, though usually just in terms of the hourly wage.

I was never turned off by a job that other people might think was beneath them. When I had the cleaning job, I was on a two-man crew with my boss. He would leave me in an office with instructions and I'd have the place sparkling by the time he got back, even scrubbing the toilets. He actually came by my dad's house a few times to tell him how impressed he was with me. I got similarly positive feedback from managers and supervisors at the bargain store. But even though I was willing to take on tough jobs, it could be hard to find the next opportunity. I often had to swing and miss once or twice before making solid contact.

In Malvern I'd connected with a few Jamaican guys about my age who'd also come to Canada from May Pen—the world is a small place sometimes. After I'd moved out of my father's house, we were hanging out together one night and I mentioned that I was looking for a job somewhere that paid better than Hurley's.

I had bills piling up. One of the guys, Steve, told me that his mom worked at Maple Lodge Farms, a poultry processing plant, and could probably get me a job there. When I said I was interested, Steve talked to his mom, his mom talked to Maple Lodge HR, and HR told her that they had something for me.

The plant was in Brampton, a suburb west of Toronto. It would have been about a half-hour drive from my basement apartment, but I didn't have a car. So, the plan was for me to catch a bus from North York to Scarborough, where Steve's mom would pick me up. I had to meet her at 6:00 a.m., which meant getting to the bus stop just before 5:30 in the morning. That's where I was waiting when a police cruiser pulled up, and an officer shone a light at me, calling, "You, come over here."

I walked over—what else could I do? When I got near the car, I was able to make him out: a younger guy, white, mid- to late-twenties, clean cut. He wasn't aggressive or even unfriendly when he spoke to me, just matter-of-fact. "I'm looking for someone matching your description," he said. "I've got to search you and ask you a few questions, so get up against the car."

I had tried to become a cop myself a few months after I'd moved out of my dad's place. He had a deep respect for police officers and had wanted to join the force when he was still in Jamaica. I saw the police academy as a potential path back into his good books. The way he tried to parent me may have triggered things I'd hoped to keep buried, but I still loved him and was grateful for everything he'd done for me. I knew he'd worried before he sponsored me that it might be a mistake, that he'd broken his own rule to do it and that he'd had second thoughts at times when he thought I was headed down the wrong path. And

I knew that when I moved out, it was like his greatest fear was coming true. I didn't want him to feel that way about me. I didn't want him to regret bringing me to Canada.

My dad had spent his whole life with the same company and never liked the way I moved from job to job, which may have been why he pushed me to consider the police force. "It's a respectable job," he'd stress to me. "And you'd have a great pension." By the time I started to consider it, I was calling the house every couple of days, asking to speak with him. My stepmom or one of my siblings would come back with the same answer every time: "He says he doesn't want to talk to you, Wes." So, one day, almost on a whim, I said, "I just want you to let him know that I'm applying to become a police officer." They did and that warmed him up.

I started preparing for the academy entrance exam with a high school friend named Danny. We had initially connected because we were both into working out, and together we trained and trained. When the day of the test finally came around, I was so nervous I couldn't eat anything. There was a written component, but the bulk of the exam was heavily physical—you had to run a few miles and do push-ups and so on. I felt faint most of the day and almost puked on more than one occasion. In one test you had to jump up to touch something high above your head. When I attempted it, I couldn't get my feet off the ground. At the end of it all, Danny passed and I failed, though I was told that if I worked on some areas, I'd likely get accepted in the future. I considered that path for a while, but ultimately chose a different one. To this day, I tell people the reason I'm successful in business is because I wasn't good enough to be a police officer.

Still, the effort I'd put in to take the test was enough to start the process of winning my dad back. I was once again allowed to communicate with him and with my siblings and stepmom. I was allowed to visit. I'd shown him that I was more likely to end up putting his friends' kids in jail than getting locked up myself. He also saw that I wanted to do right by him and was willing to work for it, and that I needed him to know he hadn't made a mistake in helping me. He saw that I was a good kid, and that was certainly worth the effort.

At the bus stop, it was unclear what the officer saw when he looked at me. I didn't try to tell him the story of my failed attempt to get into the police academy; I just silently followed his instructions, waiting with my hands on the car for him to get out and come around to where I was standing. I wasn't afraid of him or what he might do. I knew I'd done nothing wrong. I was mostly just confused by what was happening.

As he started searching me, my bus appeared in the distance. He was telling me again that I matched a description, I think, but I barely caught the words because I was thinking, *I can't miss this bus. Steve's mom doesn't play around. She's going to kick my ass if I'm late.* As the bus got closer and closer, my confusion gave way to frustration and, finally, some mix of apprehension and suspicion. When he'd called me over, I hadn't run. Would a wanted criminal have walked right up to his cruiser voluntarily? Would a criminal be waiting to make their getaway on public transit? What was actually going on here?

My bus went past. In that moment, I was more scared of Steve's mom than any policeman. As I watched the bus disappear, I thought, *Oh man, that's not good.* My distress must've shown up clear as day on my face because the officer stopped interrogating me almost immediately. "Listen, you're free to go," he said, "but I see you just missed your bus. I'll take you to the next stop to catch up to it."

Whether he'd been profiling me to that point I don't know. The offer seemed genuine, but I only wanted to get away from him. *You just searched me and interrogated me, and now you want me to get in the back of a patrol car so you can take me somewhere?* "No, I'm good," I answered. "I'll just wait for the next bus. Thank you."

He left, and that's what I did. Steve's mom had waited for me.

It wasn't quite seven in the morning when we pulled up and parked in a massive gravel lot beside a sprawling grey factory building. Steve's mom walked me to the HR office, then left to clock in and start her shift. I filled out the necessary paperwork and they put me in a white gown and white hairnet and led me down to the assembly line. I was the only Black person in the place, and the only teenager. Everyone else, as far as I could tell, was a white European immigrant—all of them men, all of them in their sixties, none of them speaking any English.

I was shown to my spot, and the supervisor pointed along the line. "Okay, you're going to see the chickens coming down the line from over there. The head's up here," he said, gesturing to the opposite side of the conveyor, "and the ass is right here," meaning directly in front of us. He took hold of a tube hanging from a stand to one side of my station. "When a chicken gets to you, you take your vacuum tube, stick it up the ass of the chicken and suck out everything inside. That's it. That's how we do the chickens here."

So, this is what I would be doing eight to ten hours a day with two fifteen-minute breaks and a half-hour for lunch every single day for the rest of my working life. "Questions?" he asked. I shook my head and he walked away. The entire training session took maybe a minute.

After two or three hours on the line, I started to feel queasy. It was the sound that got to me most of all—the wet thud as the vacuum tube went in and the awful sloppy slurp that followed. It was constant and all around me. It was the only thing I could hear. *This is my life?* I thought, fighting back the urge to be sick.

I stopped. I put down the vacuum and called the supervisor over. "I'm sorry. I can't do this," I said. He sent me back to the HR department.

When I got there, I apologized and explained my situation to the woman at the desk. "I'm getting sick," I told her. "This is just not a job I can do." She took this in stride, saying, "Okay, not a problem. We have another job you'd be suited for."

She sent me to a loading dock, where I met my new supervisor. "See those trucks coming in?" he asked. I nodded. "See those cages on the back with the chickens in them?" I nodded again. "Those are live chickens. You're going to reach into the cage and lift them out one at a time. Then you lay them on this conveyor belt with their heads hanging down over the edge here. It holds them in place and carries them down there"—he pointed into the building—"where something's going to cut their heads off." That was my new job: I was a chicken grim reaper. At least I was outside in the fresh air.

I started to get the chickens out and it was like they knew what was going to happen. They fought me. Every time I reached for one, it would scratch my arms and peck my gloves. It hurt, and I had to work fast to keep up with the belt, which meant I got scratched a lot. After a couple of hours of doing that, I called my new supervisor over. "I can't do this job," I said.

I went back to the HR department and broke the news: "I'm sorry, but I can't do that job either."

The woman at the desk said, "Well, I'm sorry too. There's no other job here for someone with your skill set."

It was noon. I sat in the lunchroom until Steve's mom finished her shift at 4:00 p.m. I waited until we were in the car to break the news, and she cursed me for the full thirty-minute ride back to Scarborough: "I worked so hard to get you this job and you couldn't even last a day? How are you so lazy? You young people don't know how to work hard. You think everything's going to be handed to you. I can't believe I let Steven talk me into helping you."

Finally, we arrived and I was able to get out of the car and away from her scolding. But then I had to wait for the bus.

I may not have been cut out for the police force or a chicken processing facility, but I did have some successes in my working life. Shortly after Steve's mom read me the riot act, I was hired as a shipper-receiver at a pharmaceutical company called Upjohn—the makers of Rogaine, among other products. The work was not all that different from loading bread trucks in May Pen. Orders would come in from doctors and pharmacies, and I would fill each one, locating the product, boxing it up and sending it out. I enjoyed my time there and was good at the job, but after a few months I left for a new opportunity with a security company, Burns.

I was hired as a security guard and manned the desk overnight at an office building. I would have to get up from my post and do rounds every hour or two, but mostly the job was me sitting around and trying not to fall completely asleep. Once a night, my supervisor would stop in to talk to me while he did his own rounds, driving from property to property. That lone bit of human interaction during my shift was a welcome thing and I looked forward to chatting with him and getting to know him better. He liked me and thought I showed too much potential to be sitting at a desk struggling to stay awake. Pretty soon he said, "You know what? You should become a supervisor." And he offered to talk to head office on my behalf.

Burns Security was headquartered on Eglinton Avenue in Scarborough. He spoke to the bosses and they okayed him bringing me in for an interview. Amazingly, I was hired as a supervisor. Now my job was to drive around in a company car all night, checking on guards posted at different buildings around the city to make sure they were doing their jobs, and to respond whenever an alarm was triggered in one of the buildings in my sector.

I'm not too proud to admit that I was scared as hell any time I found myself walking into a dark building alone to check on an alarm in the middle of the night. One of the properties I had on my route was a manufacturing plant on Labatt Avenue in Regent Park, at the time a notoriously rough low-income neighbourhood just to the east of Toronto's downtown core. I remember the alarm going off at that building one night and being *sure* I was going to run into a burglar. I was a skinny nineteen-year-old kid going in there at three or four o'clock in the morning with only a flashlight to protect me. A few of the other supervisors, all of whom were older guys who'd been doing the job for a while, had given me some advice when I was first hired: they told me to hold the flashlight, a heavy metal Maglite, up just behind its head, so that I could use the handle as a club if I was attacked. "If you get startled or you see somebody," one of them told me, "all you got to do is whack them over the head." *Really?* I thought. *Is that all?*

When checking an alarm, you couldn't just stick your head inside the door and look around. There were checkpoints in each section of the building and you had to punch in with a key to confirm you'd been there. As I walked through that Regent Park plant, I was expecting to run into somebody around every corner, my hand shaking so badly the flashlight's beam danced in front of me. But there was no one there—it turned out to be a false alarm. In a funny twist of fate, today I own that building with a bunch of partners. No one else in that ownership group can touch me when it comes to the lengths I've gone to to protect our investment.

Dishwashing at Hurley's, my one miserable day at Maple Lodge Farms, packing orders at Upjohn—all those jobs, together, spanned maybe six months of my life. Early on at Burns, though, things felt different. As scary as it could be to follow up on an alarm, I not only had a superior recognize something promising in me and take steps to improve my standing in the company, but I'd also seen those above him actually listen to him and promote me. I liked driving around in the company car at night, moving through the sleeping city with real purpose. I started to settle into the idea that Burns might be a place I could commit to in a way my dad would appreciate.

And then the discrimination started.

It was my boss who came to me first. He told me that the other supervisors had complained that I didn't put gas in the car when I completed my shifts. That didn't add up for me because I filled the tank regularly. Still, I didn't think much of it and didn't bother pushing back. I told him that going forward I would make sure the car was gassed up. And I did, often filling the tank past where it had been when I took the car out. But the complaints didn't stop. In fact, they intensified. In addition to continuing to moan about the gas, other supervisors complained about the order in which I did my rounds, the way I interacted with the guards, even how I wore the company uniform. They basically claimed I was doing every single aspect of my job wrong.

It's only in hindsight that I'm able to see that they complained about me because I'm Black. At the time, I chalked it up to my age. I figured those older guys with families to support didn't like that they were making the same amount of money as a teenage kid. That obliviousness protected me to a certain degree. In not seeing my Blackness as the reason I was being messed with, I was also managing not to see my Blackness as a limiting factor, something that would be used to deny me opportunities. If age was the issue, no problem—I was going to get older whether I liked it or not. But nothing was going to make me any less Black.

Of course, the other supervisors might very well claim that my supposed shortcomings *were* because of my age. They also might argue that I was just plain bad at the job. It would be next to impossible for me to prove otherwise, and that's the point. One of the ways white supremacy protects itself is by building in this kind of deniability. *I never said I didn't like him because he's Black. I don't see colour.*

Other white people enable this kind of barely camouflaged racism by expecting the target of it to prove that racism has occurred. Instead of trusting Black folks to know when we are being discriminated against, they search for other explanations. *Maybe he's just jealous because you're young and make the same money he does.*

But when you're subjected to racist attitudes and expectations your entire life, you develop a keen barometer for them. Black folks—in North America, at least—are never allowed to exist separate from our racial identity; every interaction we have is impacted by the colour of our skin. So, I can tell you for a fact: Black people know when it's about race. I suspect that many white people do too, whether they're willing to admit it or not.

I never found out whether my co-workers at Burns were willing to admit they had a problem with a young Black man wielding authority equal to theirs. But the way they treated me renders an admission unnecessary. In the span of a few weeks, I went from being excited at the possibilities my promotion seemed to have opened up, to seeing only one possibility: I had to find another job. Staying was making me too unhappy. I couldn't be a cop, I couldn't clean or kill chickens, and I could no longer work security. It was time to move on.

1 0

STARTING FROM THE BOTTOM

As I finished up high school and moved out on my own, I had a group of close friends who were all Jamaicans: Roger, Patrick, Steve—whose mother had set up (and regretted) my one-day career at Maple Lodge Farms—and Steve's brother Tony. Roger had grown up in Wales, but the rest of us had lived in May Pen. I'd known the others in Jamaica, but we hadn't really connected until we ended up in Canada. Our families had come at different times but had all settled in Malvern, and we were all roughly the same age. We hung out together. We went out partying together. We could open up to one another, and we were always looking to help each other out. These guys understood better than anyone where I'd come from and what I was up against in this country that was still so new to me.

Over the years I'd gotten Patrick a couple of jobs. When I was an office cleaner and my boss was looking to hire more people,

I brought Patrick in. My boss thought he was getting another me and left Patrick alone to clean an office. He came back to find it nowhere near done—Patrick was taking his own sweet time—and let him go. Then I got Patrick a job at Bargain Harolds, where he spent a lot of time talking to everybody and almost no time actually working. He was fired from there too.

When I was still with Burns Security, I talked to Patrick one day about the trouble I was getting from the other supervisors and how I was looking to leave. He called me a few days later. "Hey, I applied for this job at a law firm downtown," he told me. "They called me today to offer me the job, but I've got something else going on. I'm not going to take it. I gave them your name. They might call you."

Sure enough, later that week there was a message on my machine from the HR manager at a firm called Stikeman Elliott. When I returned her call, she told me they were looking for someone to work in the mailroom. The interview, as I remember it, was basically a single question: "Are you interested?" I told her I was, and she hired me over the phone. "Come in on Monday morning to sign a few things," she instructed.

An eminent corporate law firm with offices around the globe, Stikeman was, and is, one of Toronto's famous "Seven Sisters." When I turned up to its downtown office in 1990, in my Burns Security supervisor's uniform of a white button-up shirt and blue pants, I didn't even know that Bay Street was Toronto's equivalent of New York's Wall Street, let alone anything of the firm's history or place in Canadian business and law. Even without a history lesson, it didn't take me long to get the picture about what I was walking into.

Stikeman Elliott's offices at that time spanned the thirteenth, fourteenth and fifteenth floors of Commerce Court West at 199 Bay Street. I had ridden elevators before, but only in smaller buildings. To go that high? Feeling my ears pop on the way up? Wow.

The doors opened on thirteen and I walked into a big reception area. It was like I'd stumbled into an episode of *L.A. Law*. There was expensive art all over the place, and people in fancy suits were walking around. I was impressed and also excited by the thought of working somewhere that looked and felt so important. Whatever got done here, I wanted to help it along any way I could. I signed the papers and was given a start date.

There was no dress code for my position, but I knew I couldn't turn up to work in *that* office looking like someone who had wandered in off the street. I had to step up my game. So, I went to Goodwill and bought a navy blue suit, a shirt and tie. The jacket was nothing special, but I was proud of the pants, which had an unusually high waist, like something you'd see in a Hollywood movie from the 1940s. It gave me confidence to wear something a little different—that remains true to this day—but when I showed up to the mailroom for the first time, my co-workers, who were all dressed in jeans and T-shirts, didn't know what to make of me. When they got a little more comfortable with me, they started to make fun of my narrow waistline, which seemed particularly trim in pants that cut across the navel instead of sitting above the hips. On that first day, though, it was the decision to wear a suit at all that seemed to baffle them. The first thing I heard after "hello" and "nice to meet you" was, "Dude, what are you wearing? Why are you dressed like that?" They told me that I was going to be mistaken for a lawyer. "Maybe that's not such a bad thing," I said.

I started out as a courier, delivering legal documents to other law firms and to regulatory agencies all over the city's financial core. I did this well enough to be quickly promoted to work inside the mailroom. The job itself was straightforward. We sorted the incoming mail as it arrived, organized anything to be sent out and did the rounds delivering letters and parcels to the lawyers' assistants. I was given a map with everyone's name and office marked on it, and advice as to the most efficient route to take: a loop of the thirteenth floor followed by a loop of the fourteenth, then on to the fifteenth. No problem.

Everyone who worked at Stikeman (outside the mailroom) wore a suit, but I knew they didn't all wield the same authority. I'd never worked in an office environment before, so going in, I had no grasp on the pecking order of the firm and how it operated. Fortunately, Bay Street law firms are big on unmistakable signifiers of power, so Stikeman's basic hierarchy was laid out right there on the map I'd been handed. Each floor had four palatial corner offices. These belonged to the senior partners, each of whom was responsible for a different department—litigation, securities, mergers and acquisitions, private equity and so forth. They were the top dogs, the lawyers who ran the firm. The offices with three windows belonged to junior partners, not as important as the department heads, but still pretty important. If the office had two windows, its occupant was an associate, a lawyer who had yet to be made a partner of any kind. And anyone with a windowless inner office was either a student or a law clerk. Sorted.

But I still didn't know what anyone did. I also didn't know who was friendly and who wasn't; who would have a conversation with the mailroom guy even though they were a lawyer, and who wanted nothing to do with me; who could help me and who might be dangerous—especially if I approached them the wrong way. To me, all of this was crucial information. In any new environment, there are factors that can help you gain advantages and factors that can hurt you, and as far back as I can remember, I've tried to get the lay of new land as quickly and completely as I can, looking for possible help and harm and then acting accordingly.

I usually think of this approach as "street" smarts, but of course it applies from the sidewalk all the way up to the fifteenth floor and beyond. When I was bouncing from house to house in Jamaica, it kept a roof over my head and food in my belly. When I was hanging around United Bakery, it put a bit of money in my pocket. When I left my father's house, it helped me handle the culture shock and the back-breaking cost of rent and it helped me begin making something of myself. When I lived with my mother, it let me avoid a beating now and again.

I built an understanding of my environment both intentionally and by instinct, actively seeking out information while also listening to my gut. People think a gut feeling is an emotional reaction that has no logic to it. It is not. A gut feeling is, *Where have I seen this before? How has this affected me in a negative way?* It's your body telling you to put your antennae up and be careful, to learn the lessons of your personal history.

A lot of people ignore those messages, or quickly push them out of mind. I never do. Trauma taught me to trust my body.

When you're going through something like the abuse my mother inflicted on me, your body naturally defends you. First, it defends you by forming a kind of cocoon around that trauma and putting it way in the back of your mind, which allows you to move past what's been done to you by forgetting it, at least partially. Second, even though it lets you forget, your body remembers how to avoid those bad situations in the future or, when they're unavoidable, how to deal with them. If you don't have that instinct, or don't trust it, you will regularly walk into danger and failure. I think I've made it as far as I have in life because I listen to my gut.

At Stikeman, I also listened to anyone who was willing to talk to me. When I made my rounds, dropping the mail with each lawyer's secretary (as they were still called then), I spoke with every one of them. Soon they all knew me, and I knew them and also a good deal about the lawyers they worked for— their specialties and strengths, and maybe some of their quirks. As my sense of who was who developed, I started to chat with the lawyers as well, the higher up the pecking order, the better. If I saw a senior partner walking down the hall, there was no chance of me ducking my head and letting them pass. I looked them in the eye, said hello and asked how their day was going. I now live in the same neighbourhood as a few of those lawyers, and if we bump into each other while out walking, we still have a little chit-chat.

Corporate law firms have unwritten rules about fraternizing with the staff. As someone who worked in the mailroom, I actually had an easier time engaging a senior partner in conversation than an associate or student. The partners felt secure in their positions and didn't need to worry as much about what others at the firm might think of a friendly conversation with an underling. Students, on the other hand, might not be asked back if they got a reputation for being overly familiar with the staff. And if they did get asked back and brought in as associates, then they *really* had to worry about the way they were perceived while they fought to make partner.

The suit and tie that I wore every workday—which inspired jokes in the mailroom—turned out to be a crucial tool for getting people to give me the time of day. If I'd looked like a scrub, wearing ripped jeans and T-shirts, it would have sent a signal to everyone I greeted on my rounds that I wasn't a guy they should be speaking with. But I was in a suit, and that visual signifier alone comforted them. Never mind that I was pushing a mail cart, in a suit I was someone they could talk to without fear of being penalized for the conversation. It allowed them to drop their guard a bit. That was all the opening I needed.

As I began connecting with students, associates, law clerks, secretaries and partners, some really opened up, telling me about their jobs, their bosses' jobs, the various functions of their departments and the firm as a whole. Their stories were full of acronyms, phrases and references I didn't understand, but afterwards I would look up what an "M&A" was or read the Securities Act. Their anecdotes gave me the access points to better grasp and contextualize what I read, helping me see how business and legal concepts were put into practice. As I gradually got more and more comfortable and confident with the language and concepts they tossed around, I felt a bit like the Michael J. Fox character in *The Secret of My Success*. In the film, Fox's character is working in the mailroom and wearing a suit. One day he sees an empty office and decides to pretend he's an executive, a fantasy that spins out of control when he's genuinely mistaken for one and starts being asked to attend meetings and make important decisions. No, I wasn't getting invited into any boardrooms, but I connected to that character—someone playing at being a lawyer and sort of getting away with it.

Stikeman had an extensive legal library and I befriended Richard Dubé, the head librarian. Richard helped me pick out books to educate myself about the law. He was an amazing resource for me. That was the point at which I set the goal of becoming a lawyer for real, and it was through those friendly conversations that I became aware of a first step I could take in that direction. One of the associates told me about a program at Stikeman that allowed staff to study with the firm covering the cost. I decided to sign up and take the law clerk certification course at Toronto's George Brown College. I figured a move from the mailroom to one of those windowless inner offices would be a pretty good start. From there, I'd tackle law school and then work my way up.

As I was dreaming this dream, enrolling in night school and earning my law clerk's certification, it never occurred to me to pay much attention to the fact that Stikeman had no Black lawyers or clerks, and only a single Black secretary. That wasn't something that set off alarm bells for me back then. I applied for and got a position within the firm that took me out of the mailroom and into the corporate records department, which gave me a front row seat to the role of a law clerk. I got my certification and approached the firm's head law clerk for a position. When

I was told bluntly, "Wes, you'll never become a clerk here," it didn't cross my mind that the colour of my skin might have been a reason. The law clerks at Stikeman at the time were all women, and I assumed they didn't want a man.

Of course, I can never know exactly how much my race factored into that head clerk's decision to stamp out any hopes I had of building a career at Stikeman. Just like I can't know exactly how much of a factor it was in the hostility directed at me by the other supervisors at Burns Security or in most of the other roadblocks and microaggressions I've endured and over-come in my life. But believing that the head law clerk's refusal to even consider me had *nothing* to do with race is more naive than a Black guy in the mailroom thinking he can make part-ner in a firm without a single Black lawyer. In hindsight, this fact is plain as day to me, but back then, and for a good portion of my career, I was mercifully blind to the systemic barriers thrown in my path, because I was raised in a place that didn't have them.

I think of the differences between myself and the siblings I lived with when I was under my dad's roof. Canada is a place of privilege; Jamaica is not, unless you have a lot of money. These kids of my dad's were born into a privileged society and grew up with so many things I didn't even know I was missing because I couldn't have dreamed them up. They went to better schools, ate better food, had better access to every kind of tool a person needs to get ahead in the world and make something of themselves. But hand in hand with all that privilege, they inherited Canadian society's systemic discrimination. The jobs they could and couldn't aspire to, the neighbourhoods they could and couldn't live in, the stores they could and couldn't shop in—they were born into a place defined by these limitations and exclusions, and this discrimination was written into their DNA. Canadian racism is often called "polite racism" (as if such a thing can exist). It is a racism that is largely implied rather than explicitly written out on a sign over a drinking fountain or with a burning cross. It relies on the fact that people raised in the Canadian system will get the message—and they do. Had my siblings been told they had no future at Stikeman, they would have known why, and what's more, they would have believed that it wasn't just the one firm that didn't want them, but all the firms like it. Their instinct would have been to double back and choose a different path, one that was "allowed."

I had only been in Canada for five years, though. I hadn't gotten the message and I didn't understand that there were limitations written on my skin. I was born in a place where I saw Black police officers, Black doctors, Black lawyers and Black judges. The school principals and teachers who guided me as a child were Black. Many of the politicians who determined the policies that governed our lives were Black. So, to me, any job, any future, was fair game, and being Black had nothing to do with what *else* a person could be.

Growing up with so little had also left me with very few expectations. People raised in privilege feel a certain pressure to not only maintain their privilege but increase it. The necessities often aren't enough; they want success, not just survival. In some cases, the pursuit of success drives them into uncomfortable or unsuitable situations, and when those situations blow up or bottom out, they take it as a devastating setback. To me, failure and rejection were never reasons to feel overly disappointed or discouraged. First, because I always knew I could survive a hit. Even if I lose everything tomorrow, I've already survived worse. Second, because I don't belong here anyway, I know I'm playing with house money. Almost everyone I've worked with, for or against at every stage of my career was born with means, connections or family circumstances that gave them a massive head start on me. I never should have been able to close the distance and catch up. As a result, when I pursue an opportunity only to have it fall through, it doesn't bother me. I was never even supposed to get this far, and that's been true from the moment my feet touched Canadian soil.

With a clerk's job at Stikeman off the table, I sent my resumé to every other law firm in Toronto's financial district. Eventually, I got a call from someone at Cassels Brock & Blackwell, another blue-blood Bay Street institution, which had been in practice for more than a century. Cassels wasn't looking for a law clerk, I was told, but they had a client that was: CanWest Global Communications Corporation. Did I want them to pass along my resumé? "Absolutely," I said. I hung up and put the call out of my mind. The places I'd applied to directly hadn't shown any interest in bringing me on, so as far as I could see, there wasn't much reason to expect more from CanWest.

I always liked to work a bit late so I could spend time in the library, pick the brains of the law clerks and lawyers or ask them for some extra work to do during my spare time to gain experience. One night I was heading home around five thirty, and as I passed the receptionist, she called after me, "Wes, there's someone on the line for you." I walked back and took the phone. A woman's voice said, "Hi, Wes, I'm calling from CanWest Global. We'd like you to come in for an interview to be a law clerk."

Now, at that point my qualification for such a job was a certification course and nothing else. I'd learned the theory behind a law clerk's role, but I had no real-world experience. I'd felt like I was running my head into a wall as I searched for such jobs, but I couldn't even blame the wall. I wouldn't have hired me either. On the phone, I managed to hide my shock, exchange a few pleasantries with the woman and schedule a time to come in for an interview. The next day, I started picking the brain of every law clerk I crossed paths with—even more than I'd already been doing, given that now it felt like my whole future depended on it. I started simple: "What do you do?" When I got an answer, I worked to understand it in as much detail as I could: "How do you execute an incorporation?" "How do you do a minute book review?" It was like putting in time in a flight simulator before actually leaving the ground.

The day of the interview, I was so eager I got there early. I was sitting in the reception area in my suit and tie when a woman, who I'd later learn was the general counsel's assistant, came down the stairs, walked by the reception desk, continued on past me and stopped beside a white guy wearing jeans and a T-shirt. "Wes?" she asked.

CanWest is a media company and the dress code is more relaxed than anything you'd find at a corporate law firm, but this was still a job interview for a position in the company's legal department. If I'd been conditioned by my upbringing to expect systemic discrimination, to expect that woman to walk by me, the candidate she was looking for, sitting there in my suit and tie with my big briefcase, I would have easily picked up on the message: *This is not a job for a Black guy, no matter how nicely dressed.* Added to the typical jitters I was feeling, it would have sapped any shred of confidence I had and basically killed my chances at making a favourable impression. But at the time, I was blind to the implications. "No, this is me over here," I said, smiling.

"Oh, sorry," she said. "We're ready for you now."

On my way up, I passed a law clerk I knew from Stikeman, who had many years' experience in the field, coming out of her interview for the same job. Here was someone who actually was a law clerk at Stikeman, one of the people whose brains I'd picked. *No chance I'm getting this job,* I thought. It could have been a discouraging idea, but instead it was liberating. I thought, *Well, what do I have to lose? Nothing.* There are two ways to respond when you are up against tremendous odds: fold and give in, or muster up so much fire under your tail that you catch the competition off guard.

The interview was with CanWest's HR manager and the company's general counsel, Glenn O'Farrell. Glenn was in his mid-thirties at the time. He had a strong, square jaw, dark, expressive eyebrows, a touch of a Québécois accent, and hair that would make a bald man weep, with not a single strand of grey. After we said our hellos, he started to ask me questions and he was sharp—one of those people who instantly strikes you as the smartest guy in the room. They were technical questions about how a law clerk should handle specific situations, the same kind of questions I'd been asking the clerks at Stikeman. I started to drop the ideas I'd picked up in those hallway conversations.

I'd never actually done the things I was describing, but I surprised myself by how firmly I'd managed to grasp them. As I spoke, I kind of persuaded myself that I knew what I was talking about and became more comfortable and confident. By the end of the interview, I still knew I was an underqualified long shot, but I felt good. I couldn't have asked myself for more, and that was enough on its own.

As I walked out of the building, I found the Stikeman clerk waiting for me. "Wes, this is a *big* job," she said. "They better be paying big money for this."

"I don't care about the money," I told her. "I just want to get it."

Two weeks after that first interview, I got a call from the general counsel's assistant—the same woman who'd walked past me in the CanWest reception area. "Mr. O'Farrell would like to take you out for drinks," she said, and gave me a day and a time and the name of a nice restaurant.

I didn't know what it was like to "go out for drinks." I had never been out for drinks with anyone before. It was clearly another job interview, but I didn't know people did job interviews over drinks. I didn't even drink.

I met Glenn at the restaurant. I can't remember what he ordered, beer or wine or a cocktail, but I knew I had to fit in, so I asked for the same. From the first sip, I didn't enjoy it, but I knew I had to look like I did, so I sat there grinning and bearing it, pretending it was tasting as good to me as it was to him. We made polite small talk over that first drink and then, at the end of it, he said, "Tell me about your background."

Okay, so I told him about my background—that I was raised by my grandmother in Jamaica; that I have umpteen siblings on both my mother's and father's sides; that I came here to Canada to live with my dad but we didn't get along, so I struck out on my own; that I'd worked every crappy job you can imagine; that I got into the mailroom at Stikeman and went back to school, and now I was here.

I didn't know that you aren't supposed to be so candid in a job interview. I didn't know that people usually make careful omissions to avoid giving the "wrong" impression. Glenn O'Farrell, general counsel at CanWest Global, asked me a question and I told the truth, and fortunately, Glenn was impressed. He appreciated my honesty and saw the value in my lived experience, and he told me as much. At the end of my first time out for drinks, he offered me a job as his law clerk and assistant corporate secretary for $36,000 a year.

The Stikeman clerk had told me it was "at least" a $50,000 per year job, but I'd meant it when I told her the money didn't matter to me. I said the same to Glenn. "I don't care what you pay me," I told him. "I just want experience, and I want to prove to you that I can do this job. Once I prove my value to you, I'm sure you'll pay me more."

CanWest sent a written offer the next day. I signed it as soon as I got it and sent it back. Boom, I was a law clerk. But not only a law clerk. As Glenn later put it, I became the best law clerk the firm had ever seen. When I broke the news to my competitor at Stikeman, she asked, "How did you pull that off?"

11

LEAP OF FAITH

My grandmother was a God-fearing woman, someone who believed that each of us on this earth has a higher calling, a higher obligation. The whole time I lived with her, she spoke about her faith openly—she was never shy or quiet about it. She prayed for my grandfather while he was alive and just as often after he passed. She prayed over the major events of her life, asking for support, guidance and strength. And she prayed for us kids—with us and in front of us. Her faith was fundamental to who she was as a person, and in taking her as my model in life, I knew that faith would have the same central importance to me one day. During the same period of growth that saw me take the first major strides in my professional life—working at Stikeman, training to be a law clerk and landing the job at CanWest— I finally felt the need to make that commitment.

Church was a special occasion in Golden Grove, and the only time I'd see my grandmother in anything other than work clothes. She'd wear her Sunday best, which consisted of a white dress and white head wrap, items she kept so clean that she glowed when she put them on. We kids would get dressed up too. Early in the morning, we'd run down to the river and bathe, and then come back and sit in my grandmother's room while she fetched our church clothes out of the cardboard barrel in which she kept them safely stored away. My nice church clothes were sent by my dad. The shoes, in particular, stick in my mind, along with the process we had to undertake to get them. My grandmother would trace the outline of my foot in pencil on a piece of cardboard and mail that off to my dad. Using the footprint as a guide, he'd determine the size to buy, taking into account how much I might grow in the time between taking the measurement and receiving the package from him. When a pair no longer fit, she would hand them down to another of the boys in her care, none of whom had fathers who sent them anything. Whenever I had a new outfit, my grandmother would take a picture before we left for church. She sent the photos back to my dad to let him know that the shirt or shoes were being put to good use.

Just the act of putting on the clothes, feeling the stiffness of the shirt collar at my neck and admiring the shine of the beautiful black shoes catching the sun as I walked, was enough to make church special. My everyday life at that point was raggedy clothes and bare feet. I went to school barefoot. I went to the market barefoot. I worked on the plantation barefoot. That I turned up to God's house in shoes set Sundays apart.

The service did that work too. Even as you approached the door of the simple wooden church we attended, you could feel that it was just rocking inside. There was lots of singing, lots of clapping, lots of "Amen!" and "Hallelujah!"—lots of people getting into spirits, as they called it, jumping around and losing control of their bodies as some seemingly spiritual force took hold. It was a fun environment, and a warm one. As a kid, I found the spectacle of it all quite amusing. Everyone was Sister or Brother Such and Such, and my grandmother was looked up to, respected as an elder in the community and as a godly woman. I wasn't the only one who looked to her as a role model.

All the bells and whistles set Sundays apart, but what left a truly lasting impression on me was my grandmother's conviction. She had a look that would come over her face when she got truly serious about something. If you were horsing around, not paying her proper mind, and you caught sight of that look, you would either have to run or drop to your knees and beg for forgiveness. It was the face she put on when she was done dealing with the foolishness of the world, and especially us kids. It told us she had better things to do than deal with a bunch of kids who were goofing around. On Sundays, that look told me that she was answering a higher calling, that she was engaged in something more important than any of the other work she did through the week. Of course, she sang and clapped and danced too. She was joyous. But how much it all meant to her was always plain. Even her joy was purposeful. She was celebrating the Lord.

Her example taught me the importance of family, self-sacrifice, hard work, friendship, humility, entrepreneurship, determination, ingenuity and so much more. But above everything else, she taught me the importance of faith.

When I first went to live with my mother in May Pen, she took me to the Church of the Open Bible on occasion, but she stopped going after she caught the spirit there. I remember her falling to the floor and totally losing control of herself, wriggling like a fish. That stuck with me, both because it was such an alarming sight and because it threw into doubt my understanding of that element of Jamaican churchgoing. I'd always understood catching the spirit to be a sign of God's favour. God put His hand on you, and His touch was a blessing so overwhelming that you lost all control. But I knew my mother, and it made no sense to me that God would approve of anything she did. My stepsiblings and I discussed it afterwards and decided that she had to have faked it. But that theory fell apart when we saw how it affected her. She seemed embarrassed, clearly hating that she'd been so vulnerable. She felt strongly enough about it that we never went back.

As a child I already had a sense of faith and a tendency to think beyond myself and my day-to-day concerns—to ponder the higher obligations that meant so much to my grandmother. My stepsister, Hillary, and I had a running conversation about heaven and hell while we were both living under my mother's roof. We'd been taught that if a person was bad, they went to hell. I had a clear and terrifying image of a place where you burned in agony forever, but what it meant to be bad—and specifically, bad enough to go to hell—wasn't as easy to grasp. We knew that my mother and stepfather definitely couldn't be on the heaven side of the ledger, but we wondered whether the beatings we got meant that we were bad too. We ultimately decided that we had to do good in the world; we hadn't yet earned our final judgment and had to turn things around.

I didn't go to church regularly during the years that I lived on my own in Jamaica, but in Canada I was given the opportunity again and took it. I'd been living with my dad for a week or two when he told me that I had to go with the family to the Kingdom Hall. The name was familiar, but it took me a minute to connect the dots and realize that if we were attending a Kingdom Hall instead of church, my dad, stepmom and siblings were Jehovah's Witnesses.

I'd had no direct exposure to the faith at that point in my life, but in Jamaica we had a nickname for Jehovah's Witnesses: we called them Jehovah's Wickedness. There was a powerful stigma against them. No one actually thought they were evil or ill-intentioned, as the nickname implied, just that they were strict and didn't know how to have fun. Everyone knew Jehovah's Witnesses didn't celebrate Christmas or birthdays, and we suspected that they followed all kinds of other stringent rules as well. We knew that the Kingdom Hall didn't have the music and yelling and catching spirits found in other churches across the island. It wasn't the place most people wanted to spend their Sundays. And it certainly wasn't a place of amusement as far as a kid was concerned.

Even in the short time I lived with them, I could tell the members of my dad's family weren't severe or joyless people. That caused me to question what I thought I knew about Jehovah's Witnesses, or at least to start to recognize how little I knew about them. But I still carried an ingrained negative perception of the faith when I went to the Kingdom Hall for the first time. I was sixteen years old, a tough age for most institutions to make an impact on, especially an institution I was predisposed to dislike, but almost as soon as the service began, I thought to myself, *This is pretty cool.*

It was an inspiring and intriguing place. True, it wasn't exciting in the way my grandmother's church could be—there was no band, no choir, no yelling "Amen" and "Hallelujah" and definitely no catching spirits—but it was far more engaging. I found it engrossing in a way that didn't require all that fanfare.

I'd had a reverence for the Bible instilled in me from a very young age, but I'd never really *used* the book in church. The Sunday sermons I'd heard to that point involved plenty of instruction from pastors on what to think and how to act, but I'd never once been urged to read a Bible passage and think for myself, or to get up in front of the congregation and share any of my own understanding of Jesus Christ's teachings. When my first Kingdom Hall service began with a man stepping up to the lectern and clearing his throat to speak, I assumed that he was the pastor and I was in for more of the same kind of preaching, only without the hymns. I was wrong. The man was a congregant. He'd been assigned a subject to study and then share his thoughts on, and he was expected to present for forty-five minutes. That caught my attention, but what really pulled me in was the subject of his talk: hellfire.

I didn't think of myself as a bad person, but I'd been taught my whole life that if you don't do exactly what the Bible says, you

will burn for eternity. There are a lot of rules in the Bible. I figured I'd slip up and miss one and that would be it, I'd be cast into
the flames without even really understanding why I was burning.
As a result, I'd been petrified of going to hell even before Hillary
and I began trying to make sense of good and evil. But when the
man at the Kingdom Hall began his talk, he explained that there
is no such thing as hellfire and that bad people do not go to hell.
Hold on a second there, I thought, leaning forward in my chair.
*You're telling me that the thing I'm terrified of, that I'd hear about
every time I set foot inside a church, is just a misinterpretation?* Then
he started to walk us through his argument.

We all opened our Bibles, and he directed us to read certain
passages of the scripture and to think about what they meant. It
was revelatory to me to be actively involved in the sermon. I wasn't
just sitting there passively listening to someone tell me whatever
they wanted to tell me. Instead, there was this urging: *Look at it
yourself.* And all around me, everybody was engaged in this process
of discovery. My brothers were looking the passages up; my sisters
were looking them up; my stepmother was looking them up; the
stranger in the seat in front of me was looking them up. You could
hear the thin pages of Bibles constantly turning throughout the
man's talk like wind blowing through leaves as everyone acted on
the invitation: *Don't take my word for it. Look at the Word itself.* It
was physical and mental gymnastics.

I connected with what was said just on its own, but this open
pursuit of truth is what drew me to the Jehovah's Witnesses. As
I learned more about the guidelines the faith offered—the "rules"
that had sparked so much derision in Jamaica—they seemed
pretty reasonable to me. But I was still a sixteen-year-old kid,

and I wasn't yet ready to dedicate my life to a faith, any faith. I attended the Kingdom Hall with my family every week while I was under my dad's roof, but after I moved out and no one was telling me I had to go anymore, I stopped. There were other things I wanted to spend my time doing.

When I first left my dad's house, my older sister Marcia would regularly encourage me to do two things: make amends with my father and go to the Kingdom Hall. After giving me the family updates and asking what was up with my work and dating life, she always took some time to stress the importance of fixing what had gone wrong with my father and re-engaging with my faith. She wasn't pushy; she just spoke her heart, telling me what she genuinely believed was best for me. I knew she was right, on both counts. Where my dad was concerned, I immediately started scheming with her as to how I could get back in his good graces. But the truth of my feelings about dedicating my life to Jehovah was buried deeper. When Marcia would invite me to go with her on a Sunday, insisting, "Wes, you need to go to the Kingdom Hall," I would tell her, "Yeah, one of these days. One of these days." It might've sounded to Marcia like the type of meaningless promise you make to get someone off your back, and that may have even been what I thought I was doing—just trying to change the subject—but deep down I meant what I said.

Because of my grandmother's influence, I knew that religion was going to be a part of my life, but when I was young, I think I wanted to cheat that effort a bit. I didn't want to put in the work true faith demands. I never imagined that it would be the Jehovah's Witness faith that would end up speaking to me. It was a denomination that didn't let you coast. You couldn't just say you were a believer and turn up every other Sunday. The gift of God's Word had to be met with a genuine effort to understand it and apply it in your life. I think that commitment scared me.

At the same time, though, what I'd been taught at the Kingdom Hall resonated. I was persuaded by the teachings that the Witnesses presented, and that continued to be the case. When they knocked on my door, I invited them into my tiny apartment to talk and study the Bible, and I read the issues of *The Watchtower* and *Awake!* magazines that they handed me as they left. I just wasn't yet ready to jump in with both feet.

While I was working in the mailroom, though, I got to the point that I wanted to dip a toe. I wasn't ever a smoker or a drinker, but in the time I'd lived on my own, I'd started to do things that I knew weren't cool: I swore a lot; I lived with my girlfriend, one of the receptionists at Stikeman, despite the fact that we weren't married; and I went out to the clubs every weekend, coming home at three in the morning. I'm not sure what exactly sparked my change in attitude, but one weekend when Marcia called as I was getting ready to go out, she asked, "Are you going to the nightclub?" and I said no.

"Where's your girlfriend?"

"She's gone to the club."

Marcia called again the following week and we had the same exchange. After a few weeks of me staying in while my girlfriend went out, Marcia came right out and asked me why I'd stopping going to the clubs. I told her I just wasn't into that stuff anymore.

"Right," she said. "Then you better come to the Kingdom Hall with me tomorrow."

But it wasn't until after the Stikeman office Christmas party a few weeks later that I agreed to go. I'd gone to the party even though doing so went against what I felt in my heart. I tried to skate by on the technicality that I wasn't yet a baptized Witness, so I wasn't breaking any rules by heading to a Christmas celebration, but I woke up the next morning knowing I hadn't convinced myself. When I next spoke to my sister, I told her I was ready to go. But I warned her that all I was going to do was tag along to check out the congregation she was attending in Markham.

The drive from where I was living in downtown Toronto took about an hour. As we walked in, people at the door warmly greeted us, instantly setting me at ease. Then my sister took me around to meet all her friends. As she introduced me, she explained that I was coming to a meeting for the first time in a long time. Everyone I met was welcoming. I felt like I was a part of the congregation from the moment I walked in, and when the meeting began, I thought, *Oh, I get it now. I'm ready to do this.* I decided that day to commit to the faith, 110 percent.

That meant making some changes in my life. I stopped swearing overnight. I was surprised at how quickly my friends and the guys I worked with in the mailroom noticed and started asking me to bring "the old Wes" back. But those conversations were nothing compared to the one I had to have with my girlfriend. She and I had spoken about the faith earlier in our relationship. I'd told her that I planned to return to it at some point, and she'd said she was interested in joining me when that day arrived. So, when it did, I told her I was ready.

"What do you mean you're ready?"

"I'm ready *now*," I said. "I went to the Kingdom Hall today. I want to go back every week."

She said, "I'm not ready yet."

I said, "Well, the problem is that we're living together and we're not married. I'm going to start studying to become a Jehovah's Witness, so I can't live with you while we're not married."

"What?"

"Yeah, I can't live with you. Either you've got to move out or I've got to move out, but we can't live together now that I'm serious about this."

It wasn't that I didn't care for her, but she was still busy with partying and having fun, and she wasn't someone I could see spending the rest of my life with unless she wanted to change along with me. When she made it clear that she was not ready to settle down, the decision for me was easy. In the end, she was the one who moved out. Things got a little complicated at work for a time, but she was very independent-minded and eventually she moved on from her job too.

Everyone who is new to the Jehovah's Witness faith is given the opportunity to study scriptures with a baptized Witness. I was paired with a member of my sister's congregation, but it didn't take me long to discover that he wasn't as serious about my studies as I was. We had a regularly scheduled meeting time at his house after Sunday service, but he started to cancel on me here and there. He told me he was busy, and I understood, but I was eager to move ahead with my studies and wanted to work with someone who could match my drive and intensity. I went back to my sister and said, "Listen, I think I need to be working with someone who is more engaged and more interested in teaching me." She talked to one of the elders about my situation, and he agreed to study with me. He was deeply dedicated. He held me to the exacting standards I was seeking and never missed a session. He also taught me more about the workings of the organization. I realized that Jehovah's Witnesses are encouraged to join a congregation close to where they live, rather than commute almost an hour each way to attend Kingdom Hall like I was doing.

Closest to my apartment was the Gerard Congregation, on the east side of downtown Toronto. I told my sister that it was time for me to make the switch, given that I wanted to continue my journey in the right way. The following Sunday, I walked into the Gerard Kingdom Hall, identified one of the elders and introduced myself. "I'd like to study with somebody," I told him.

It's unusual for someone to do that. If a person outside the faith knows only one thing about Jehovah's Witnesses, it tends to be that we're the ones who knock on people's doors and offer to help them study the Bible. I've spent most Saturdays for the past three decades of my life doing exactly that, and most people I've spoken to have declined the opportunity, sometimes politely, sometimes with aggressive intolerance. Very rarely does a stranger walk into a meeting and ask for guidance.

The gentleman I approached was Andy Zoutman. After he'd given me a chance to explain a little about myself and my experience with the faith, he told me he was a little too busy to study with me himself but would introduce me to someone who could. That person turned out to be his brother-in-law Ed McCarthy, another elder in the congregation. I began my studies in earnest the following week.

There's a process to becoming a baptized Jehovah's Witness. It's a bit of a stretch to make this comparison, but imagine something like the study prep ahead of major exams like the SATs or LSATs. Such study is preparatory work that establishes the foundation of knowledge you need to enter the faith. It's also a minor test of your conviction, a bar that requires enough effort to clear that it winnows out anyone who isn't serious. I worked with Ed and his wife, Andy's sister Judith, and joined the book study group they were part of, which met weekly at Andy's house. That study group would ultimately play a key role in two of the most significant moments of my life: my baptism as a Jehovah's Witness in July 1991, and my marriage the following summer.

Andy Zoutman came from a family of devout Jehovah's Witnesses. He and his seven brothers and sisters were born and raised in the faith in Walkerton, Ontario, a town of less than ten thousand people two and a half hours northwest of Toronto. When the Zoutman siblings came of age, they moved to the big city. Andy, the oldest, was the first to leave home. As each of his brothers and sisters followed, they tended to spend some time living with Andy and his wife, Susan, as they got their feet under them. When I joined the book group in the early months of 1991, the sibling who was staying with Andy and his wife was his eighteen-year-old sister, Christine. She had recently moved down from Walkerton, got a job and joined the Gerard Congregation. For obvious reasons, she was assigned to Andy's book study group.

In the meetings, Christine remained quiet. At first, I took that to mean she was timid or nervous, maybe overwhelmed by the thought of speaking in front of a group or by her new life in the city, or both. Eventually, though, we started talking—just friendly conversation—and I realized that Christine was someone who didn't need to fill the air to feel like she belonged. At eighteen she was already confident in who she was and what she wanted from life. Her silence was a sign of strength—she felt no need to prove herself to anyone, only to God.

I was impressed by that maturity. The way she carried herself reminded me, in some ways, of my grandmother. But Christine was also a beautiful young woman, with long blond hair and an athletic build, and had been a top competitor in track and field in high school. After we'd gotten to know each other a bit, I asked her out. She said no. She was not interested in a relationship. If you have read this far, you know that I am not deterred by a challenge.

Christine was very particular about her faith—she still is. At the time, she was what's called a Pioneer, someone of uncommon commitment, who spends ninety hours each month going door-to-door to talk to people about the Bible. Pioneers only work secular jobs part-time, making professional and material sacrifices in order to better serve God. I was a new guy in the faith who worked full-time and had lofty professional aspirations, even though I was still a records clerk at Stikeman. Christine was a legal secretary who made more part-time than I made working full-time. She looked at me and said in effect but with kindness, "I don't want a guy like you, because you're not as serious about your faith as I am about mine. I want someone who fully shares my values."

That was okay with me. I could understand why someone would doubt my ability—anyone's ability—to balance a career and a deep commitment to God. I hadn't yet proven that I could do that or that I was in it for the long haul. To me, that just meant I had to show her what was in my heart. When I asked her out a second time, she turned me down again. So, the third time, instead of asking her out, I asked if she would let me go with her to knock on doors, as we call it in the faith, "the door-to-door work."

You may have wondered why Jehovah's Witnesses always appear on your doorstep in pairs. There are two reasons: The first is safety, plain and simple. The second is to deliver our message more effectively; we can step up or step back depending on whose words and energy are having the greater impact. Working with Christine would give me a chance to show her my passion for the faith by the way I presented it to other people. It would also give us a chance to feel out how well we clicked. Telling her why she should give me a shot wasn't going to work; I had to show her. Fortunately, she agreed.

We put in a full afternoon together, going door-to-door and talking about the faith with whoever was willing to hear us out. We found our rhythm quickly, and it turned out that our person-alities meshed quite well. I was very outgoing, a life-of-the-party type, and that helped with the initial greeting and setting the person at ease. Christine brought a calm, measured confidence. Her words had a weight that resonated with people if they were open to them, because she clearly cared.

The person I'd met and started to get to know at book study behaved in the same manner beside me on every walkway and doorstep, in every sitting room and at each kitchen table. She didn't change to suit her surroundings, to deliver what people expected of her or in reaction to how they treated her. She was firm in herself. I admired that, and it felt right to me to be working alongside her.

When we were finished for the day, I said, "Why don't I take you out to dinner to say thank you for the time we spent together?"

She said, "Sure, fine."

I could work with that.

We went to an Olive Garden restaurant near the waterfront. Over dinner we loosened up with each other, talking and laughing about some of the standout moments of the day. After the cheque came, I said, "Why don't we take a walk on the boardwalk? It's just down the street."

Again, she said, "Sure, fine."

And I could work with that.

So, we strolled along the boardwalk, talking and looking out at Lake Ontario. Next thing I knew, my hand bumped against hers and she didn't pull away. That bump soon turned into a clasp. We started dating that night. When her parents found out, they were concerned that I might pull her away from the faith. Just as Christine had at first, they doubted whether I was as serious as she was and wondered if I'd only joined the congregation in order to find a wife. Under the pressure of their scrutiny, we broke up, but only a month later we were drawn back together. As we got to know each other more deeply, I realized that Christine was someone I could see spending my life with. She anchored me in ways I needed to be anchored. Her parents were right about a couple of things: I wasn't Christine's type in any way and I wasn't particularly strong in the faith because I was new to it. Christine herself said I was conceited, and I was a little. Well, maybe a lot—remember what I said about a young Black man trying to prove the world wrong? But that walk and the time we spent together in the door-to-door work showed her a whole new way of looking at me. Walks can do that. I knew that together we had a foundation on which to build something truly beautiful. We were engaged six months after that walk on the boardwalk and were married six months after that. She was nineteen and I was twenty-two.

We have been together more than thirty years now. We have five children. Always trust your gut.

Before I finally agreed to go with my sister to that first Sunday meeting in Markham, I remember telling Marcia that I wasn't ready to get baptized as a Jehovah's Witness. I needed to get the major fundamentals taken care of first, the things I felt I needed from the world: I wanted to own a house and a nice car. I wanted a good job with a promising future. And I wanted to be married. That was what I thought I needed.

When I did become a baptized Jehovah's Witness, all I had was a car—and it was only an okay car. I was still working in the mailroom, still living in a small, rented apartment, and still single (though I guess I was working on that last part). Success and real fulfillment, both personally and professionally, all came after my faith began shaping my life—in how I studied and prepared, how I conducted myself in my work, what kind of work I wanted to pursue, what I valued in a romantic partner, everything. The biggest factor in these changes was, of course, the joy of reconnecting with Jehovah and the deep peace of mind, the comfort and steadiness, that came from living my beliefs. But there were also tools that the faith equipped me with that, though intended for higher purposes, proved useful as I worked to achieve my goals.

One of the central aspects of being a practising Jehovah's Witness is attending what is now called the Life and Ministry School (formerly the Theocratic Ministry School). The essence of the faith is that everyone is a student and learning never ends. The Life and Ministry School teaches us to study the Bible, understand what the scripture says and how to apply it, and then share what we discover. There are many elements to that process, and one of them (probably the most daunting for some people) is that every man, woman and child in the congregation is given the opportunity to select a subject to study and then develop a short presentation to share what they've learned. The elder in the congregation who oversees the school helps you decide on a topic and then guides you to the necessary source material. After that, it's up to each individual to do the research, prepare the talk, and then stand up and deliver it in front of the entire congregation.

Being made to do such work was invaluable for improving my presentation and communication skills, but I also learned a lot from the public critique that happened at the end of each talk. In front of everyone, an elder would walk you through your strengths and any areas that still needed work. Anything was fair game, from your interpretation of the scripture, to the way you structured your argument, to more technical aspects such as the volume and modulation of your voice, your eye contact and whether you used the microphone properly. You may have held the Bible too close to your face or kept your head down and read your talk without once engaging with the congregation. You may have spoken too quickly or too quietly. The elder would also point out areas in need of improvement in your grammar and enunciation. In my earlier days in the faith, they would give you a grade at the end of the critique (this is not done anymore). You hoped for a "Good," which meant you automatically moved on to another topic, or an "I" for Improved, which meant you could repeat the same presentation until you got a "Good." If you got a "W," you'd have to keep working, and head back to the drawing board to start over. Eventually, as I progressed in my studies, I was preparing and delivering forty-five-minute lectures at the Sunday meetings like the man I'd seen speak on hellfire the very first time I set foot in a Kingdom Hall. At the end of those lectures, there was no critique; instead people clapped to show their appreciation.

Life and Ministry School also taught us how to present the Truth at the door. We would act out improvised scenes with someone playing the householder, and then we'd be critiqued in much the same way as after our talks. The focus was on how to become a better teacher and communicator. The lessons made it much easier for us to handle some of the considerable challenges that arose when going door-to-door.

I joke with people nowadays: "You think it's tough being Black on Bay Street? Try being a Black Jehovah's Witness knocking on doors in a rich neighbourhood." When I started the door-to-door work, I didn't think at all about the racism I faced. But it affected me the whole time just the same. People would follow me through wealthier neighbourhoods, not directly confronting me but obviously keeping an eye on me, as though they were waiting for me to choose a house to break into. Similar suspicion greeted me when I knocked on doors. At the time, not knowing any better, I thought I was only receiving the cool and distant greeting people saved up for Jehovah's Witnesses. Looking back, I can see, plain as day, the expressions of mistrust and the quiet aggression that came from the belief that a Black man had no good reason to be in their neighbourhood. I must be up to something, and possibly something criminal.

My territory included extremely wealthy neighbourhoods and also under-resourced areas like Regent Park. With Christine, or whoever else I might be partnered with that day, I went up to drug dealers and gang members on the street to talk to them about the Bible. They usually assumed we were undercover cops. When they realized we were Jehovah's Witnesses, they would go back to selling their dope right in front of us. We tried to find ways to let them know that what they were doing was wrong without chastising them or turning them completely off our message.

To be at all successful at this, I had to learn how to get people interested in something they automatically assumed they didn't want anything to do with. In one of Toronto's roughest neighbourhoods, I had to be able to approach the toughest-looking person around and engage them in a meaningful conversation about the Bible, about life, about the future. And in some of Toronto's wealthiest neighbourhoods, I had to navigate my way past security gates and entrenched racial prejudice to get a chance at changing someone's mind and opening them up to God.

To say the least, these were unique challenges. And though selling a boss or client on a particular business strategy is obviously not the same as sitting down to study the Bible with someone who's just felt their first spark of interest in tackling life's biggest questions, there are aspects of the skill set I learned that transfer to the boardroom. But beyond all the tools that allow me to present to executives and investors in a compelling manner, or thaw out and win over a cold and combative client or advisor, I've seen far greater impacts from the deeper lessons my faith has taught me about how to carry myself in the world—namely, the value of humility and how to deal with rejection.

A lot of people can't deal with rejection. That's not an option as a Jehovah's Witness. I have spent more days than I can count heading out into the world to share my faith and the teachings of the Bible. I walk up to people's doors carrying something I know has the power to change their life forever. I knock and offer them the most valuable thing I could imagine. More often than not, they turn it down without even considering it. Sometimes they tell me to get lost, to get a life; they slam the door in my face. On more than one occasion, I have been threatened with violence.

Then I have to go on to the next door. I can't let the insults, the threats and the slammed doors affect my attitude. I have to get a smile back on my face and work my energy back up, because if I don't, I might stumble with the next person I talk to and spoil *their* chance to find faith and meaning. It is not my place to take that risk.

What I learned in Life and Ministry School is that when somebody says no, they're not saying no to me. When they get upset, they're not getting upset with me. Their quarrel is with the message itself. My only obligation is to deliver it. We present an opportunity, and if they aren't interested, then, as it says in Matthew 10:14, "wherever anyone does not receive you or listen to your words, on going out of that house or that city, shake the dust off your feet."

I have never presented an idea to a boss or a strategy to a client that was even a fraction as valuable as the wisdom of the scripture. So, when I present my best advice and a client refuses to take it, it feels like nothing compared to the experience of a door slamming in my face. And that is something I've survived hundreds of times. In business my job is also to present an opportunity. If the client ignores my counsel and goes in another direction, that's fine; it's their choice. When they lose as a result, there's nothing to be gained by saying, "I told you so." I have learned to leave my ego out of it and just move on. They will come back to me on future deals, and the next time, they'll listen.

About the ego: It is humbling to have doors slammed on you, but that is the price of sharing the faith. It is humbling to take criticism in front of an entire congregation, but that is the price I pay to gain the wisdom that allows me to grow and improve. It is humbling to be the CEO of Kingsdale, advising on billion-dollar transactions all day, and then be assigned to clean the Kingdom Hall's toilets that evening, but that is the cost of keeping God's house in order.

Humility reminds me to do as Jesus said and abandon myself and my ego, to put the community first and remain open to other people's ideas. Humility reminds me that my successes don't exempt me from hard work or set me above anyone else. And humility means that, even though I've given thousands of presentations, I still feel butterflies in my stomach when I get up at the front of the boardroom and begin to speak. We are taught at the Kingdom Hall that having butterflies in the stomach during a presentation is normal. Having them fly in unison is the trick.

I'm thankful for the ways I am humbled, and I'm thankful for those butterflies. They tell me that after more than twenty years in the business, there are still things to learn in my work—I don't have all the answers. And they tell me that I love what I do, and that I still care deeply about getting it right.

1 2

"I'M AFRAID FOR YOU"

On my first day at CanWest, I was shown to a beautiful, empty office and handed a catalogue. "Pick out whatever furniture you like from the catalogue," I was told. "It should get here by about the middle of the week." I had just started thumbing through pages of desks, chairs and bookshelves in disbelief, when I was handed another catalogue full of televisions. "The executive offices all get a TV. Yours will go in the corner there." I couldn't stop grinning. Not that long ago, I had been working in the mailroom, and now I was going to have my very own office with a TV.

I still remember the reaction I got when I told a Stikeman senior law clerk that I got the job. "Wes, are you kidding me?" she said, not actually asking. "They're going to fire you. You don't know what you're doing. This is a big job. You're not . . . I'm afraid for you."

But I wasn't afraid for myself. Sure, I didn't know how to do the job, but the opportunity was a blessing and I had nothing to lose. When I'd been invited to live with the Grahams after years spent bouncing from house to house, I didn't stress about the risk of getting kicked out, even though it was a possibility every day. When my dad brought me to Canada, I didn't worry about leaving everything I knew behind and starting a new life in an unfamiliar country. The job at CanWest was the same kind of situation as far as I was concerned. The worst that could happen was I'd end up back where I was. Okay, so they might fire me. What was the sense in being afraid of something I knew I could survive?

Soon my furniture arrived and people started turning up at the door with requests. Because CanWest was a major media conglomerate and broadcaster, they needed me to review and sign off on various types of contracts, including employment contracts for on-air personalities, to review transmitter licences, to assist with CRTC applications, to review scripts for defamatory content, to draft corporate resolutions and to undertake minute-book reviews. I needed to figure out what all of this involved. My only option was to teach myself how to do the job by doing the job. For instance, the minute-book review: Every time a company either holds an in-person meeting or agrees on a certain action, it must create and keep minutes of that meeting or decision, and all of those minutes are held in the records of the company, in a form that is called a minute book. Periodically, someone in the legal department needs to review that minute book to make sure that everything has been properly recorded and documented. Google didn't exist yet and there was no way I could easily search for document templates and precedents. To get that stuff, I needed to find or create a network of people who could help me. So that's what I did.

I first reached out to lawyers and law clerks I knew at Stikeman. They were an invaluable early resource and helped me as much as they could, but that tactic had limits. They were working for an external firm while I was working in-house, where I always had to take into account the internal workings and dynamics of the place when it came to advising on a course of action. What we were doing was similar, and some of the tasks were even identical, but Stikeman approached everything from the opposite direction, which could translate into very different processes and practices.

I realized pretty quickly that I had to start building a network of in-house law clerks and corporate secretaries, people who were doing exactly what I was doing. So, I found other companies in the broadcast media sector and looked up the governance professionals in their corporate directories. Sometimes I'd reach out just to introduce myself, but mostly what I did was fax people questions. If I needed something, like terms of reference for an audit committee (basically a constitutional document defining the committee's scope, powers and responsibilities), I'd send a fax out to a bunch of in-house legal department staff in other companies, and amazingly, people would send me back answers—a template to work from, for example, or some other bit of useful information or advice. In this way, I gradually crowdsourced an education in corporate governance practices, with a specialization in the broadcast industry. After a year or so on the job, I could execute most of my responsibilities in my sleep, and if I did still occasionally run into an unfamiliar challenge, I knew exactly who to reach out to.

Having felt the impact of such a network in my own career, I knew that everyone in the profession would benefit from the support and collaboration it made possible. I'd taken all the certification courses I needed to call myself a law clerk, but it wasn't until people who were already on the job shared their knowledge and experience with me that I got to a place where I truly *became* a law clerk. I knew of an existing body that facilitated that kind of networking, the Institute of Chartered Secretaries and Administrators, but it was a global entity with few, if any, Canadian members. I felt we needed an organization for Canada, so I co-founded the Canadian Society of Corporate Secretaries (CSCS). Today it's known as the Governance Professionals of Canada, and it's one of the largest professional associations in the country—this group that I initially co-founded to help me do my job.

I wanted the CSCS to be a network of in-house people who could share resources and best practices, an organization that recreated the village that had raised me. I became its first president and formed the board. The following year, I organized its first conference. It was modest, just a half-day long, but it was my vision come to life, the whole network right there in the flesh, shaking hands and trading jokes. I'd organized the agenda and arranged all the speakers myself, so while it was happening, I was mostly busy running around and seeing that events went smoothly, but I do remember the few times I got to pause and take it all in. I felt pride, satisfaction and happiness in knowing the good this organization could do for our profession. And I felt something else too, something that had likely been building for a while but was only just coming to the surface: *Now what?*

By that point, I had been at CanWest for five years. Glenn O'Farrell had turned out to be the best mentor I could ever have asked for, someone who'd been kind and patient with me, and who'd offered guidance in the right spots and at the perfect times. Every meeting he brought me into was a learning opportunity. If we were getting together to discuss a contract with a third party, for example, he would ask me to do the first draft of the contract. When he reviewed my draft, he would be kind with his edits, using them as a way to teach me. Over time those edits got fewer and fewer, until I was taking the meetings on my own. Glenn encouraged me to take on additional challenges and not be afraid to fail. He was always there to provide guidance, but he never micromanaged me. There had been much to learn, but I'd learned it. I'd proven my value. And now, I felt like I'd run up against the limits of what could be accomplished in my role. The next challenge? What could be more logical than to go from law clerk to lawyer?

I decided to apply to law school as a mature student. I prepped profusely for the LSAT, got excellent reference letters from Glenn and the CEO of CanWest Global, and sent applications to law schools all over Canada. None accepted me. That was a huge disappointment, but I also took it as a sign that it was time to reinvent myself. I had to move on.

I started speaking with friends about my interest in pursuing opportunities beyond CanWest. One of those conversations was with a gentleman who worked in the stock transfer industry. He told me that CIBC Mellon Trust Company, an agency in that business, was hiring. "You should think about going there," he told me.

When I started at CanWest, I may not have had the practical knowledge to do the job, but I *did* have a basic grasp of the work and the theory behind it. When it came to a stock transfer agency, I didn't have the faintest idea what they did. All I knew was that I had this one friend in the industry who seemed to be doing well for himself and enjoying his work, and he had recommended CIBC Mellon. That was enough for me to at least have a conversation.

I learned that a stock transfer agency works with public companies to balance their stock registers. Companies issue shares to all kinds of different investors, and somebody needs to keep everything straight and ensure that certain obligations are met—coordinating annual meetings, acting as scrutineer for those meetings, collecting proxies, and the rest of the nitty-gritty. It was CIBC Mellon Trust's job to handle all of the administrative crossing of t's and dotting of i's. That sounded all right to me.

I met with the person in charge of hiring, Laurel Savoy, and had a great interview. She said there were several positions open, but she thought I would be best suited for one in a department they were restructuring, though the role hadn't yet been created. The solution she proposed was that they hire me for a job lower down the organizational chart with the assurance that they would move me into the new job as soon as it was created. I didn't like that idea. It would take months to restructure a department, and by that point, they might decide that I wasn't the guy anymore and give the job to someone else. "Look," I said, "I'm not in a rush to leave where I'm at. So, when you've got this sorted and figure your structure out, just give me a call."

We hung up on good terms. Six months later, Laurel called to offer me the job that we'd discussed in the interview, senior manager of relationship management. I accepted, gave my notice at CanWest, and set out to see if I could figure out another job on the fly.

I returned to Bay Street in 1997. Five years after I'd left the mailroom, I was back as a senior manager. I was twenty-eight years old and had eleven people reporting to me, all of them older than me. And I really didn't know what my department was meant to do.

Unlike when I started at CanWest, there were no practice runs, and I didn't have anyone I could call to answer my questions and help me get my bearings either. I had to dive into the deep end and figure out how not to drown. And this time I was responsible for more than just my own performance. I couldn't dial in on myself and focus exclusively on working to fill the gaps in my own knowledge because I was accountable to and for my team. Also, I had to face the fact in the beginning that my team didn't show much interest in making my life easier, especially a guy who would for a time become the bane of my existence, Warren Jensen.

Warren was in his mid-fifties and had worked in the stock transfer business for about thirty years. I later found out that he had run his own department at CIBC Mellon at some point in the past and been demoted. But when I started the job, all I knew was that he didn't think much of me. Clues about the way he felt were there in his body language and cold demeanour—I didn't need to be Sherlock Holmes to figure it out. But he also told me he didn't like me directly to my face.

Warren had an annoying habit of setting an alarm for 4:45 p.m. every day, fifteen minutes before closing time. We were in a section of the building where only flimsy cubicle walls separated our workstations. When Warren's alarm went off, it reverberated throughout the entire office. Then the man would stand up and loudly begin packing up to head home. I watched him do it every afternoon for a few weeks, and then one day, just after his alarm sounded, I walked over and asked him for a word.

He was stuffing items into his bag as I approached. He paused briefly when I first sat down in his cubicle, but then went back to it, perhaps wanting to send me an even more pointed message by refusing to stop and talk to me. I waded in anyways.

"Warren, I don't mind you leaving early," I told him. "You get your work done, so I'm not going to make a fuss over fifteen minutes. But could you not set that alarm? When it goes off, it not only interrupts everybody else, it sends the wrong message."

All the anger he felt at having to answer to a twenty-something was in his face as he stared me down. He was standing and I was sitting, and so he actually loomed over me as he said, "You're the most arrogant son of a bitch I've ever worked with." Then he grabbed his bag—I'm not sure if he'd finished packing it or not— and stormed off.

Maybe he was trying to get disciplined in a way that would bring heightened attention to the situation and to me, or maybe he was trying to get fired. I wasn't going to fire him or recommend his transfer or dismissal, though. I could see how frustrating it would be for a guy like him to lose his department and end up reporting to a Black guy half his age who didn't even know the industry, let alone his job. Any hard-working person would find that off-putting. I wasn't even mad. I just thought, *Okay, I've got to win this guy over.*

Warren had something valuable that I didn't: experience. He'd been there and done that in his thirty-year career, and he'd likely forgotten more about the stock transfer business than I would come to know in my lifetime. He had more to offer me than I had to give in return—and I also had more to lose. If I could break through his anger, he could be a huge help in getting me up to speed.

When Warren and I went to meetings together, they were supposed to be my meetings. I was the boss, so I was expected to run the show, especially if we were meeting with clients. What I decided to do instead was ask Warren to take the lead. He was a fifty-five-year-old, grey-haired white guy, and I was a young Black guy who'd had a woman walk past me and my briefcase and suit to ask a guy in a T-shirt if he was there for the job interview. Who looked the part of a Bay Street boss? Who better matched clients' expectations? Warren did. That was the system and I could either choose to fight it or play the game. Not only did Warren look the part, he was better informed and more intelligent than me on the subject at hand. My street smarts were telling me that I needed to be the one to adapt.

So, as we were walking to a meeting one day soon after that 4:45 p.m. confrontation, I casually told him, "Warren, I want you to take the lead on this one." He looked a bit surprised, but he quickly agreed. When we got in there, he did all the talking as I sat to one side and took notes. To anyone who hadn't seen our org chart, I looked like his subordinate. He did an excellent job.

Meeting after meeting, I asked Warren to run point as I sat quietly and took notes. By refusing to let my ego get the better of me, I learned so much so quickly. I also empowered Warren. He felt useful and engaged, and when he saw that I respected his expertise and what he'd accomplished in his career, he loosened up. Pretty soon, he started to outright train me, the boss: "So, in that meeting, when he said all that stuff in the middle, here's what he was telling us. And when I came back at him, this is why. When we get back to the office, we're going to talk to this particular person, because they can do this and this and that." He literally led me to each of the department heads who were critical to supporting my department and helped me develop relationships with them. He pointed out their strengths and weaknesses, and identified the people working for them who were key so that, if I needed to, I could bypass the department heads and go straight to the key employees. This information you cannot just pick up by osmosis. Banks are extremely bureaucratic, so learning their internal politics is just as important as knowing the job.

I continued to listen and nod and take notes. Eventually, my trust and the space I gave Warren to do what he did best won him over. And once I got him on my side, the rest of the team followed suit. Pretty soon, they would run through fire for me. Warren Jensen went from being the bane of my existence to the best thing that ever happened to me.

One of the key responsibilities we had at CIBC Mellon was running various companies' annual general meetings (AGMs). We took attendance, tabulated votes and provided a report to the chairman of the AGM that covered how many shareholders had turned up, who they were, and what the vote counts were on various issues, both by proxy and in-person ballot. It sounds fairly straightforward, and it is in a way. You're following a rule book that offers very precise step-by-step instructions, but as anyone can tell you who's read a book on parenting or puppy training and then tried to apply its teachings to the cutest member of the family, getting the real world to conform to a rigid set of guidelines is no mean feat.

At the beginning of every AGM, the chairman would announce, "We appoint CIBC Mellon Trust Company as scrutineer." Then they would read out the names of the two CIBC Mellon employees who were assigned as agents to everyone assembled—often a group two to three hundred people strong. As the manager on the file, I had to be there to supervise the agents, and I witnessed many times how uncomfortable that reading of names could be for my people, who were being made personally responsible for the smooth functioning of such a large event. Even laying that element of personal accountability aside, running AGMs was a very stressful part of the job.

Say, for example, that the chairman calls for a vote on a particular issue. All two to three hundred people in the room need ballots. And given that the meeting can't proceed until the results are in, they want their ballots as soon as possible. A big lineup forms, and it's the scrutineers' job to determine who should be given a ballot and which type of ballot they should be given based on the category of shareholder they are. The speed and seriousness with which you have to work your way through the line is stressful to begin with, but the intensity really spikes when someone argues with your decision. It happens to some degree at every meeting. The most common complainant is a beneficiary, someone who owns stock in the company through a broker but doesn't understand that they aren't entitled to a ballot. To vote at an AGM, you have to be a registered shareholder or duly appointed proxy holder. People who own stock through a broker aren't registered; their broker is and votes on their behalf. That can be hard to grasp for people who've come to the meeting because they saw in the latest report from their broker that they hold the company's stock. While most people will quietly accept reason when the situation is explained to them, every now and again a guy (in my experience, it is always a guy) will fly off the handle, waving his broker's report around to show he owns the stock and insisting he needs a ballot. Anytime someone argued with one of my agents, I would get involved—especially if they argued loudly enough to make a scene.

In business, as in other parts of life, people have a tendency to get locked into a certain way of doing things. This is especially the case in an environment as prescribed as an AGM, and even more so when they're under pressure. The rules, procedures or workflows tell them how to do something, and they do it that way time after time. When something comes along and throws a wrench in those works, they don't know what to do. They hunker down inside the box they're comfortable in and point at the rules. It's a way of dodging both blame and ownership: *Don't be mad at me; I'm just following orders.*

If you're willing to take ownership and risk blame, though, the solutions are often simple. Whenever someone was refused a ballot and started to make a scene, I told my team to just give them the ballot. Most of the time, the agent would be thankful I gave them an out, but occasionally someone was so stuck in the usual way of doing things that they'd start pushing back as if I was making a mistake: "Wes, we can't give him a ballot. He's not on the register." Then I'd have to take that agent aside and explain.

Once all the ballots are cast, the AGM adjourns while the vote on that issue is tallied by scrutineers in a separate room. During that count, ballots are invalidated for a variety of reasons. A shareholder may not have signed their ballot, for example. In that case, it isn't counted toward the final tally. If the name on the ballot doesn't appear on the stock register, the ballot is also invalidated, whether someone made a scene before the vote or not. So, if someone is yelling for a ballot, give it to him, let him fill it out and give it back to you. When the counting begins and the name is cross-checked against the list, the scrutineer won't find it, the vote will be invalidated, and it'll be as if you never gave the guy a ballot at all—except that it will have been resolved without disrupting everyone at the meeting.

As I ran more of these events, I developed a reputation within CIBC Mellon and with our clients for that kind of problem solving, for not losing my cool in stressful situations, for always seeming like I'd been there a thousand times before, and for being both proactive and considerate. If a vote was underway, and we were preparing to tally in-person ballots but the proxies—cast ahead of time—had already arrived in large enough numbers for the issue to be settled, I would let the chairman know they could proceed with the meeting before we finished the count because the outcome wouldn't change. A decision like that could save everyone at the meeting an hour of their day or more—a small efficiency always appreciated by the people on the receiving end.

All these small calls of mine not only didn't go unnoticed, they eventually laid the groundwork for my next opportunity— the one that introduced me to the secular work I believe I was put on this earth to do.

1 3

VP OR BUST

Georgeson & Company had been in business in the United States since 1935, but they'd only recently opened Georgeson Shareholder in Canada. The move north of the border came after they bought out a fellow named John Ross, an entrepreneur who'd literally run his business out of the shoebox in which he kept all his bills and receipts. Ross's company was called Proxy Solicitation, a name that doubled as a description of what he did: solicit proxy votes.

Every company has a quorum requirement for its AGM, a percentage of shareholders that have to participate for the meeting to be valid. The number is generally quite low—in some cases less than 10 percent—but some companies have trouble clearing even that bar. Others are driven by pride or the desire to get as many shareholders as possible to participate to pursue a 40 or 50 percent return. Ross would approach prospective clients and ask, "Do you have a problem getting your shareholders to vote?" If they did, he would offer to call everyone on the company's register and encourage them to vote, and he would charge five to ten thousand dollars per meeting.

Georgeson was doing the same thing in the United States, on a bigger scale. After they bought out Proxy Solicitation and its client list for about a million dollars in 1997, they set out to bring a little more oomph to the business in Canada. Their sales team pursued new clients a bit more aggressively than Ross had, and they had call centres they could lean on to handle files with much larger groups of shareholders than Proxy Solicitation had been able to take on.

I first became aware of them when their people started turning up to meetings I was scrutineering, wanting to know how the vote turned out. Most folks working at transfer agencies thought they were kind of a pain in the arse. They would pester us for a sense of how the proxy votes were coming in before the meeting too, meaning that in addition to preparing a report for our client, we would also have to prepare a report for Georgeson outlining how many votes had come in, so they could go back out and keep soliciting if they hadn't yet met the quorum requirement. The extra work prompted some grumbling, of course, but not from me.

To my mind, we had all been hired by the same client and our goal was a shared one: to deliver a successful meeting. Since we each served a purpose that ultimately helped the other, we might as well play nice in the sandbox. As a result, I applied the same attitude, effort and attention to detail to the reports I sent to Georgeson as I did when dealing directly with the client.

Georgeson staff appreciated that, and they were also present for the meeting itself, giving them ample opportunity to see how I handled myself in that environment. They must have liked what they saw, because eventually I got a call from the president and CEO of Georgeson Shareholder, Glenn Keeling, who asked me to lunch.

I knew it had to be about a job and, to be honest, I wasn't particularly interested. It was 2000 and I'd been at CIBC Mellon for three years, long enough to get a clear sense of the future I could make for myself at the transfer agency. CIBC Mellon was bank-owned, and Georgeson was a small entrepreneurial shop working in an industry that was new enough in Canada for most people on Bay Street, myself included, to not really know what they did. I couldn't see myself forgoing the security of the bank job for the unknown, but I still agreed to the lunch. A lot of people look at an opportunity that doesn't fit the path they imagine taking in their professional life and refuse to explore it. A door opens, but when they can't see all the places it might lead, they pass. I've never been one to do that. I may not be able to imagine myself on the other side of the door, but I don't fault the door. If someone wants to talk to me about an opportunity, I'm glad to be talked to. So, even though I didn't really get Georgeson's business, this was a chance to find out more about it. Plus, the last time I'd met a guy named Glenn for an informal interview at a nice restaurant, it had resulted in the biggest break of my career.

We met at Mercatto, an Italian restaurant in the financial district. Glenn Keeling was a heavy-set guy with a shock of red hair and a red beard to match who'd spent his career in the newswire business before moving to Georgeson. Glenn is a larger-than-life character, a consummate salesman who can sell anything to anyone. Even if you already have a dozen of the same item gathering cobwebs in your garage, he will sell you a dozen more. He saw opportunity in the nascent proxy solicitation industry, and he was looking to professionalize it by bringing in people who could find new ways to grow the business.

"I've heard a lot about you, Wes," he said. "My guys tell me that you're really good at what you do, and I've heard the same thing from the clients we've shared. You're smart and we like the way you carry yourself. Have you ever thought about coming to work for us?"

"Glenn, thank you for the kind words, but I don't even know what you guys do," I answered, laughing.

He gave me a quick explanation that didn't reveal much more than what I already knew, but Keeling's energy and interest were enough to stoke my curiosity. As it happened, I was due to fly to San Francisco for a conference put on by the Canadian Society of Corporate Secretaries' American counterpart. Even though I was no longer working as a law clerk, I'd stayed on as president of the CSCS because so many of CIBC Mellon's clients were corporate secretaries and general counsels. My continued work with the CSCS allowed me to maintain a strong understanding of life in our clients' shoes. It also sent the message that, in a way, I was still one of them, and certainly someone who valued their work. At some point during our lunch, I mentioned the conference to Keeling, and he told me that staff from Georgeson's U.S. offices would be there too, looking to wine and dine existing clients and woo new ones. "This is great," he said. "Meet some of our guys when you're there."

After San Francisco, he said, we'd circle back and check in on things. The trip would give some other Georgeson folks a chance to feel me out. It would also give me a first opportunity to see them in action and figure out just what they did.

Christine and I flew down to San Francisco for the conference a couple of weeks after my lunch with Keeling. Georgeson was an exhibitor, corporate secretaries making up a key portion of their client base. I went over to chat with the guys staffing their booth, all from the company's New York office. They told me that Keeling had put us on the guest list for a client event they were throwing the next night, a big dinner at a fancy hotel, and personally urged me to come.

The dinner was designed to win over clients, but it worked on me too. The food was good and the hall was beautiful, but what I loved was the energy the Georgeson guys brought. There was schmoozing and business talk, of course, but they also did their best to make the night fun. There were about 120 guests, and at one point the hosts moved around the tables offering a hundred bucks to anyone who could do a celebrity impersonation. When they got to our area, I stood up and did my Mike Tyson, with the high voice and everything: "I'm going to gut him like a fish. I'm going to rip out his heart and show it to him." I cracked everyone up and got the hundred too. Later I got up with a group of Georgeson's head office guys to sing some R & B.

Shortly after we got back to Toronto, Keeling called me up and said, "Wes, the guys loved you, man. You've got to think about joining the team."

"I still don't really get what you guys do," I told him, "but if you have half as much fun in your office in Canada as those guys in New York do, and if you're half as cool as them, I want to come work for you."

He emailed me an offer letter within a few days. It was a single short paragraph: "We're pleased to offer you the position of Director of Business Development for Canada at a salary of $75,000 per year."

There was no job description, no non-compete clause, nothing. I still didn't know what the company wanted me to do, but the salary was hard to ignore. When you work for a bank, they treat you well, and you get stability, great benefits and plenty of perks. But banks don't generally pay you enough to afford the kind of life I'd been working toward. The Georgeson offer was almost 40 percent more than what I was making at the time.

When I went home that night to discuss it with Christine, the home in question was a 1,100-square-foot semi-detached on Marigold Avenue, in a transitioning neighbourhood just east of downtown Toronto. Our first child, Darian, was eighteen months old, and Christine was pregnant with our second son, Brentyn. We were living in what was basically a construction site. We were renovating the place, but our contractor had quit on us, and since I couldn't afford to hire another, I was doing the work myself. (It nearly did me in, but I'm proud to say that I built sections of that house that are still standing all these years later.) But even with me doing the work, we couldn't cover our bills, let alone buy decent furniture.

When Keeling called a few days later to check on the status of his offer, he caught me in the bedroom, where Christine and I were sleeping on a mattress on the floor because we didn't have a frame, box spring or headboard. "I just want to make sure you got the offer okay," he said, then delivered it again almost word for word. "You'd be our director of business development. And we'll pay you $75,000 a year."

"Glenn, I don't have a problem with the compensation. The money's not a big deal to me, and it seems fair," I said. "But the title doesn't work. My next move has to be to vice president. I'm happy here at CIBC Mellon, and I'm not leaving the firm for anything less than a VP role."

"Wes, the job's supposed to be director-level," he said. "I don't have the authority to offer you vice president."

"Well, it's the only thing holding me back, Glenn. I'm ready," I answered. "When you have the authority, call me."

After we hung up, I turned to find Christine looking at me like I'd grown another head. We couldn't even afford our mortgage, we'd been talking about how cool this $75,000 offer was for days, and I'd just turned it down. She was pretty upset with me— justifiably. I hadn't necessarily planned in advance to turn Keeling down, but in the moment, I had my reasons. I explained it to her this way: In a sense, I was bluffing. I wanted the $75,000 salary and I'd already seen how well I might do working for a company with the attitude I'd witnessed in San Francisco. I'd asked for the title, hoping he'd just give it to me. But when you negotiate with somebody, you have to be prepared for them to call your bluff. A lot of people who demand things as a ploy aren't actually willing to follow through with the threat, and when there's push-back they fold. But for your reputation to stand for anything and for your play to work, you have to be prepared to be denied, and you can't beat yourself up when you are. If you're making a play just to try to squeeze the person you're dealing with, you're going to fall apart when the deal does. You have to have real reasons.

My biggest real reason was that the title meant more to me than the money. If I was brought on as a VP, no one in the larger world would know I was only making $75,000. It would open up the possibility of going back to the bank or another firm at the VP level and earning some real money. Since I was happy at CIBC Mellon and confident about my ability to gradually move up, I had no need to agree to any opportunity unless it took me up a level and added to my skill set, resumé and worth. "I can't leave for a lateral position, especially to go to a part of the industry no one knows anything about," I told Christine. "It's got to be something that will give me a title I can use for leverage someplace else."

"Okay," she said. "I just hope you know what you're doing."

Two weeks later, Keeling called again. "Wes, I've been given the authority to offer you what you were looking for. How does vice president, business development, sound?"

I told him it sounded great.

I'd gotten breaks before—my friend Patrick not wanting the mailroom job; Stikeman paying tuition costs; Glenn O'Farrell seeing my potential at CanWest—but the Georgeson job felt like my first *big* break. *Vice president of business development.* In the early days, I'd say the title out loud to myself now and then, to enjoy the ring of it and marvel at how far life had taken me. There would be no more worrying about money. Christine and I would be able to pay our mortgage and bills, and maybe even afford some furniture. I'd also finally be able to do something big for my grandmother: bring her to Canada and get her out of poverty for good. I couldn't wait to share my success with the person who'd laid the foundation that made it all possible. But I wouldn't get the chance.

On September 20, 2000, about three weeks after I signed the Georgeson offer, Mama fell in her house in Golden Grove. My sister found her, but though she did everything she could to help her, Mama died from her injuries days later. My sister had wanted to call me right away, but my grandmother had said, "Don't call. It will worry him. I'm going to be fine." She spent her whole life putting other people's needs before her own, making sure all of us were okay, and that stayed true until the moment she died.

She and I had remained close even after I moved to Canada, writing letters back and forth because the houses in The Barracks didn't have telephones. I started sending money to her as soon as I started earning some, even if it was just twenty dollars here and there. I told her that I dreamed of bringing her to Canada to live with me one day, but I hadn't followed through. I'd wanted to get more established in Canada before moving her, for one. I'd also worried about pulling her away from everything she knew. A life in poverty surrounded by her friends might be better than a much more isolated life with me in Canada, where she'd be stuck inside all winter while I worked long hours. But after she passed, all of those reasons struck me as thin excuses. Filled with grief over her loss, I also felt incredible guilt and regret. I'd let her down. I hadn't worked hard enough to help her, to repay her for the sacrifices she'd made.

I also beat myself up for never just asking her whether she wanted to stay in Jamaica or be with me in Canada. I'd made the decision on her behalf, guessing at what would make her happiest. When I travelled to Jamaica to bury her, I found out I'd guessed wrong. After the service, I spent some time in her place, thinking about her and beginning to get her things organized. At the foot of her bed, I found a suitcase. When I opened it and began to unpack its contents, I realized it was the bag she had planned to bring to Canada. She'd had it there ready, just waiting on a call from me that never came. She'd also told people in The Barracks that she was moving to Canada to live with her grandson. I was that grandson, and letting her die in poverty is the biggest regret of my life.

That discovery undid me for a long time. It is still painful to think about. I'd worried about taking her away from her friends and community, but when I saw that bag, I knew that the only thing she'd really wanted was to be with me—and I didn't give it to her. In my grief, I used that thought against myself like a weapon: *Why did I wait? Why didn't I work harder to repay all her sacrifices?* Eventually, though, I realized that beating myself up wasn't doing justice to my grandmother's memory. I was dwelling on the ways I'd failed her rather than celebrating who she was and how she lived. Finally, I came to see that in her death, as in her life, she still had important lessons to teach me.

Yes, she died in poverty, but she never resented her place in the world, or me for not rescuing her from it. She never complained about being poor and, I had to remind myself, when she was dealt a blow, she never sat and sulked and said, "Why me? Why me?" She loved her family and lived a life anyone would be wise to admire, and even envy. She knew what to value in this life and conducted herself accordingly. Her bag was packed not because she was looking forward to hot showers, electricity, restaurants, nice cars and cable TV, but because she was looking forward to time with a boy she had raised who'd been through some tough times but had come out the other side, happy and successful. Thinking on all of that was what finally started to bring me some comfort.

I still kick myself for not bringing her to Canada. That mistake cost both of us the time we would have shared in her golden years, and there's no way to get that back. But it also taught me one of the most important lessons of my life: don't wait for the "perfect" time to do something good. I think I might have been prone to that kind of thinking my whole life if not for the burning regret I experienced after missing my chance with my grandmother.

In business, my philanthropic work and my personal life, I don't let opportunities pass because I'm not sure I'm ready to seize them. I say yes and then figure it out. I will never be able to fully shake off the regret I felt when I lost Mama. One way I can honour her memory is to remember that there is no "perfect" time, and that there is no time like the present. If a door cracks open, it's up to me to see where it leads.

14

BEING BLACK IS

MY SUPERPOWER

Georgeson Canada was headquartered on the fifty-second floor of the TD North Tower on King Street West in Toronto's financial district. It was a beautiful space, looking south and west toward Lake Ontario, but it was also a fairly boutique operation with about fifteen people working there. On my first day, it didn't take long for me to do the rounds, introducing myself, and end up back at my desk, shuffling papers around and thinking, *Okay, what* is *my job?*

I knew four things about my new role: the title, the pay, the fact that it was a sales job and that I was selling proxy solicitation, which seemed to boil down to calling shareholders and encouraging them to vote. Nobody came to me with any pressing requests, as they had at CanWest. There was no orientation, and the inbox connected to my brand-new Georgeson email address was empty. *What is my job?*

Look, I was a sales guy, right? So, my job had to be to sell, so I could bring in clients. That meant that the first thing I needed to do was work my Rolodex. (For you millennials out there, that's a contact list, an actual physical one, composed of little cards that spun on a little wheel.) I figured I'd make some calls to clients of mine from CIBC Mellon, people who knew and respected me, and get them interested in this new industry I was a part of, and then I'd be up and running. I started to do just that, calling or emailing former clients to say, "Hey, I've left CIBC Mellon and I'm now with Georgeson Shareholder, doing business development. I'd like to talk to you about what we bring to the table"—not knowing exactly what we brought to the table.

I think there's a natural tendency to come into a new job wanting to prove yourself as quickly as possible. We all have a little anxiety when we take on new challenges—some of us just disguise it better than others. Speak to the CEO of any Fortune 500 company and if they are truthful, they will tell you that the day before their big first day they did not sleep. They lay awake all night with their stomach in knots and planned and then rehearsed every aspect of their debut. They will tell you how they agonized over their first meeting with the board, their first investor call, their first AGM.

It's easy to forget that in all your previous jobs, the process of familiarization took time—weeks or months, as it should. Especially when you've been given the top job, you want to come and make a splash, leaving no doubt in anyone's mind that you're the right person for the role. You put that pressure on yourself, and when things don't play out like a movie, you get even more stressed out. Here I was calling all my old clients, and no one picked up. I left messages and sent emails, and no one got back to me. Even though this was only day one, even though it wouldn't have bothered me at all to wait for a response when I was at CIBC Mellon, I started to second-guess myself and the decision to join Georgeson. *Nobody's calling me back. I know these people and they won't even return a call. Did I mess up here? I should've just stayed at CIBC Mellon. Why am I here? What am I doing?*

Eventually, I had to interrupt that thought process. I went into my new boss's office and I levelled with him: "Glenn, nobody's calling me back. I don't know what's going on, man." I started to run through all the calls I'd made, everyone I'd reached out to. He let me go on for a little while and then held up a hand to stop me. "Wes," he said, "just take your foot off the gas for a minute. Keep doing what you're doing, but take your foot off the gas."

It may seem silly, but that was all I needed to hear. With that one line, Keeling gave me permission to cut myself a break. It was probably the best advice he ever gave me, and I took it. I kept making calls and chasing leads, but I stopped stressing about whether or when people would call me back, and I put my faith in the work and in myself. I would put in the effort, I knew, and eventually it would pay off. Almost as soon as I relaxed my grip on the steering wheel and settled back in my seat, people started to return my calls. My inbox started filling up too. Old clients sent congratulations and asked about the new job—they didn't know what Georgeson did, either. *I can do this*, I told myself. *I can figure it out.*

It was right about then that I saw the first person go by my office with their personal effects in a banker's box. In my memory, it feels like that happened on day one, but it must not have been quite that quick. I'd had a chance to not only introduce myself to everyone in the office but also to start picking their brains about proxy solicitation and what they did. In those conversations it became clear why I'd had to push Keeling to bring me in at vice president. Like in most small shops, many of these staffers wore multiple hats. People stepped up when there was a hole to fill, taking on tasks and responsibilities that technically lay outside their job descriptions (assuming they had job descriptions). As I would see when I started my own company, leaving room for that kind of initiative can breed a feeling of agency, dedication, corporate pride, loyalty and fulfillment in employees. But when people feel like all that extra effort isn't recognized and rewarded, it instead breeds resentment.

When I walked in the door, Georgeson already had a group of people who seemed to be unhappy with their place in the company, including the guy who ran the business development department I joined. He was in a director-level position, which is what I'd initially been offered, and then I came in as a VP, a title change he'd wanted for himself. My appearance had to have triggered a new level of resentment and dissatisfaction. My office was the closest one to the entrance—I joked to Christine that it was for maximum convenience if I didn't work out—so I saw him passing my door as he made his exit. Next, the director's right-hand person in business development headed into Keeling's office, closed the door, then came out, gathered up his things and headed past me and out the door. After him, the director of finance did the same. All told, four people left for good, one after the other—nearly a third of the staff, and all senior people.

Panicked concern about the future of the business spread like wildfire. We'd just lost basically the whole sales department and our head of finance—the guys who brought in the deals and the woman who transitioned the financial workings of the company from John Ross's shoebox. I'd been asking these people how to do the job, and now they were gone, leaving me a one-person business development department.

Keeling hadn't come out of his office, and no one who hadn't quit that day had yet gone in to see him. So, I went and knocked on his door. When he looked up, his face was redder than his hair and I could tell I was the last person he wanted to see. He'd been brought in by Georgeson to overhaul this company and take it to another level. I was the first person he'd hired specifically to help him do that, which triggered the senior people he'd worked most closely with to leave the company. And they did so, it turned out, with plans to set up their own competing shop.

"Listen, man, we're going to be okay," I said. "We don't need those guys. We're going to do better without them."

He didn't answer, but the look on his face said, *This is serious. You just cost me my job.*

"We're going to be okay," I told him again. Then I turned and left his office.

I was just trying to calm him down by saying he hadn't made the wrong decision, and that I was going to make sure he would be okay. I had no plan, no idea how I was going to make good on what I'd said, but I felt a responsibility to deliver. He'd put his faith in me and now he'd put his job in my hands—unintentionally, but still. I decided it wasn't going to be a decision he would live to regret. I just had to figure out how to land a deal.

When I joined Georgeson in 2000, proxy solicitation was still a relatively new thing in Canada, and not just as a stand-alone business. Some bigger companies—banks mostly—had departments that touched on some of what we did, but basically they were just there to answer shareholders' questions, or to direct them to the transfer agency if they wanted information about a specific stock. No one really bothered to solicit votes, because they didn't think they needed votes. The only reason to invite such participation, as far as they could see, was if you were worried about failing to get a quorum. Because the quorum requirements were so low, that was rarely a concern.

If they'd looked to the United States, they would have realized that down south, the climate around these votes was getting more and more contentious. With activist investing percolating in a real way and hostile takeovers becoming a much more common phenomenon, American AGMs were beginning to take on the dynamics of political campaigns. But Canada's business world was extremely cordial. Everybody knew everybody else, and no one was all that interested in ruffling feathers or disturbing sleeping dogs. That attitude would shift pretty drastically in just a few years. In the meantime, however, all that seemed to be at risk when people started to return my first Rolodex calls was quorum. If they weren't worried about hitting that number, I had to find another way to sell our services.

At first I concentrated on booking the client meetings we called "sits." My goal became to get as many companies as possible to simply agree to hear us out. Every time I landed a sit, I would call in Keeling and another guy who had stuck with us, the granddaddy of the proxy business, Roy Shanks. Roy had been in the business almost fifteen years and knew everything. Roy was old school. His filing cabinet was his desk, and on it he had newspaper clippings, transaction documents, takeover circulars, every industry-related piece of paper you could imagine, piled to the ceiling. If you sat in the chair across the desk from him, there was no way you could see Roy behind all those piles. If you asked him for a takeover bid circular on a particular deal, he would close his eyes, shift in his chair to get at one of his stacks of paper and pull the exact thing you needed from a seemingly random spot in the middle of the pile. "Here you go, Wes." He was also particularly good at reciting the details of deals he'd done as many as fifteen years earlier. He was just an amazing resource.

So, I would book these client meetings for Glenn and Roy and then, just as I had in my early days at CIBC Mellon, I would sit off to the side and take notes. As I watched them work to make sales, the framework of the pitch revealed itself.

Why do you need proxy solicitation?

You need it in order to form a relationship with your shareholders. By soliciting them, you're showing them you know who they are and you believe their vote matters. The effort gives them a point of contact to the company and that builds loyalty. If they're ever unsure how to vote on a particular issue, they're more likely to reach out to you if you've taken the time to establish a real connection—and they're more likely to hear you out if you ever have a case to make.

Say you need a stock-option plan approved. There are a lot of ways a vote like that can go against you, but they all boil down to enough of your shareholders deciding they don't like the plan and refusing to green-light it. For example, at the time I was learning the business, there was a powerful third-party advisory group called Fairvest (it later became Institutional Shareholder Services, better know by the acronym ISS), which institutional investors would hire and lean on for advice. If Fairvest didn't like your stock-option plan, your institutional investors wouldn't vote for it, and that could result in 20 percent of your shareholder base turning against the plan you put forward. Not good. But if you'd taken the time to build relationships with your shareholders through proxy solicitation, then you'd be able to counteract that institutional swing by appealing to your retail investors—the "moms and pops" who own stock individually and tend to listen to and support management. When you've created that loyalty among your retail investors, they will help to offset any negative votes.

At some point early on, I booked a sit that neither Glenn nor Roy could attend. I went in, delivered the pitch and closed the deal. It was the first client I landed on my own, and that small victory did wonders for my mojo. I spent some time working on the pitch I would use next time, crafting it, making it my own with little tweaks and additions, and then I started calling *everybody*.

I kept the two major newswire services—Canada Newswire and Business Wire—open on my computer, refreshing both feeds literally ten times an hour. As soon as I saw a deal announced, boom, I called the company contact listed in the release. If no one was listed, I'd look the company up on the System for Electronic Document Analysis and Retrieval (SEDAR), a database for all securities filings from public companies. I would find the name of the person who did the filing—almost always a corporate secretary or general counsel, and sometimes a person I already knew from the CSCS—and then I would give them a call: "Hey, it's Wes Hall from Georgeson Shareholder. I understand you have a meeting coming up to seek shareholders' approval for this deal. We do proxy solicitation and can help you get your deal approved. We'd like to talk."

Some of them would call me back and some wouldn't bother. Most of these people had never heard of Georgeson and didn't have a clue about proxy solicitation. They'd been doing deals forever, and no one had ever told them they needed what I was telling them they needed. So, they didn't think they needed it. I needed to survive hearing no twenty times in a row and keep pushing for the yes. That wasn't a problem for me. But being able to keep my energy up and my attitude positive didn't mean I enjoyed being turned down. I knew that a big part of the problem in getting people to say yes to proxy solicitation was that we were the only ones making the pitch. I had to find a way to change that.

In addition to going to companies directly, I started to book meetings with securities lawyers and investment bankers, who already had the ear of their clients and were expected to give them advice and direction. If I could get them on board, I would be creating advocates who could tell clients, "You need Georgeson."

I pitched them using the same arguments I'd been delivering directly to companies, only through the lens of "this is what's in your clients' best interest." I still had to deal with rejection, but less of it—it turned out to be easier to get someone to judge our services on their merits when they knew they wouldn't be the ones footing the bill.

The investment bankers were a tougher sell than the lawyers. They saw the value in proxy solicitation but got hung up on the idea of their client paying someone else to do it. "We know the shareholders. Why don't we just do this ourselves?"

My counter-argument was built on respect and valuing their expertise, but it didn't hurt that it played to their egos as well. "Listen, you're a highly paid investment banker," I said. "Do you really want to be calling Mom and Pop and telling them to vote? Don't you want us doing that grunt work so you guys can focus on closing the big institutions?" I also pointed out that if they tried to free themselves up by dropping the work on junior employees, they'd mostly succeed in upsetting and then losing a bunch of very talented people they'd painstakingly recruited out of the best business schools. My points were taken.

The strategy drew on everything I'd done in my career to that point, all the way back to the mailroom. We got the bankers and lawyers feeding us deals, and that brought clients in the door, while also building the company's brand. We became a name people had heard *before* I called them up to talk, and they'd usually heard it from someone they trusted who was telling them they needed us on board. After building some momentum to close out the last quarter of 2000, we took off in 2001. My first full year with the company was by far its best year to date.

But there was still plenty of room to grow, and also grow our revenue. When I'd first started, I'd been given a breakdown of Georgeson's rates. Clients were charged a flat fee per contract that ranged, depending on the size of the company, from $10,000 to $35,000. On top of that fee, we charged six dollars for every call we placed or received from a shareholder. We rarely pulled in a company large enough that we could charge the high end of the range. Most of our contracts brought in between fifteen thousand and twenty thousand dollars.

In March 2001, I was working on a deal to bring in an energy company out of Australia—let's call it Australian Energy. They had just announced a hostile takeover bid for a Canadian oil company—let's call that one Canadian Energy. I'd booked a call with Australian Energy's CEO, but because of the time differ- ence, it was happening at 1:00 a.m. for me. It was nearly four in the morning by the time we got all the details hashed out. Just before he agreed to hire us, the CEO told me, "Wes, anyone who works the kind of hours that you do is going to be fine working with me." I signed Australian Energy for $125,000.

When I presented the deal to the leadership team at Georgeson, instead of greeting me with champagne and fire- works, they looked at me like I'd grown another head. According to the business model Georgeson had inherited from John Ross's Proxy Solicitation, we basically operated as a call centre busi- ness, dialing up all those mom and pop investors. When I came to the end of my Australian Energy presentation, there was an awkward, you-could-hear-a-pin-drop moment in the room. The person who was to work the mandate broke the silence. She asked, "Wes, what are we going to do for $125,000?" She was right to ask. For that kind of money, a client would be expecting a lot more than some phone calls to shareholders. In order to avoid disappointing them and damaging our reputation, Georgeson was going to have to evolve. "We'll figure it out," I assured her and all the other skeptical faces in the room. "I'm going to work with you to figure it out, okay?"

I already knew that Canadian business was an insular world that became more and more tight-knit and closed off the higher I climbed. I was now a vice president talking to lawyers, investment bankers and executives about how best to sell a big deal to investors, but nearly everyone I dealt with—both clients and in-house at Georgeson—had the same backstory. They grew up in the same neighbourhoods, had the same kind of families, went to the same schools and followed the same career paths. I don't mean to strip away anyone's individuality or diminish their lived experience here. I did come across people who'd come from lower-income families or gone to less stuffy schools, but even those "outliers" tended to have enough in common with the rest of the room to mostly fit. And when someone mostly fits, the things that make them different tend to be sanded away over time. Unsurprisingly, these people with so much in common tended to think similarly. They all had the same basic sense of what was possible and what was acceptable or allowed. And that meant that when business problems arose, they were all likely to come up with the same kinds of solutions.

I was never going to fit. The path I'd taken to get there was too different: it was dirt and I'd walked it barefoot. Since I was usually the only Black person in the room, I was never even going to *pass* at fitting. That had consequences, of course. It put barriers in front of me that no one I worked alongside or against was forced to deal with. But I'd overcome more than any of them before I even set foot on Canadian soil, and I believed there was nothing anyone could throw at me that I couldn't turn to my advantage. From Stikeman to Georgeson and beyond, I was regularly underestimated by people who assumed they'd be able to roll right over this dumb Black guy who grew up in a shack and never went to Harvard. Their racist and classist confidence in their own superiority made them cocky and caused them to drop their guard. And when I got the better of them, that same blindness left them wondering what on earth had just happened. If I had perceived my Blackness as a disadvantage or weakness, then it would have been exactly that. If I'd tried to ignore who I was and be more like them, I would never have accomplished what I have. To me, being Black is my superpower. I brought something no one else in those rooms did: a different perspective earned through different lived experience. There's no telling what someone who sees things through a new lens can add to your business. In my case, I didn't just add to the proxy solicitation industry in Canada, I reinvented it.

When you boiled it down, Georgeson's goal in most cases was simply to encourage shareholders to vote. So, callers would be given a simple script and they'd dial the first name on their list, deliver the script and then move on to the next name and number. "Hello, my name is Wes Hall. I'm calling from Georgeson Shareholder, and we would like to get your support in connection with the bid by Australian Energy for the outstanding shares of

Canadian Energy." You couldn't charge a $125,000 management fee for that.

In order to earn the fees we wanted to be charging, Georgeson would have to offer advisory services, not just the grunt work call-centre stuff. We had to bring the same level of expertise that lawyers and investment bankers brought to the table and apply it to *selling* the deal. Why was it that these two companies were coming together? We had to know who the shareholders were, what they wanted and how they thought. Then, working with everything we knew about them, we had to be able to craft a narrative to explain and endorse a course of action that would be persuasive to both retail and institutional investors.

Scaling up in that way meant moving well outside our comfort zone. We needed to know the deals we worked on at a much deeper level than the call-centre model had demanded, and we needed to have an active say in the messaging around them, including the language of the deal itself. That meant fundamentally altering our relationship with our clients, asking them to trust us with more responsibility and give us more agency so that we could deliver a greater return.

It started with revising the call-centre scripts. There was a regulatory requirement that prevented us from discussing anything with shareholders that wasn't contained in the information circular that was sent out to them in advance of the vote. Once the circular was mailed, you had no wiggle room at all. You couldn't even paraphrase a section, let alone help an investor interpret its impact on their holdings. Everything our people said had to come word for word from the circular. To me, that meant we had to write enough of the circular to be able to tell people what we needed to tell them.

To that point in time, Georgeson usually wasn't even sent a rough copy of the circular before it was finalized. Now I began advising companies that not only did we need to see it from the first draft, but they had to build time and space into their process for us to offer edits and suggestions so that the arguments we needed to sell the deal made it into the circular. There was a bit of pushback from the lawyers, but it was almost entirely on the grounds that they'd never had to do this before. Routine and complacency are powerful forces, but they don't stand up all that well against a logical argument for trying something new. Lawyers and investment bankers thought about the deal from their client's perspective, so the circulars were written with that mindset. If we could make sure that the concerns of shareholders were also reflected and addressed, and their common questions were asked and answered, it would make a huge difference come the day of the vote. That was enough to get everyone on side.

Once we started being able to shape the narrative of the deal before it was done, we also needed to make sure that anyone looking for information about the deal and the vote came to us to get it. Information circulars tend to be large documents, commonly upwards of two hundred pages. The majority of retail investors don't do anything more than skim them ahead of a vote, and the same is probably true of a lot of company board members. It was certainly true of the shareholders' financial advisors, and yet the circulars always told people to contact their advisor if they had any questions. It wasn't helpful for anyone in this situation that a person who hadn't read the circular was directed to seek context or advice from another person who hadn't read it. I am not suggesting that financial advisors were abdicating their duty to their clients here, just that you'd need to deploy an army to keep up with the needs of hundreds of clients with multiple stock holdings receiving hundreds of pages of circular on each investment. So, I brought another suggestion to clients, aimed at making the whole process more intentional and beneficial: "Put Georgeson's logo and phone number on the back of the circular."

The response was swift: "We'd be advertising your company. We don't want to do that."

I had a counter, though. "A shareholder's financial advisor is no help," I argued, "and if shareholders call your investor relations department directly, they won't get answers to their questions there, either. They're not going to go digging through a two-hundred-page book to track us down, so put our information on the back and tell them to call if they have any questions. Let us take on the whole mess."

After the first client agreed, it became that much easier to push for the same placement with those that followed. We developed a template for the back of circulars, and to this day, if you flip to the back of one of those documents, you'll see the proxy solicitation firm's contact information.

We shifted to this new model on the Australian Energy deal. Though we charged the company three and a half times our top rate to that point, we delivered at least that big a multiplication of the quality and effectiveness of the work we did. The client came away both happy and praising our brand. From there, things took off like a rocket. We approached our existing clientele and told them our rates were increasing dramatically, but that we'd deliver something new and improved for the money. They bucked, but I gradually convinced all but one client to stay with us. I finally started to feel comfortable with the VP title and to consider that by hiring me at a $75,000 salary, Georgeson had gotten themselves a bargain.

On the strength of my ideas, we more than doubled company revenue in a year. My ambition, and the results I was delivering, didn't go unnoticed, either by my boss, Glenn Keeling, or by headquarters in New York. But the rough lesson I was about to learn was that instead of recognizing and rewarding me, the powers-that-be began to treat me with a mixture of disbelief and quiet hostility.

Shortly after a new CFO was brought on for Canada, he came to tell me about a phone call he'd had with his boss in the New York office. They'd been reviewing some of the clients and deals I'd recently landed, and the American had said, "Despite the fact that Wes is Black, he's doing really well." My Canadian colleague was bothered by this framing of my race as though it were a disadvantage or disability. He told me about it because he felt I had a right to know. I appreciated his openness, but what was I supposed to do with the information?

Still, at this point in my career, I'd never thought of my race as a limiting factor. I thought that every roadblock put in front of me (which I later realized had been screaming systemic racial prejudice) had other possible explanations. I may have known the score subconsciously, but that comment, received second-hand, was the first time I recognized blatant racism. I didn't yet have the tools to do anything with the knowledge other than move on, so that's what I did. I put the exchange out of my mind and kept on doing my job. But even though I wouldn't face another instance of overt racism while I worked there—at least not in-house—that backhanded acknowledgement of my success was a kind of trail marker. My relationship with Georgeson's management, and especially my boss, was about to get a whole lot worse.

15

THE END AND THE BEGINNING

As Georgeson Shareholder's business shifted toward the model I had created during the Australian Energy deal, my approach changed with it. Instead of being a guy who only sold our services, I started to think of myself as operating the way investment bankers do: I would first sell a client on the need for strategic advice and then be one of the people who provided it. Of course, that meant a mountain of additional work, but I felt we needed to have at least one person doing *both* sales and execution. Once I got into this kind of holistic approach to our work, I couldn't imagine doing it any other way.

When you have to execute a deal, you are immersed in every nuance of it. You learn the technical and procedural elements involved and develop a much better sense of the pain points and human failings that can undo you in a crucial vote. Working on deals made me a much, *much* better salesman. It gave me a much stronger sense of who to pitch and how to pitch them—which later evolved into a sense for who to take on as a client and who to avoid—and it really deepened my relationships with clients. Now I wasn't just the guy enlisting them; I ran them through boot camp and then climbed into the trenches alongside them. When they saw me in action, I was able to prove my value directly. As the bankers and lawyers who worked with us advocated for their clients to shell out more to get me in their corner, I was able to raise my fees. They knew what I could do and what my value was, and they couldn't say the same for anyone else selling them shareholder services. They knew Glenn Keeling and went out for drinks with him, but once the contract was signed and the work changed gear and shifted focus, he was no longer involved. When they had a deal in the works, they didn't call Glenn or any other salesperson at Georgeson. Instead, they called me, and they paid what I asked.

As the contracts I brought in skyrocketed in value, and more and more of our clients sought me out personally, my relationship with Glenn deteriorated. There were many disagreements and disputes as we rode toward our inevitable parting, but there is not much point in laying them all out here. To sum it up, I felt that the company consistently attempted to undervalue and limit my work—even as I hit the ball out of the park again and again—so they could get away with paying me as little as possible. When I stood up for myself and pushed back, I believe they saw me as a brat or a diva or a pain in the behind, or all three.

From my earliest days with Georgeson, Keeling enjoyed telling me about the biggest deal in the company's history. It started out as a way to pump Roy Shanks's tires, but over time I began to hear it as a poke at me: *You think you're such a hotshot, but you still don't have a bigger deal than Roy.* According to Glenn, Roy had once signed a major Canadian airline for $300,000—presumably when the airline was fighting a hostile takeover attempt back in 1999. I have no idea what Georgeson delivered for that money, especially given the anxiety around how we were going to make good on $125,000 worth of services for Australian Energy, but Glenn often pointed to Roy in front of me and practically shouted, "The biggest deal in the history of the company? Signed by this guy!"

It burned me up every time he said that. I wanted him never to have an excuse to say it again, and I constantly pushed the envelope trying to do just that. But I was between a rock and a hard place. I wanted to sign something way bigger than the Australian Energy deal, but I couldn't see how Georgeson would muster the horsepower to back me up. But I found out that surpassing Shanks's biggest deal only seemed out of reach until I figured out how to do it.

In early December 2002, a Canadian financial services company—let's call them Bidco—submitted a hostile takeover bid of $6.4 billion to buy a competitor we'll call Targetco. By that point, my title and responsibilities had changed: instead of heading up business development, I was overseeing national sales for Canada. Even so, when Bidco approached Georgeson ahead of the deal going public, Keeling decided not to bring me in to pursue the file. Instead, he reached out to the New York sales team. He was the CEO and it was his prerogative to leave me out.

A group from New York flew up to Toronto, and they went with Keeling to Bidco without me to finalize terms. They reached an agreement and started conducting secret strategy meetings with Bidco. It must have felt like they'd really won something big—until the day they launched the takeover attempt. After it went public, and Targetco saw that Georgeson was working against them, Targetco went nuclear. What Glenn and the New York team had either forgotten or never known was that Targetco was one of our clients. That meant that we had inside information on all their shareholders. When Targetco called up threatening to sue Georgeson into bankruptcy, Keeling and New York decided they had to make a decisive move. So, they switched sides.

Now it was Bidco's turn to lose it, given that Georgeson staff had been sitting in closed-door strategy sessions with them during the leadup to the bid announcement. They'd laid their entire playbook out because they thought they were dealing with a teammate, and then Georgeson switched jerseys and headed to the other locker room. They were furious, but to Keeling and the Georgeson people, that seemed better than working against an active client. Then things got even messier.

After agreeing to quit the Bidco team and work the other side, Keeling and the New York group sent a proposal to the VP in charge of investor relations at Targetco, asking for $650,000 to help defend them against the hostile bid. They pitched the proposal via conference call in Keeling's office, which was beside mine. Our offices had very thin walls, so I could hear the whole thing. Still, I was only half paying attention until the Targetco VP started yelling. To paraphrase: "You guys are out of your minds. There's no way. We're not paying you $650,000 to call some shareholders." He refused to put the proposal in front of his boss, the CFO. "You go back and rework this proposal so that I've got something I can actually bring to him," he said, and hung up.

The group in Keeling's office stuck around for a little while, talking in lowered tones. After they all filed out, Glenn came into my office and dropped a stack of papers on my desk. "Hey, here's a proposal for Targetco," he said. He was about to go on vacation and it was on me to come up with a deal they would sign while he was away

I took a look at the proposal and couldn't argue with Targetco's VP: we really were asking for $650,000 to call the shareholders.

It seemed to me that Keeling's basic issue with the way I approached building the business was that he thought the extra work I took on interfered with my ability to sell. In his view I would be bringing in even more clients, if I wasn't spending so much time paying extra attention to the ones I'd already signed. But it was precisely because I'd worked on the deals and understood how they were structured and how they played out that I was able to rework the Targetco proposal.

What I came up with was a stepladder approach whereby our fee would grow depending on the length and intensity of the fight. It worked like this: If Targetco accepted Bidco's $6.4 billion initial bid, they would pay Georgeson $350,000. If they turned it down and chose to fight, they would pay us an additional $350,000. If Bidco amended the bid and Targetco turned it down again, they would pay us again. There was another bump if a white knight (a bidder friendly to the company and approved by Targetco), entered the fray, and another if the sides couldn't reach an agreement through that process. The final tier was a success fee triggered if Targetco got a higher offer from somewhere else and Bidco's bid collapsed. If we got that far, our fees would total $1.25 million.

I sent the proposal to the VP who'd yelled at Keeling. After he looked it over, he called me. "Wes, I don't think you guys understood what I asked for," he said. "They wanted a fee of $650,000. I told them they were crazy. And here you are, asking for $1.25 million."

I said, "Listen, why don't I meet with you and your CFO together? Let me be the one who explains my fee to him. That way, if he doesn't like it, it's not on you."

He thought that was a reasonable request, so that very day I went over to Targetco's offices. The meeting was in the CFO's office. The room was huge, with mahogany panelled walls and elaborate mouldings—a big, intimidating place. The three of us sat at a round table. I handed a copy of my proposal to the CFO and another to the VP, and then I started going through it. The CFO remained quiet as I spoke. When I finished explaining step one, he just said, "Okay." After explaining step two, there was another "Okay." I went through steps three to six, and after each, his response was "Okay." When I got to the end, he said, "That seems reasonable." Then he turned to the VP and asked, "You okay?" The VP said he was, and the CFO signed the proposal unamended.

I was ecstatic and, once again, assumed that everyone else at Georgeson would be too, especially Glenn. But when I called him at his vacation spot, he said, "Wait a minute here. We wanted $650,000. We figured you'd be able to get us $500,000, at least. You only managed to get $350,000?"

"How do you get only $350,000 from this?" I asked him.

"Because if these guys accept the first bid, it's only $350,000."

"But they're not going to accept the first bid."

"How do *you* know that?" he asked.

I explained. Bidco had already gone public with their bid, and in response Targetco had put out a press release saying the price offered was "inadequate." They weren't going to turn around and accept an offer they'd already called inadequate. Keeling countered that the even-handed language in the press release made him nervous, that it basically committed them to analyzing the full offer when they received it, after which they'd make a recommendation to their shareholders. What if they recommended accepting the offer?

To me, that language was just a formality. The official response had to come in a directors' circular within ten days of the offer. Not only did directors' circulars (effectively statements from the board) usually recommend rejecting initial takeover offers, but Targetco's executives had already been quoted being heavily critical of the deal. In addition, the price offered put management's stock options underwater—the price for them to exercise their stock options was higher than the price Bidco was paying, which rendered the stock options useless. If you want management to support your bid, this is not a good way to start. They'd also just *hired* us, which wouldn't make much sense if they planned to take an offer they'd already received. By law they couldn't reject it until after they received the official offer and the board met and voted, but they were clearly going to say no. Without having to lift a finger to make even one phone call to a shareholder, my deal meant we were guaranteed $350,000. As soon as they formally refused the offer, we immediately stepped up our earnings to $700,000.

I had already heard from a financial advisor that Targetco's board was consulting on their response to the bid, and I was confident we'd get to step three at least, or even step four. When a company is faced with a hostile takeover, they often seek a white knight, a friendly bidder that will offer a higher price. Ultimately, everything I'd laid out in the proposal came to pass, including the white knight. The deal ultimately netted Georgeson every single penny of the $1.25 million I'd negotiated as our top fee.

When the money came in, I didn't expect a fuss and I didn't get one. Still, no one would ever be able to make the claim that somebody else had signed the biggest deal in the history of the company. I'd wanted to prove that I was as good or better than anybody who'd ever worked in proxy solicitation, not just in Canada, but anywhere, including those company hotshots in New York. Also, I'd wanted to make good on the promise I'd made to Keeling after the walkout during my first week on the job. I'd told him that we wouldn't need those guys, that I would figure it out, and I did.

Given the history of the Targetco and Bidco deal, I could understand that it was wishful thinking to hope that my boss would recognize what I'd done on Georgeson's behalf. But I did think he'd want to talk through the possibilities my stepladder idea opened up for the company. So, I went to him soon after we closed the file with an informal proposal.

"We need to change the business," I said. "We need to hire ex-lawyers and ex–investment bankers so we have the in-house expertise to push for bigger fees. There's a lot more money to be made here; just look where we came from and where we are now. We need more people who can do what I'm doing on these deals. We need to go out and find those people."

"We're already the best game in town, Wes," Keeling said. "In fact, we're the only game in town. We don't need to go out and find a bunch of new staff. We're good."

I left that meeting feeling frustrated with the company's lack of vision, which compounded my growing resentment that I had basically already reinvented the business and brought in the biggest contract in the company's history, but I wasn't being compensated for my work. Christine and I were living in Newmarket at the time, which is about an hour's drive north of Toronto. We had three children and were renovating a house to accommodate our growing family. I was working brutal hours trying to do everything I could to support us, and had finally reached the point where what I was getting back from Georgeson just wasn't worth the time away from my family and the extra weight Christine was having to carry at home.

I knew I was headed for a confrontation at work. The big blowout came after I'd recruited a new client at the gym. While I was working out, I'd got to talking to a gentleman at the next machine. I found out he was a senior Bay Street lawyer, so I pitched him on our services. It turned out he had a deal he was working on, and he thought we'd be an asset. I signed him the next day and then walked into Keeling's office, tossed the papers on the table and told him, "I did this deal at the gym. You have to start paying my membership."

The gesture didn't go over well. Keeling rose to his feet as he replied, "Who do you think you are? You don't even give us a heads up when you're doing deals. You just come in and throw them on the table—no advance warning, no plans, no projections. I can't run a business like that."

By now he was really hot. "You know what your problem is, Wes?" he yelled. "You want my job."

That would not be my first reaction if a subordinate threw a million dollars on my desk. I would be more likely to hug them than chastise them.

The truth is he was partially right. While I didn't want his job and I wasn't gunning to oust him, I did want the freedom and agency to pursue and execute deals the way I knew it *had* to be done. I felt I'd earned that, and that feeling, combined with the lack of appreciation I got from him and the company, *had* made me arrogant. Sales is about pride; you have to believe in yourself and your product to really sell it. But in that particular environment, my pride had made me bitter, even spiteful. As I reflected on our fight in a quieter moment, I knew I had to get out of that place.

Still, as we neared the end of 2002, Keeling and I reached an unsteady peace. Then rumours started to circulate that even though company revenues were up, Georgeson wasn't going to pay bonuses, which they'd done in one of my earlier years at the company. I didn't know what to expect when Keeling called me into his office, but he told me that only "over-performers" would receive bonuses that year and I was one of them. I found that it didn't really make a difference as to whether I would stay.

My boss was on vacation the day my $100,000 bonus was paid, and he'd left me no contact information. Once I'd confirmed that the money was in my account, I went to the CFO's office, told him I was resigning from the company and asked him to forward my resignation letter to Keeling.

All hell broke loose. The CFO asked me to wait in my office. "Don't touch your computer; don't do anything," he said. He then got Keeling on the phone and delivered the news. The two of them called New York and their lawyers and I don't know who else, and then the CFO came and told me I had to leave immediately.

I'd given two weeks' notice in my letter of resignation. "Does that mean you're not taking my notice period?" I asked.

"Yes."

"Okay, I need that in writing. And you've got to pay me in lieu of notice." He quickly agreed.

When I got to the building's ground-floor lobby, I took out my company cellphone to make a call and found that it had already been disconnected. I went into the first wireless store I came across and bought a flip phone. Walking out with it, I said to myself, "What these guys didn't want, I'm going to build. I'm going to professionalize this industry. I'm going to bring in the exact people I told them to go out and get. I'm going to build the team I've been dreaming of, and we're going to create a business unlike anything anyone in this industry can even imagine."

Me and that new phone—that was the birth of Kingsdale Advisors. I still have that phone number today, though the phone has been upgraded.

I often say to my wife that I would hate to be my boss. I was a young Black man with a chip on his shoulder out to prove the world wrong. I know that some of the decisions I made came from that resentful place, at a time when I didn't have the maturity to handle things differently. Don't get me wrong— that attitude has gotten me this far. But if I had to do it all over again, I would have behaved with more grace and patience.

16

THE FOUNDER

The proxy solicitation industry in Canada began with John Ross, the guy Georgeson bought out as they looked to expand north of the border. His company had been a one-man show. In 2003, as I prepared to produce my own one-man show, I was returning to the industry's roots. But unlike Ross, I didn't want to run my company out of my house or keep my accounting department in a shoebox. My only competitor wasn't a huge outfit, but it was backed by an international firm. If I wanted to survive, I couldn't emulate Georgeson's model. An advisory business was what I was best-suited to deliver, and that didn't require a network of call centres. I wasn't a total unknown. The reputation I'd built in my three years at Georgeson would get me in the door with some prospective clients.

I put together a comprehensive business plan, including financial projections, clients I would target, potential employees, a marketing strategy and other elements. I shopped my plan to investors I was aware of and to all the major Canadian banks, and everyone turned me down. I really didn't know what my next move was. Then I walked into the main branch of the CIBC in downtown Toronto and amid the sea of staff I saw a Black man behind a desk. His name was Lancelot Dey. I pitched my plan to him even though his bank had already said no. He loved it, and suggested I come back to see him in a week. I did, and he was able to get me approved for a $100,000 loan. Now I had some fuel for this rocket of a company I was about to launch.

But if I hoped to compete, I needed to establish instant credibility. I needed a proper office with a Bay Street address, so that was the next task I set for myself.

Through another conversation at the gym, I found out that the man I got talking with about setting up my own business was part of a group called Kingsdale Capital. It was looking to assemble a coalition of businesses under its umbrella that could offer companies soup-to-nuts service, from financing to investment banking and beyond. "Whatever a company is looking for, we want to be able to provide it," he said. "It sounds like what you've got planned could be a great fit. Why don't you talk to our guys and see if it makes sense for you to join the group?"

I was determined to have full control of the company I built, but I could see the benefits of being under a bigger umbrella. I also wanted that Bay Street address and I liked the name. "Okay," I said. "Let's have a conversation." I went in and chatted with the chairman and vice-chairman. I laid out my vision for the company and how I saw it fitting in the market, and I ran them through my background and expertise. They loved it.

They immediately set me up with their CFO to negotiate terms.

The deal I ended up making was one of the worst of my career, my judgment clouded by my eagerness to lock in that Bay Street office and get to work. Though my insistence on the company remaining *mine* drove me to turn down their first two offers— they'd asked for 70 percent ownership and then a 50-50 split—I ultimately agreed to give them 25 percent equity and 25 percent of my topline revenue. That meant Kingsdale Capital would get a quarter of the revenue I brought in each year regardless of whether I turned a profit, and if I sold the business, they'd get a quarter of the proceeds. In exchange, I got to use the Kingsdale name, an office and a second desk outside my office, which meant I wouldn't have to worry about the furniture if I hired employee number two. I also got to set up shop inside their existing operation; if I brought a client in to meet with me, it would look like I had a team. I decided to name my venture Kingsdale Shareholder Services. With my new address, I was truly ready to become the King (Kingsdale) on Bay Street.

It was a steep price, but it didn't seem like such a big deal to me in the moment because I honestly didn't think I was going to make all that much money. When I was at Georgeson, I had a global brand behind me, and I was able to leverage that brand to open doors and demand premium pricing. When Kingsdale's principals had asked me for financial projections, I'd been uncharacteristically conservative, forecasting about half a million dollars in revenue per year. They pushed me for an aggressive projection, so I'd raised the target to $1.4 million in revenue. But I really did think half a million was the number. Paying 25 percent of that didn't seem so bad to me.

It would end up being an expensive lesson. Recall my earlier vow that I was going to set up my own firm and it was going to be different from anything anyone in this industry could even imagine? Clearly, I didn't truly believe in my own vision.

That deal was me at my most Canadian. I think we are mostly a contented people, and that can lead to dreaming small. Once we get a bit of business that we like, we don't feel an immediate impulse to grow it, to take it international—or even to another province, let alone national. We settle, thinking, *This is good.* It's admirable in a way, I suppose, but also frustrating. I saw that thinking constantly at Georgeson. *We're number one. Why take a risk? Why get uncomfortable?* I find it almost funny to realize that after fighting that exact brand of thinking for so long, when I finally set out on my own, I immediately fell straight into it. Maybe I made my break just in time—the attitude was contagious, but the case I caught was mild and temporary.

I got set up in my new (soon to be wildly overpriced) office and once again started working my Rolodex. I hadn't been able to reach out to clients while I was contemplating leaving, or in the two weeks I'd spent on Georgeson's payroll after I was gone. That would've been a good way to get sued. Being careful on that front didn't stop Georgeson from coming after me, though. From the second I was officially in business, I started getting letters from their lawyers telling me I couldn't launch a competing firm and threatening legal action. They took particular exception to a phrase in the initial emails I sent out to prospective clients: "I will continue to provide the great service that you expect of me." I was referring only to my personal reputation, but they argued that I was inviting clients to jump ship to

Kingsdale. Ultimately, it was nothing more than an intimidation tactic. And while it did make for some tense moments at home—the letters were sent to my house, and Christine had to sign for them—they couldn't sue me for competing with them because they'd never asked me to sign a non-compete. They had no legal way to stop me from starting Kingsdale. If they wanted to shut me down, they had to beat me fair and square by offering their clients a better, more appealing product.

I trusted my expertise and believed I could outsell anyone at Georgeson, but there's a unique kind of pressure to embarking on an entrepreneurial venture. *You* may trust your skills and your product, but you don't know whether anyone else will, until they actually do. If the first day of unreturned calls and emails at Georgeson had made me panicky, what I was experiencing now was that feeling on steroids. And this time I was the boss, so there was no one to talk me down.

Not only was I dealing with my own doubts, but also those heaped on me by pretty much every colleague and friend I'd worked with at Georgeson. They knew what I could do better than anyone, but none of them had been willing to come over to join me. I'd even offered a few whose work I truly valued equity in my company as a signing bonus. Worried about mortgages and their kids' educations, they'd all turned me down.

True, there was a historical precedent that fuelled their skepticism. The folks who'd quit Georgeson so dramatically when I was first hired started a competing firm that went out of business in eighteen months, creating the impression that no one could compete with Georgeson. As far as I was concerned, that other firm had failed because they'd tried to do exactly what Georgeson did, rather than change the business. Even so, people still expected Kingsdale to fail, and I couldn't prove I wouldn't until I didn't.

The call that finally let me exhale came within a month. It was from a Canadian aircraft maintenance firm dealing with an outside investor who didn't like the company's top three executives and was looking to replace the board. The firm hired me for $250,000 with a mandate to defend them—half of my small-dreams annual revenue projection.

I was thankful for the money, but the real blessing was the chance to stop dialing for dollars and get to work on an actual file. There was still pressure, of course. I had to deliver for my client. But it was the type of pressure that I thrived under, pressure you could actively deal with as opposed to just sitting by the phone. I stepped up to work closely with the three senior executives to defend them and the company. Soon we were gaining traction, and I was certain we were going to be successful. Then I received a call from the chairman of the board. "Wes," he said, "you are working for the board, right?" When I replied that of course I was, he said, "Great! The board has reached a settlement with the dissident shareholder, and I want you to tell the three executives that they should expect a letter from the board shortly terminating their employment."

This I did not see coming. But I made the call, my three friends were terminated, and the fight was over. A quick way for my company to make a quarter of a million, but not a way to build a reputation.

That was the deal that got Kingsdale into the market. My second deal showed me that I was going to own it.

I'd started chasing a piece of one of the earliest, if not the first, tech fights in Canada after seeing a press release announcing that the company's former CEO was coming after the current leadership. The company designed and built technical components for the film and TV industry, and since the former CEO had left, its performance had been all over the place. The CEO had solid backing and looked like the favourite to come out on top, so I reached out to pitch the company, thinking they'd need all the help they could get. Kingsdale was still so new that they didn't want to risk throwing their lot in with me. Then the former CEO hired a top Bay Street law firm to represent him and went with Georgeson.

Literally left with no other option, the tech company defaulted to me. The fee was pitiful—just $75,000—but who was I? This was Kingsdale's first full-blown activist fight. The previous deal had been a pillow fight in comparison. And I had to work it on my own, against my old, well-established firm and excellent counsel. The former CEO was loved by the shareholders, and the existing management team was out of favour. The company usually holds some measure of power and authority in a proxy fight, like the incumbent in a political race. We were an exception, true underdogs. I went into the fight with one thought: *I must win.* And I worked my butt off.

I personally called anyone with a significant stake in the company to sell our story to them. I made calls all day at the office, and once I got home after my two-hour commute to the suburbs, I continued to make calls. I remember one call in particular, which was to a French-speaking shareholder. My French is bad now and it was worse then, and we just couldn't communicate. I urgently called out to my eldest son, Darian, who was in grade two French immersion. When he came running into my home office, I held the phone out, my hand over the receiver. "Darian, I need you to say something for me in French," I said. "Tell this woman I need her to vote her yellow proxy for the management slate of directors at the upcoming AGM."

I was so driven that I didn't even register how unreasonable my request was. Darian was eight and didn't have any corporate French. I put the call on hold as I tried to coax the words out of him. "Come on, you're in French immersion. How can you not know this?" When he started to cry, I came to my senses. I ended the call, apologized to my son and helped him calm down. The next day—literally the next day—I hired a bilingual representative for my team. My early hiring often went like that: it addressed an immediate need rather than a grand plan. Darian still remembers that day and we often laugh about it. He teases me, saying, "I knew you when Kingsdale was *primitive*."

As hard as I worked, and as much as I asked from the people around me, things weren't going our way. Everybody I talked to hated the management team. Some of the bigger institutional investors didn't even want to take a call. As the AGM approached, the company hired a new CEO, which armed me with fresh material about how shareholders should give his new vision for the company a chance. But the move came so close to the vote that it felt like it might be too little, too late. The shareholders seemed to have made up their minds.

My life has taught me again and again that you keep playing your pieces to the best of your ability no matter how hopeless a situation seems, and you play until the end. As long as you still have a move, there's hope. Something the company side has some control over ahead of an AGM is the proxy deadline—the cut-off point for proxy votes to be counted. Usually, it's forty-eight hours before the start of the meeting, in order to give the scrutineer time to process the votes, but the company can extend that deadline or waive it entirely, allowing votes to be counted right up to the start of the meeting. If you're ahead in the voting, you stick to the deadline in order to lock in that advantage and limit last-minute flip-flopping.

I came up with a strategy as a direct result of lessons learned on this campaign: when working to defend a company in a proxy fight, always hold the meeting on a Tuesday. If the meeting is Friday at 4:00 p.m., the forty-eight-hour proxy deadline is the preceding Wednesday at 4:00 p.m., which gives the company two days to change shareholders' minds if the company is losing the vote. If you call the meeting for a Tuesday at 4:00 p.m., then the proxy deadline is the previous Friday at 4:00 p.m. This gives the company Friday evening, Saturday, Sunday, Monday and most of the day Tuesday to persuade shareholders to change their minds, or to come up with a Hail Mary strategy.

A few days before the AGM, I advised the company to waive the deadline so that I could keep working on the shareholders right up to the start of the meeting. I had one option left to try, and I wanted to buy as much time as possible in case it actually worked.

The company's largest shareholder owned 15 percent of the company. I figured they were staunchly supporting the former CEO, even though they hadn't said so publicly or privately. They had to be, because they wouldn't give us a meeting. If we could flip them, it would mean a thirty-point swing in the race overall—it was basically the only way we could win.

Two days out from the meeting, I still hadn't had any luck getting them to talk with us. I kept on calling other share-holders. It was American Thanksgiving, a Thursday, but I'd forgotten the holiday and didn't think twice about making calls to the States. One American gentleman picked up just as he was about to sit down to dinner. He was by himself, though, and didn't seem to mind letting his food get a little colder as we talked about how he might vote his shares. Throughout our conversation, he seemed receptive to the points I was making. Then, toward the end, he blew my mind when he said, "By the way, beyond the shares I own, I'm a portfolio manager and my firm owns 15 percent of the company." This was the 15 percent owned by the shareholder who'd refused to speak with us.

"We've had a great conversation today," I said. "Why don't you let me set up a meeting tomorrow with the company's man-agement team? Just to give you a chance to hear what they have to say, and what the new CEO has to say, before you make up your mind for good."

"Fine, I'll talk to them," he said.

I could have done a backflip. I called my client. "Guess what?" I said. "I've booked us a call with the portfolio manager for the 15 percent shareholder." They were shocked.

We had that call on the eve of the meeting. The new CEO did a fantastic job of presenting his vision and making a case for him-self. We threw everything we had at the portfolio manager and his team. At the end of the call, he said, "Listen, I appreciate you guys talking to us, but I think we're going to stick where we are."

I said, "I'm sorry to hear that, but thank you for taking the time to hear us out. I'm going to give you guys my cell number.

If anything changes and you want to make something happen tomorrow, just give me a call. Okay?"

The next morning, I made sure that if the 15-percent guys changed their minds, we'd be able to register their votes in time. We were still communicating with faxes at the time, and since we were meeting in a hotel conference room, I went to the hotel manager and asked if I could take over the entire business centre, commandeering all the fax machines so no one else could use them. The manager was fine with that. Afterwards, I went up to the suite where the company's management team was camping out. Losing seemed like a sure thing. I remember the newly hired CEO saying, "This is the shortest I've ever served as CEO of a company." Then he left to take a long walk.

Just before the meeting was to start, while the CEO was still out walking, I got a call from a guy on the 15 percent team. "We're changing our votes," he said. "Where do you want us to send the fax?"

Holy crap. I didn't stop to ask why; I just gave them the fax number and took off running for the business centre. Then I remembered to detour to the conference room first. Once the board chairman called the meeting to order, the voting would be over. When I burst into the conference room, the chairman was walking to the podium. I rushed to the front of the room and asked him to delay the meeting for half an hour.

"Why? What's going on?"

"There's no time to explain," I told him. "Just delay for half an hour."

As I turned and hustled back toward the business centre, I heard him on the microphone: "Ladies and gentlemen, thank you for coming today. We're going to start the meeting in half an hour."

I stood sentry by the fax machine, and then breathed out a big sigh of relief as a stream of paper began pouring from it. The full 15 percent was changing from the former CEO's side to ours, one proxy vote at a time. It took ten or fifteen minutes for it all to come through. Then I gathered up all those pages of faxes and ran to the scrutineer's table. "Here's a revocation of 15 percent and it's coming over to our side," I said. That was one of the most satisfying sentences I've uttered in my entire career.

Keeling was at the meeting, along with the army of lawyers representing his client. They'd watched me tear into the conference room and catch the chairman; they'd listened to him delay the meeting; and they'd seen me run out and then back in and over to the scrutineer's table. They had no clue what was going on, but I bet they knew that me running around couldn't be a good thing.

Those final votes were tabulated, and when the scrutineers gave us the proxy vote count, we were ahead by enough that the in-person vote wouldn't change the outcome. The chairman walked back onto the platform, cleared his throat at the microphone and announced the result. We'd won. The whole room was stunned. You could feel everyone thinking the same thing: *What just happened?* When the CEO, back from his walk, heard the results, he asked the same question.

I hadn't had a moment to stop and find out why the 15 percent group had changed sides. The reason turned out to be simple: they wanted to give the new CEO a shot. They'd liked what he'd said on our call, but then they had to get their heels undug and rethink their position. Which they did in the nick of time.

That was my first victory with Kingsdale, and it showed me

what my company was going to be: we would be fighters for our clients, we were going to think outside the box, and we were going to leave no stone unturned. It was the case study I used when I started building and training my team: This is why you make the extra call. This is how you execute, how you win. That win showed me how to create opportunity, and victory, out of nothing.

Of course, beating the competition once didn't mean I'd beaten them for good. But beating them so dramatically may have gotten into their heads. After that proxy fight, Georgeson started to slip up. It was like when a boxer who has never been beaten is solidly trounced by an upstart. It shows that boxer he is vulnerable, which plays with his psyche. I'd been the guy who set their fees for three years, so I knew what Georgeson should be charging on a job. After that loss, they halved their fees. Friends still inside the company told me they did it to starve me out. It was a siege tactic: If they could snap up all the available business long enough for my capital to dry up, I'd be forced to fold. So, they underbid me.

The problem was that cutting their fees in half was too radical a move. If they'd come in under me by twenty-five or even fifty grand each time, they would have won everything we were bidding on in a heartbeat. But by cutting their fees so drastically, they created such a disparity between their fees and mine that prospective clients began calling me up to yell, "Wes, what the hell is this? Why would you charge so much more than Georgeson? Georgeson's willing to do it for half."

Once I got a client on the phone, even an upset one, I could start selling. They gave me the perfect opportunity to make a case for why they should go with me anyway. Because I'd been turned down when I tried to transform Georgeson from a sales operation into one that could also execute, I knew what I was up against. I could execute, so that's what I sold. I walked each client through the whole deal—what I was going to do and how I'd do it. Once they'd heard me out, people started to say, "Okay."

Since the fees charged by proxy solicitation firms have to be publicly disclosed in the circular published prior to the AGM, Georgeson could see in every situation that I was charging double, and then triple their fees, and then the sky was the limit.

I soon heard from clients themselves that Keeling had started to badmouth my new business directly in the pitch process. Rather than hurt me, the things he said made clients more likely to choose me. Which didn't stop him from letting rip.

After a year or so of this, I called Keeling and told him I wanted to talk things out.

"You haven't reached out in all this time and now you want to talk?" he responded.

"I just want to bury the hatchet between us."

He said he could meet me the next night at Canoe, a fancy restaurant at the top of TD Bank Tower in the heart of Toronto's financial district.

The next night, I took the elevator up to the fifty-fourth-floor restaurant and found him already sitting at the bar. Georgeson had recently been purchased by Computershare, a huge international transfer agent, and now he had a much bigger war chest. As soon as I sat down, he told me what he planned to do with it: put me out of business.

Then he paid his bill and left me sitting there. I hadn't even ordered.

It was the worst thing he could've said to me. He wasn't threatening me, he was threatening my ability to put food on the table. By threatening my livelihood, he was threatening my family. No one should do that. And you *really* shouldn't do it if you can't deliver on the threat—like those athletes you see trash-talking their opponents ahead of a big game who then go on to lose. I skipped dinner, went back to the office and got to work, more determined than ever to evolve the industry and create something new.

Georgeson had a number of call centres and made six dollars each time one of their staffers picked up the phone. Even with a war chest big enough to destroy my new company, they wouldn't abandon this model they'd invested so heavily in, although the industry was leaving them behind. As a result, Keeling was never able to make good on his threat. On February 5, 2015, a *Financial Post* headline read, "Proxy Solicitation Firm Georgeson to Exit Canada." The paper went on to report: "Sources have estimated that Kingsdale, founded by Wes Hall, has more than 70 percent of the proxy solicitation market."

Still, I always remember how great my relationship with Glenn Keeling was at the start. He aggressively pursued me to join Georgeson. When I turned down his initial offer, he went back and made the case to the higher-ups that I deserved the opportunity. Almost a third of his team left after I came on board, and he stood by me. We had lots of laughs while travelling for work—he was a fun guy to be around. And for quite a while, he was pretty patient in his dealings with a rookie with a chip on his shoulder. I was grateful then and I am still grateful to him today.

My aggressive revenue projection for Kingsdale Capital been $1.4 million. In year one, we brought in $2.5 million. Well before we hit that number, I realized just how bad the deal I'd signed was. I'd already had to hire some staff, and it was clear we'd be expanding more in year two. The only contributions that Kingsdale Capital had made were the single office and the second desk. I had to pay them for every additional workspace as new employees came on board, on top of the 25 percent topline royalty and the equity that was increasing in value by the second. This was not viable for me, but they were adamant about not renegotiating our agreement.

After three years, the "rent" on my office must have been the most expensive per square foot in all of Toronto. We were up to twenty employees and over $7 million dollars in revenue. At that point, I told Kingsdale Capital I had to buy them out.

Buying my company back was the most difficult deal I've ever closed. They didn't want to sell—they were making a fortune off me in exchange for basically nothing. They refused to play ball at all. Finally, I gave them an ultimatum: "Either you take the deal that's on the table and I buy you out, or I fold Kingsdale, go across the street and set up Wes Hall Proxy Solicitation." I'd built the Kingsdale brand so effectively that people assumed that the principals of Kingsdale Capital worked for me. If I left, it would deal the Kingsdale brand a significant blow.

That did it. In January 2007, I gained full control of my business. From then on, I dedicated myself to pushing the industry to new levels.

17

I'VE BEEN WORKING
ON THE RAILROAD

Public companies are mandated by the Toronto Stock Exchange to hold their AGMs within six months of their fiscal year end, which means that most AGMs fall in the first half of the year. Effectively, proxy season runs from January to the end of June. It is an extremely busy time—at Kingsdale we generally make 80 percent of our revenue in those months. A person has to be unusually driven, focused and energetic to survive it and come back for more. Part of my job is to find ways to spread the work out, getting as much done in advance as possible to ease the strain of our busiest months. But it's also my job to make sure we stay busy, preferably year-round. The technology proxy fight I'd help win marked a shift in the Canadian business environment that made keeping busy a lot easier.

When I got into the industry, many of my early clients were mining companies. I love mining CEOs and executives, and there were a lot of colourful characters in that sector at the time—bold, brash personalities who made bold, brash moves. Those moves had a tendency to spark drama and a lot of infighting. If a board fired its CEO, for instance, the CEO was likely to want their job back and make a play for the company. If a board had a dispute with a major shareholder, the shareholder was more likely to try to replace the board than to go away. Mining was also the Canadian industry that took the earliest and most aggressive dive into hostile mergers and acquisitions (M&As). A mining company would find a nice asset, its stock would start to climb, and one of its competitors would make a bid for the company in order to get the asset—it's more of a sure bet to buy than to explore. When the competitor was turned down, the hostile takeover would start. Any of these conflicts, from dysfunctional squabbling to hostile bids, could lead to a proxy fight, and all those mining industry fights played a huge part in Kingsdale's growth.

For proxy solicitation to explode the way it did, people had to be rocking the boat. Early on, the people most willing to do that were in mining, and that made sense to me: hostile takeovers were kind of un-Canadian, but these were companies whose major assets tended to be situated outside of Canada, often in some very dangerous places. To go after another company is an aggressive, risky, often uncomfortable act. In my experience, most executives in this country wanted, above all else, to stay comfortable. They were not interested in making waves.

So, what changed?

For one thing, the rest of the Canadian establishment saw that the miners were building world-class companies through risk and acquisition, which lit a bit of a fire under everyone else. But I think the biggest motivator wasn't growth potential; it was fear of losing what they already had.

Activist investors had been on the move in the United States for a while. They were outsiders who bought a significant stake in a company and then pushed for significant changes to the way it was run in the hope of improving performance and turning a profit. At the time of the tech proxy fight, this still wasn't a common dynamic in Canadian business, but it did reveal the potential power shareholders possessed if they could get organized. Until that point, the boards of most big Canadian companies had taken for granted their ability to dictate terms to their shareholders. The attitude was, *Hey, if you don't like my company, sell your stock and get lost.* In the early to mid-2000s, it became clear that that attitude wasn't going to cut it anymore.

Though our client won the technology proxy fight, they came out of it still wiping the nervous sweat off their brow. Everyone watching knew they shouldn't have survived—and wouldn't have if the other side had hired me. It was a sign to other companies, who weren't used to a serious challenge, let alone being the underdogs, that this could happen to you if you failed to build a relationship with your investors. The message was hammered home even harder in a few other proxy fights that came soon after, in which former management came after companies the way the technology company's former CEO had done, but actually won.

Whereas in year one of Kingsdale, I had to explain to prospective clients why we were useful, by year two everyone had realized that if you fell into a major dispute, you needed someone on your side who knew how to navigate the conflict. When American activist investors finally started looking north of the border for opportunity, things became so unsettled that publicly traded companies no longer knew when a potential conflict might hit them. Instead of calling us only when they were facing something aggressive and un-Canadian, they began to think it made sense to give us a call for advice before they knew the specific challenges they needed us to address.

Of course, that meant we had to be ready at a moment's notice to give our clients advice they weren't already getting from their lawyers and investment bankers. To get to that level, I adopted the strategy I'd once recommended to Keeling: I hired a lot of former lawyers and investment bankers who knew deal execution front to back and down to the smallest detail. They could hold their own in any conference room, whether they were meeting with a client and their other advisors or selling a deal to a major institutional investor.

I also started to collect case law from other parts of the country. When we started out, every single lawyer would refer to the same case, *Blair v. Consolidated Enfield Corporation*, a 1995 Supreme Court judgment on a dispute between a management group and a major shareholder that dealt with the validity and scope of proxy votes. It seemed like any time people in a strategy meeting had to make a tough decision, the lawyers would invariably say, "Well, in *Blair v. Enfield*, the court ruled . . ." It was the first and best-known case in the field, and it became the benchmark, because people were hesitant to take these disputes to court and make new case law.

There *was* case law being made, though, so I began to create a proxy-specific database of precedents. I signed up to receive reports from law firms all over the country. When a firm won a case, especially a precedent-setting one, it wasn't shy about advertising it. I'd read judgments from the west coast or the Yukon and file them away for future use. When a lawyer brought up *Blair v. Enfield* to add context to a decision, we could add another perspective: "You're certainly right that *Blair v. Enfield* was resolved on that issue, but there's this other provincial case where the judge ruled a little differently."

I was careful in these exchanges not to show anyone up. I wasn't trying to pretend I was a sharper legal mind than the best lawyers in Canada, but I was taking the opportunity to demonstrate Kingsdale's expertise and the value we brought to a proxy fight. Thankfully, I didn't run into much ego. The lawyers we worked with were almost always receptive to any new and useful information—they were even excited by it. Sharing case law became another way to win over and build relationships with people well positioned to champion our work in the future. As my relationships with various law firms deepened, I started encouraging lawyers to try to make their own case law, and not to be afraid to lose in the effort. Once they saw the scope of my knowledge on proxies, if I said, "You should go to court on this because the other side's wrong and you'll win," they took my advice seriously. One of the lawyers who was eager to make new case law from the day we met on our first proxy fight was Walied Soliman of Norton Rose Fulbright. And each time he followed through and went to court with his litigation colleague Orestes Pasparakis, new case law was created.

Soon, we had no trouble staying busy all year long. But being so busy was its own challenge. In every one of our proposals, I included a written assurance to our clients that our team was available twenty-four hours a day, 365 days a year. I guaranteed that kind of service when the company was just me, and we still guarantee it today. In an industry where the hours are long to begin with, I wanted us to be known as an especially hard-working firm.

I led by example on that front for years. It didn't matter if Christine and I had been planning a family trip for months; I would cancel my vacation to work for clients. When we did take vacation, Christine would usually run off with the kids while I stayed in the room to take conference calls. Sometimes I missed being with my family at Kingdom Hall because of work. Once, I was in the delivery suite with Christine, who was giving birth to one of our kids, and in between her contractions, I was on a conference call because we were in the middle of a large hostile takeover deal. No, I'm not proud to say that.

But I believed I couldn't ask people to do something I wasn't prepared to do myself. They had to see me leading and making sacrifices, and so I did. That inspired many of the people who came aboard to buy into that strategy and adopt that work ethic, but there's no getting around the fact that it was a recipe for burnout. When people have quit Kingsdale, it has almost always happened just before proxy season—the worst time to lose staff—when they've decided they just can't handle another year of it. One of the biggest blows the company ever took is one I now attribute almost completely to burnout.

It happened very early in our growth. I had about ten employees at the time. An office that small meant that everyone wore multiple hats, and everything was out in the open. We were working non-stop and only getting busier—my staff would double in size in the next twelve months. Everyone was exhausted and stressed and getting on each other's nerves, and there was no end in sight. One day, I was sitting at my desk when one of my people came in and handed me their resignation: "I'm leaving."

"What do you mean? We have all this stuff going on."

I didn't get an explanation. As soon as they walked out, the next person walked in to resign.

It was a replay of my first week at Georgeson, except I lost half of my staff, not a third. It was a massive setback, and one that required a difficult on-the-fly rebuild. In the moment, I took it as a coordinated attempt to take my company down. But once I got a little distance, I chalked it up to stress and burnout. My people were moving at a pace they couldn't sustain with no sign that the pace would ever slow. Resigning was simply their way of yelling, "Stop the bus. I need to get off."

Kingsdale is a people business. My biggest assets ride the elevator up to our office every day. To be successful, I need the right team, and back then I didn't yet have it. As I rebuilt, I paid much more attention to the hiring process. Ex-lawyers and -bankers are not hard to find, but I needed people who shared my drive, who could not only handle being busy all the time but also *wanted* to be busy all the time. I looked for people out to prove that they were the best of the best. And I was able to find them, because it was a bit like looking in a mirror.

I am lucky to have found something to do with my life that I have a unique talent for. Some people who end up in that fortunate situation coast on their talent, having found that they can put in half the effort and still get by okay. Others see it as an opportunity to prove they are the best in the world, maybe even the best ever. They start with the talent but also bring the work. And they thrive in situations where they have to overcome others' doubts about how good they are.

There's a famous sequence from a 1987 game between the Chicago Bulls and Utah Jazz in Salt Lake City. The Bulls brought the ball up the court, and Michael Jordan caught an entry pass deep in the post with John Stockton guarding him. Stockton is a Hall of Famer, a very good basketball player, but he's only six foot one and 170 pounds. The much bigger and stronger Jordan easily overpowered him for an uncontested dunk. After the basket, Larry H. Miller, then the owner of the Jazz, yelled at Jordan, "Pick on somebody your own size." As soon as Chicago got the ball back, they kicked it to Jordan in the Utah half, and he drove and dunked over six-foot-eleven centre Melvin Turpin. As he was running back on defence, Jordan called to Miller, "Is he big enough?"

That's the spirit I bring to the proxy business. The money has never been the motivation. If I was in it only for financial gain, I would've burned out or lost interest long ago. It's about proving I'm better at this than anyone else and then working to widen the gap. It's about setting records so outlandish that they will never be broken. It's about giving my all to every client, so that even if we lose, no one can say I didn't do everything possible to win. It's about taking on the most impossible mandates, winning them and then saying to the world, "Is that all you've got?"

This attitude did not square with my commitment to humility through my faith, but I was a young Black man out to prove the world wrong. It has been a conflict throughout my career. But what my faith does reaffirm in me is that you don't win at all costs. Some people win by cutting moral corners. That is something I would never do. No matter the joy I find in proving that I am the best at what I do, and in winning, my faith grounds me as to what is ultimately important.

Talking about impossible mandates? So far in my career, there has been no better example of an impossible mandate than Canadian Pacific Railway (CP).

Bill Ackman hired Kingsdale in October 2011 to consult on his dealings with Canadian Pacific Railway. Ackman is the CEO of Pershing Square Capital Management, an American hedge fund known for high-profile activist campaigns. He brought us in right around the time he crossed the 10 percent ownership threshold, requiring him to publicly disclose his CP holdings. He was already in talks behind the scenes with CP's chair, John Cleghorn, about changes to the business that Pershing Square thought could drastically improve its efficiency. The talks had shown early promise, but Ackman's Canadian securities lawyer, Patricia Olasker, suggested he hire Kingsdale as a precautionary measure.

As I do with most activist clients, I advised Ackman to take things slowly. Activist investors have a tendency toward impatience. It's a tendency I can understand and even relate to. If you look at a business and see obvious ways to make it more efficient and effective, you're excited to share those ideas, and you kind of expect management to instantly see that you're trying to help them. I felt the same way when I brought suggestions to Georgeson's management, and I remember my frustration when I met resistance.

But the best-case scenario in any potential proxy fight is that you never get to the fight at all. Pointing that out might seem to run against my best interests—the longer a dispute plays out and the more intense it gets, the higher my fees climb—but my end goal is to leave my clients happy. When things go public, there is almost always some ugliness, something that gets taken personally by both sides. Working issues out behind the scenes and finding a solution that's satisfying for all involved is the surest route to coming away with a smile on your face. But such a bargaining process takes real patience.

An activist investor can become so wrapped up in the work they've done on a file that they forget that from the company's perspective, their suggestions might be coming out of left field. Most management groups feel they are already doing the best possible job for shareholders under the circumstances. It can be a serious blow to the ego to have some outsider appear on the scene and point out all the ways they could be doing better. Good executives will come around to sound arguments, but they have to be given time to adjust their thinking, and maybe lick some wounds. Someone who has just sunk a billion dollars into a company can find it very hard to give management that time and space, but it always yields a better result.

In the case of CP, I felt that patience was particularly important. The company had the bluest of blue-chip boards in Canadian business. Being named to its board was almost like a lifetime achievement award, a golden handshake after a stunning career. Of the board's fifteen members, six were Order of Canada recipients. Cleghorn was the former chairman and CEO of Royal Bank, the biggest bank and the biggest public company in Canada. The former CEO of Suncor, Canada's second-biggest public company, was also a member of CP's board. This was a group that believed itself to be unassailable, for the good reason that everyone else believed it too. At one point during negotiations with Pershing Square, Cleghorn was going around town telling anyone who was interested that no shareholder would ever vote him off the board. Who was this American bull-in-a-china-shop activist guy to tell them how to run their business? It was an attitude that prevented the board from seeing the sense in Ackman's proposals. Their arrogance made it hard for Ackman to be patient with them, or even believe that they'd ever get over themselves to the point where they would consider some new ideas.

In November Ackman flew to a private airstrip in Montreal to meet Cleghorn in person. Sitting in a room in the terminal building, he shared Pershing Square's analysis and recommendations in a book-length document that laid out every change he hoped to see at CP. He boiled the big ones down for Cleghorn: He wanted to replace CEO Fred Green with E. Hunter Harrison, who'd been CEO of Canadian National Railway (CN) and whose non-compete clause with CN was set to expire in January. And he wanted two seats on the board.

Given Ackman's reputation for shaking things up, and the fact that Pershing Square owned 15 percent of the company, it wasn't that much to ask. With just two seats on a fifteen-member board, Ackman would still have to do a lot of persuading of other members to get anything done. But Cleghorn was opposed. "That's not going to happen," he told Ackman. "We love Fred. Fred's a great guy."

They went back and forth for a while, but it was clear to Ackman that they weren't getting anywhere, so he decided to leave. He said his goodbyes and went back to his plane. As they started taxiing to the runway, his pilot told him, "There's an elderly gentleman chasing the plane." It was Cleghorn, in his seventies, in the middle of a Montreal winter with no coat on. Ackman got off the plane to talk with Cleghorn, who told him he'd spoken with Fred Green as soon as Ackman had left. It turned out that Green was okay with stepping aside. Cleghorn assured Ackman they had a deal. They shook hands and Cleghorn said, "Welcome to CP." They agreed to sort out the paperwork in the coming days.

Ackman told us the story in our strategy meeting the next day. He was in good spirits at that point, but when two weeks went by with nothing further from Cleghorn, he started to get agitated. Ackman didn't have a cell number for Cleghorn, only his email address. I don't know whether Cleghorn had been advised by someone to keep most of his exchanges with Ackman in writing, or it's just his old-school nature not to hand out his number, but it's my position that in a situation like that, you want as much verbal communication as possible—the more you talk, the more likely it is you'll come to terms on a deal. Since Ackman didn't have the option to pick up the phone, he sent a note to Cleghorn to say, "Listen, I thought we had a deal. Why am I hearing nothing from your end?" Cleghorn's response was basically, "I don't know what you're talking about." It was like the conversation at the airport had never happened.

Ackman lost it. He called me up and told me he'd drafted an email to send back. He knew that Cleghorn was something of a war historian, and so his subject line was "War and Peace." Ackman wrote about the "border skirmish" happening between the United States and Canada and his desire to avoid a "nuclear winter." He wrote that if a battle happened, CP would lose, and he demanded that Cleghorn live up to the deal they'd made. He said that if CP didn't honour the agreement, he would rent the largest hall in the city of Toronto and host an event to expose and embarrass the company. He would publicly air every misstep and poor decision the board and its chairman had made.

"I wouldn't send that email," I told him, when he finished reading it to me.

"Okay, why not?"

"Because it makes you sound like a bully."

"Well, it's already sent," he said.

CP immediately leaked his email to the media in order to make Ackman look like the bad guy in the battle that was about to begin.

Despite my opinion that Ackman shouldn't have sent it in the first place, the email ended up being a positive development, because it forced us to follow through on his threat. No one in Canada had ever launched a proxy fight with a public town hall. It was fitting that we would venture into that unknown territory for the first and (as of this writing) only time, given that this was the biggest and most public proxy fight the country had ever seen.

We scheduled the town hall for February 2012, but before we could get to planning the event itself, we had to deal with a significant technicality. As I'd pointed out to clients in my Georgeson days, you can't make any argument to shareholders ahead of a proxy fight that isn't contained in the information circular. In effect, you can't solicit votes, or even talk about the fact that there's a vote coming up, until the AGM is called, which is what triggers the deadline to release the circular. We didn't have a meeting date yet. How were we going to hold a town hall if we weren't allowed to say anything?

The solution we came up with was to publish our own circular. Generally, the target company of a proxy fight issues the first circular and then the activist side follows. We decided to turn that order around (I believe for the first time ever on a high-profile campaign). It was no simple task—it involved an incredibly detailed legal vetting process—but we got it done and got it out to shareholders, effectively saying, "We don't have a date for the meeting yet, but we know there will be a meeting on this at some point, and here's what you need to know."

As Ackman had promised, we rented the Hilton Toronto's biggest banquet hall. Now we had to fill it. We invited every investor and we invited the press, but since we didn't know if they'd come, we enlisted every Kingsdale employee and every employee of the other advisory firms Ackman had hired to be ready to attend. It turned out we didn't have to use any of them. Four hundred and fifty people came in person, with hundreds more online. Bill Ackman and Hunter Harrison got up in front of them and did a fireside chat. They first spoke about mismanagement and inefficiency at CP, highlighting failure after failure on the part of the board and management team. Then they presented a vision of how the company would run under Harrison. Ackman made good on every threat in his email to Cleghorn. It was a heck of a way to kick off a proxy fight.

There is no template to follow in a proxy fight because every deal is different. It's one of the aspects I like most about the work. You get dropped into a situation where so much is unfamiliar: The management culture of the company, the personalities, drama and infighting are all new. The threat you're defending against or the case for making change is new. Even the industry itself might be something you have no real experience with. You need to get the lay of the land as fast as possible in order to understand what will speak most powerfully to shareholders, and that process of learning is always invigorating. It's a work environment that my early life prepared me for. I may now be consulting on multi-billion-dollar mergers, but on a personal level the stakes are actually lower than when I was figuring out how to fit into the dynamics at United Bakery or the Grahams' home.

As I travelled the country speaking to shareholders alongside Hunter Harrison and Pershing Square's Paul Hilal (who sub-sequently left to set up his own firm) in the months after the town hall, the learning process was one of the most enjoyable and enriching of my life. Harrison, who passed away in 2017, was brilliant. Watching him make our case and then, afterwards, lis-tening to him talk through the particulars of why he did things the way he did them was like taking an MBA. I got lessons in management, the railroad industry and precision scheduled railroading that no one else on earth could have given. Harrison was in his mid-sixties and had spent his entire career working for and eventually running railways. I was in awe when I listened to the man winning over shareholders. It was a master class.

We flew to those meetings in Harrison's private jet, and one day I asked him why a retired person owned such a plane. In his Southern drawl, he told me that he'd gotten used to the company jet he'd had at CN. "After I retired, I just had to get me one. Wes, you're such a hard-working guy, you will get your own one day." I loved that he had that kind of confidence in me, even if owning a private jet has never appealed to me.

As deep as Harrison's knowledge was, the argument we were making to investors was a simple one. No one doubted that the company was inefficient—you could see it right there in the numbers. What most people couldn't wrap their heads around was the idea that anything could be done about it. Railroads use something called operating ratio—operating expenses as a percentage of operating revenue—to determine their success and the effectiveness of their management teams. The lower the number, the better. At the time, a good operating ratio—like the ones posted year after year by Canada's other major railway, CN— sat in the low sixties. In 2011 CP posted an operating ratio of 81.3 percent; it would climb to 83.3 percent in 2012.

Clearly there was an issue if the company was 20 percent less efficient than CN, but CP's management team argued to shareholders that the difference came down to the fact that they were focused in Western Canada. (CN had lines that ran all the way to the Pacific but was more focused in the eastern half of the country.) Western Canada gets a lot of snow and the terrain is more difficult, at least west of Calgary. Steeper grades and the need to clear the tracks more regularly meant slower service with more interruptions. That's what was to blame, they claimed, not mismanagement.

It's hard to imagine that excuse holding water with investors, but it did because of who it was coming from. The CP board was an all-star team. Those folks were capable and talented, and their reputations were impressive. How could anyone do better than those people? Shareholders were willing to buy the weather and terrain excuse because it didn't seem possible that those superstar executives were running the business poorly. But that was the case—the wrong person was running the company and reporting to the wrong people. Though we had to work much harder than we should have to get that message across, I watched Harrison change the minds of shareholder after shareholder. It also didn't hurt that he guaranteed that he could get the operating ratio down to the low sixties within three years (though we persuaded him to tone down that prediction to four or five years, because some shareholders had trouble believing anyone could be that effective).

Harrison basically sold himself. Anyone who spent half an hour in a room with him could see there was no one on earth you'd rather have running a railroad. But replacing the CEO wasn't the only change Pershing Square was pursuing. Ackman had initially asked for two board seats, one for himself and one for Paul Hilal. (Harrison would automatically get a seat when he was appointed CEO.) He'd fixed on that number assuming he'd be working with people who were open to friendly conversation and ways to improve the company's performance. But after

Cleghorn denied all knowledge of the private airport meeting and CP turned hostile, he realized he wasn't going to be able to accomplish anything with only two directors and the rest of the board fighting him tooth and nail. We ended up going for seven seats, enough to have a strong voice at the table without going so far as to take control of the board.

To convince shareholders to give us those seats, we had to identify the directors most likely to be voted off the board and then make a case against each of them. We did what we call a Kingsdale vulnerability analysis. This isn't digging up dirt for a smear campaign; it's an evaluation of a person's current and past performance in their jobs. If they're a former CEO, we look at that company's performance under their leadership. If they're on the board of another company, we look at how it's doing. We're looking for a pattern of underperformance that points to an individual either not doing their job or not doing it well. Those are the grounds on which we go after them. We did that for every one of CP's directors, and we liked the results when we pitted them head-to-head against our candidates. I thought our chances looked good, but it was a call from CP that finally convinced me we would win.

Toward the end of January, someone from CP called the Kingsdale offices asking to speak with us about potentially working with them on the defence against Ackman. The AGM was scheduled for May 17, only three months away, and here they were, not calling to hire us, but to talk about *maybe* hiring us. We'd been working with Pershing Square since the previous October and were in the middle of putting the finishing touches on the town hall exposé. Yes, our work had largely been behind the scenes, but Kingsdale's name and logo had been printed in plain sight on the information circular we sent out before the town hall. I don't know if CP was just not paying attention or what was going on. The fact that they hadn't secured proxy advisors despite the threat they were facing showed me, more than anything else, the level of arrogance and privilege on that board. They were so sure they were untouchable that they weren't even bothering to defend themselves. I politely responded that we were advising Pershing Square in the matter. They later hired Georgeson.

As the clock ticked down to the May meeting, both the management group and the activist group sent out full ballots. Unlike in the United States, in proxy fights in Canada, each side only sees the votes on their own side before the meeting. Votes usually start to come back about a week before the meeting, and though we only got to see the votes cast for our side, we could tell that we were absolutely destroying them. The outcome was not in doubt—it wasn't even close. CP had to know that too.

We figured a settlement phone call would follow in short order, but it never came. Instead, CP waived the proxy deadline, a sign that they intended to keep fighting or attempt to create enough chaos to justify postponing the meeting. If they postponed the meeting, they would be able to delay announcing the results of the vote, which would lead to uncertainty and could compromise the integrity of the process. I suspected it was a postponement they were after, and so I recommended that we keep the deadline on our side, getting all our proxies in forty-eight hours before the meeting so we had our votes nailed down. We did that and then called CP and asked for a conversation to plan the meeting, which is the common practice with a contested AGM—both sides establish the ground rules so it's not a disorganized mess. CP turned us down. Instead, they suggested that we exchange voter information. We agreed, provided they sent their numbers over first. When they did, it confirmed what we already knew.

I called their proxy guy. I told him we were about to send over our numbers. "Just make sure you're sitting down when you get them," I said. After I'd given him a chance to review everything, I called him back. All he could say was, "Uh, wow." He was stunned. Our slate was ultimately elected with 90 percent of the votes cast.

I still consider that deal the biggest win of my career. By far.

At that 2012 town hall, when Harrison had guaranteed he could get CP's operating ratio into the low sixties within three years, he'd told the shareholders in attendance that they didn't have to pay him if he failed to deliver. By 2015 CP's operating ratio was 61 percent, down more than twenty points from when he took over as CEO. The man knew what he was talking about and more than earned his compensation.

The stock price, meanwhile, doubled in the year after he took over. I remember chatting with Harrison at CP's AGM in 2013. He told me that the improvements he'd made to that point didn't even qualify as the low-hanging fruit. "We haven't even started on the tree yet, Wes," he said. "We're still picking stuff up off the ground." I said, "You know, Hunter, I went with you to all those meetings, and even after listening to your great pitch, I didn't buy the stock. Had I bought the stock, I would have my own plane by now." He said, "No, Wes, you would have had two planes by now." Bill Ackman would ultimately make a reported $1.8 billion in profit on his investments.

In a sense, after the AGM is over and the deal either happens or it doesn't, my job is done. But there's massive value for Kingsdale's brand and future business if our clients not only win but also deliver on the vision we sold to shareholders. We had tied ourselves to our clients' message and worked our butts off to persuade shareholders that Hunter Harrison and Bill Ackman and their crew could do a better job than CP's bluest of blue-chip boards. When they did, the next time I went to those same investors on a file, they were much more open to what I had to say.

The real win for me, though, was accomplishing something everyone thought was impossible, and what it meant in a bigger-picture sense to prove them wrong. Here was a group of executives who thought they could win on reputation and status alone. Their experience in life had taught them that just showing up was enough. To me, that attitude spoke to so much of what was wrong with corporate culture, and society more broadly—and it still does. They were some of the most respected figures in the country, and instead of seeing that status as coming with duties and responsibilities, they saw it as bestowing privileges and advantages. Even worse, the system had conditioned them to think that way. Instead of questioning their superiority, everyone had just accepted it as an immutable fact.

Our winning blew that reputation to pieces. Not only was CP's board no longer untouchable, we'd sent the message that no board is untouchable. Privilege alone is not enough; you have to do the work. If you don't, someone who is willing to do the work will come along and unseat you—even if you imagine yourself sitting on a throne. The shift in thinking opened up many new possibilities, in business and outside of it. It changed the old refrain, "There's no point; it'll never happen," to "What have we got to lose?"

I'll die happy if that win inspired even one person who never thought they'd get a chance to step up to the plate to swing for the fences.

18

THE RUNNING BACK

In 2009 I was named the Ernst & Young Entrepreneur of the Year in the financial services sector in Ontario. There had been 130 nominees longlisted in my category, and that had been whittled down to four finalists for the awards gala. The other three nominees all ran very successful companies. They'd gone to the best schools and worked at the most prestigious investment banks prior to striking out on their own. I was flattered just to be nominated alongside them. When my name was called in front of nearly a thousand attendees, I was genuinely shocked. Kingsdale was doing well, but those other companies were much bigger than my shop. How was I the one on stage accepting the award?

I got the chance to have lunch with a couple of the judges later on, and I asked them directly why I'd won. "When I look at the names I was up against, there's no way I should have received the award. Why did you guys give it to me?"

"Wes, if those other finalists didn't do what they're doing today, they would be considered failures," one of the judges answered. "They were groomed to do it. Their whole life was planned out: *You're going to go to a prestigious school, you're going to work at a big bank until you learn the ropes, and then you're going to run your own firm.*

"You didn't have any of those tools or advantages. The spirit and the work it took for you to create your company, that's what *entrepreneurial* means. And that's what we were rewarding."

There are a lot of successful people who fall into the trap of believing in their own specialness. I can understand why it happens. You hear someone say something like the explanation that the judge gave me, and it's hard not to start patting yourself on the back. *Look at everything I've accomplished and all that I had to overcome to get here.* You find yourself in a place where you're the exception, and you think the reason must be that you're exceptional. From there it's a short leap to thinking that the only reason other folks aren't there with you is they just aren't special enough.

I have accomplished things in my life that shouldn't have been possible, at least not for someone who started where I did. I was a barefoot boy in The Barracks, and now I'm known as the King of Bay Street. Make no mistake: I am special. But what does that really mean? I've never claimed to be the smartest guy in the room, or the most knowledgeable. So, what sets me apart? For me, *specialness* means that I fight. I get hit, I get knocked down and I stand up again and say, "Is that all you got?" A barrier is put in my way and instead of feeling defeated by it or sorry for myself, I start looking for a way around, over or through it. I am not easily discouraged, and I'm not easily stopped.

Now that you've read the story of my early life, you can see what made me this way. My grandmother's example, my mother's abuse, my time surviving on my own, my faith—each of these things, whether through love or through pain, taught me to face hardship, to drop my shoulder and push toward my goals. They taught me to get up.

The other kids are making fun of you for being poor? Get up. Your mom beats you? Get up. She kicks you out? Get up. Your dad beats you? Get up. You're on your own again? Get up. You have a door slammed in your face by someone who doesn't want to hear the Truth? Get up. Half your staff quits? Get up.

That's what's special about me. For a Black person in the corporate world, my willingness to fight was far more valuable than being the smartest person in the room, and more necessary for survival. Being Black in business is like being the running back of a football team. Running backs get worked harder than any other player on the roster. Every time they're handed the ball, they know they're probably going to get hit, and when they do, it's their job to get back on their feet as soon as possible. To make any real progress, a running back needs to spot the smallest hole in the defence, a brief flash of daylight, and dart through it into the open field. You get hit no matter what, but to move the chains, you need to find a hole and get through it before it closes. Football is a game of inches and so is life. We cannot always score the touchdown on the first play. Sometimes it takes ten plays. If we look at life the same way, we will take advantage of every opportunity, no matter how small.

I may be able to exploit a smaller hole than someone else or rack up more yardage once I get free, but the hole still needs to be there. My dad bringing me to Canada, Patrick getting me the mailroom job, Glenn O'Farrell seeing potential in me, Keeling bringing me into the field of shareholder services—take away any of those chances and Kingsdale probably doesn't exist. In other words, I may be special, but I wouldn't be where I am without opportunity and good fortune. Some people take hit after hit before even the smallest hole appears. Some people never get any opportunity at all—that flash of daylight just isn't there. But other people don't expect to take a hit at all. Like a quarterback, they're protected in the pocket, and they get to throw the ball. When they get hit, they don't easily bounce back, because being hit is not part of their game.

When I think of that judge's words now, what stands out for me is the inequality she described. I had to struggle and fight for everything, while the other finalists were given so many advantages that they would've been seen as failures if they hadn't matched my success. What would their careers have been if a teacher at one of their elite private schools had taken a look at them and decided, *I'm going to make sure you don't succeed*? What if they'd graduated Harvard, right on track, entered the work-force and a superior had told them they would never advance in the company? If they had faced even one devastating setback or barrier, how many of them would be CEOs today? What would their lives have been like if there'd been people telling them they couldn't do it every step of the way?

For most of my career, I didn't really think about the system that put so much in my way even as it gave so much to the people I had to compete against. I was used to being unsupported. I was used to having to fight for things that other people took for granted, including food and shelter and shoes. I was used to being the outsider, the immigrant, the person who didn't belong. Encountering those challenges in the workplace didn't set off alarm bells for me. I didn't brood about who got to move easily up the corporate ladder and who had to fight and claw for every rung. I didn't think about the fact that I was almost always the only Black person in the room, especially once I'd made it to the executive level. I didn't think about why. Instead, I devoted my energy to solving whatever problem was in front of me, getting around the obstacles, and beating my opponents. That was more than enough to keep me occupied.

In the process, I ignored the system every time it told me where it thought I belonged. I didn't get the message; instead, I came up with explanations that didn't involve my race. When I was told I'd never be a law clerk at Stikeman, I decided it was because I was a man and all the other clerks were women. When I was dressed up for my interview at CanWest and the white guy in jeans and a T-shirt got asked if he was the candidate, I thought, *Well, it's the entertainment industry and they have a different dress code.* Anytime I walked into a boardroom and felt the uncomfortable attention familiar to every Black person who's ever been in that situation, I shrugged off the feeling—I had more important things to worry about than who was looking at me and why.

Once I'd achieved real success, I ran out of excuses. When I walked into an office to advise the CEO of a company and someone assumed I was there to clean the conference room, it was impossible to keep ignoring the message. If you think someone in a bespoke three-piece suit is there to empty the wastepaper basket, it's because you didn't even see the suit; the skin was enough for you to make up your mind. When an executive paying me fifty thousand dollars a day to consult on a proxy fight talked slower and louder and used simpler words every time he addressed me, it wasn't hard to figure out why. Both of those situations happened more than once. But at the end of the day, I collected my fifty-thousand fee and never saw those people again.

There was a time when our family lived in a beautiful French château–style house outside of the city. We were there for five years, but none of the neighbours spoke to us. The properties were big and people would drive right into their garages, so it wasn't like there were a lot of opportunities for chit-chat. But Christine and I had a bunch of kids and were often out walking around the neighbourhood or playing on the lawn. Neighbours would drive by and we would wave, but they wouldn't wave back. Christine often commented on their bizarre behaviour.

One day, I entered a boardroom to discuss a new proxy fight, only to find one of my neighbours there. It turned out he was the CEO of the company I'd been hired to defend. He came over to me and said, "Hey, what are you doing here?"

"I'm Wes Hall. I'm the CEO of Kingsdale," I said. "I'm here to help you on the proxy fight."

He'd known I was successful, but he'd clearly assumed my place wasn't on Bay Street. Maybe I was in sports or entertainment, but I wasn't someone he'd turn to for help with his business. That was how I finally met the man I'd lived right next to for years.

Another time, I was working on a fairly big merger that involved a huge team. Early on, there was an all-hands video conference call to discuss strategy, and each advisor took their turn to offer insight on their aspect of the deal. My turn came and I gave my advice, and immediately afterward, one of the other advisors said, "That was the dumbest advice I've ever heard anyone give a client in twenty years of being in investment banking." Did the advisor really think the advice was dumb or that the Black person giving it had to be dumb? Would he have come out and said such a thing at all if I'd been another white guy? In fact, he made no comment after the other advisors gave their opinions.

As a Black person, when you have an interaction like that, you don't necessarily know how much of a factor racism is in the other person's behaviour, but you always know it's a factor. That idea can be difficult for white people to take on board, but when you've dealt with racism your entire life, you have no trouble identifying it—even when it's the quiet, deniable kind. Every time you take a walk through a nice neighbourhood, every time you go shopping for anything from a car to clothes to a candy bar, every time you sit down in a nice restaurant, you encounter looks, comments, actions and assumptions that tell you where people think you belong. Injustice finds Black folks even when we're not looking for it. When someone calls me out in a meeting, I can tell whether they're questioning my work out of genuine skepticism or attacking it because it came from a Black man.

Maybe it was dumb advice. Even if it had been, that's not how you criticize a person you have any respect for. That advisor was grandstanding to provoke a reaction, trying to get me to take the bait and act in a way that confirmed the image of me he was trying to paint: a dumb Black guy who couldn't control himself in a professional setting. His comment really hurt my feelings. But I just bit my lip and let my work speak for itself. And that's what it did: the advice I gave the company turned out to be right.

When that became clear, the guy apologized, and to his credit he did it in an email to everyone who'd worked on the deal. He also invited me to lunch. I accepted.

Someone asked me later why I was willing to hear the guy out. I told them that the only way to heal is to move on. I might get upset in the moment, but if I take it personally, I won't be able to get past it. If I go to the next meeting still wrapped up in what that guy thinks of me, worried about the fact that everyone remembers what he said and is looking at me in a different way, I won't have the confidence I need to do my job. I feel my anger and then let go. My healing is to move on, and if I do that successfully, it's no big deal to hear his apology in person. Actually, even if he never apologized, it wouldn't matter, because I'm already over it—*he* doesn't matter anymore. I already proved him wrong.

As incidents like that kept happening, with no explanation for people's behaviour that didn't involve my race, the way I looked at my early career changed. The Stikeman clerk, the CanWest interview, the hundreds of microaggressions—all these incidents that I'd explained away took on a new dimension. I realized just how many times people's biases could have derailed me, how many times I ignored the writing on the wall that told me my goals were impossible for someone with skin like mine to achieve. And I realized in a whole new way just how lucky I've been.

When I joined Georgeson, shareholder services were still so new that no one on Bay Street even understood what we did. Activist investing and the types of proxy battles that I built my reputation on hadn't really made their way to Canada yet—they were just peeking over the horizon. It wasn't an established industry; it was a frontier, and its newness made it possible for me to avoid so many of the institutional barriers that would've slowed or stopped my success in a more established field. The major players, the big banks and legacy firms, weren't in the field yet, so they didn't have their people locked in. The Georgeson office had just fifteen employees and we were the only shop in the country. As a result, I was able to quickly establish myself as the best, and then build on that reputation with Kingsdale. By the time bigger companies realized the importance of shareholder services, I was already the guy you went to if you wanted to win your proxy fight. And once I was the guy who won, no one cared if I was Black or cream or Popsicle. *Just go get me the guy who wins.*

I was able to see a lot of the biggest trends in my industry coming before they arrived, but it wasn't until I got to the top that I fully understood my own place in it, and how fortunate I'd been to find it when I did. There's that x factor again, right? Good fortune. Opportunity. A fighting chance. In case it isn't already clear, I'm not one of those people who thinks that everyone coming up behind me needs to struggle the way I struggled and overcome what I overcame. First of all, almost no one would make it. Everyone thinks they're the first-string running back until they get hit, but there aren't too many people built to endure what I've endured and stay on their feet. Nor should there be. And even the few who could take the hits would still need the opportunities. To get a sense of the odds on that, look around for another one of me and see if you find any.

In the summer of 2020, the Diversity Institute at Ryerson University (which changed its name to Toronto Metropolitan University two years later) released a study of 178 corporations based in Montreal, Toronto, Calgary and Vancouver. Of those companies' 1,639 board members, the institute found that 1,483 were white and just thirteen were Black—90.48 percent versus 0.79 percent. So, the makeup of today's senior executive class is basically as homogenous as it was when I began my career. If no one ever expected me to make it, if my journey was an impossible one, how could I expect anyone to follow in my footsteps?

The more I thought about all this, the more I felt something had to be done. There were so many ways to address systemic racism and improve the lives of Black people. To borrow a phrase from Hunter Harrison, the fruit was right there, just lying on the ground. All that was required to get that work started was to convince the right people to buy in. My *job* is to win people over, and my conscience was pushing me to do something. I had doubts and reservations, but I knew I wouldn't be able to look myself in the eye if I didn't take action—if I didn't at least try. So, I did what I do: I picked up the phone.

Taking on a challenge as big as ending systemic anti-Black racism might seem daunting, but only if you look at it the wrong way. First, it's not a burden; it's an opportunity. The chance to make meaningful change is everywhere in the world, and that's an energizing idea. Second, you don't have to fix everything all at once—it doesn't even make sense to try. Working on hugely complicated multi-billion-dollar mergers has taught me that regardless of the scale of the problem, you've got to focus on one step at a time.

I decided to begin reaching out to politicians in positions of authority. They were the ones making the laws and deciding how public money was spent to tackle important issues, so who better to spearhead change, right?

My first call was to Ahmed Hussen, a friend who also happened to be minister of immigration, citizenship and refugees in Prime Minister Justin Trudeau's first Liberal government. This was in September 2018. I told Ahmed I wanted to speak to the prime minister about improving the lives of Black Canadians, and he agreed to coordinate an initial discussion between my office and Trudeau's. The proposal was simple: I wanted to organize a private event with Black business leaders from across the country. There would be a fireside chat between myself and the prime minister, and then we'd open things up to questions and a larger discussion. No public, no media, no gotcha moments—just key stakeholders discussing necessary changes and the best ways to achieve them.

There was interest on the prime minister's side, so I started organizing. On September 12, 2018, I sent a note about the event to prospective attendees on the networking site LinkedIn. "As you may know, I am a Jehovah's Witness and I do not vote or politic. I support no party. However, I support the Black and Caribbean community," I wrote. "We have no voice at the federal, provincial or municipal levels of government. As a result, things affecting us take place without our input. I have taken it upon myself to put on this event because I believe it to be important to our community. I am personally extending an invitation to you."

We scheduled the event for early November and capped attendance at eighty people. I asked every guest to make a $1,500 contribution to the Liberal Party. (For religious reasons I was restricted from writing a cheque myself, but I stressed that this was "about letting people know we have a voice and we're willing to write a cheque to support people who support our community.") There was healthy interest. There was also pushback from people who told me they wouldn't attend because of their particular political stripes. I reminded them that this was about supporting the Black community, not any one party, and that politicians only pay attention when you show up with a cheque. I spent the better part of a month chasing people and nailing down the guest list. Then, a couple of days before the event, the PMO reached out to say Trudeau wouldn't do a fireside chat. They proposed that he deliver a speech instead.

I had no way of knowing their logic, but based on what I could see, that didn't make much sense. The event was already in his calendar. Whether he came with prepared remarks or sat down and spoke with me, he would be there for the same two hours. There would be no media, just the people in the room. Was he nervous to have a real conversation and be put on the spot about issues affecting the Black community? I responded that I wasn't interested in the prime minister giving another speech, that the whole point of the event was to create a discussion where questions could be asked and we could have a proper back-and-forth. At that point, I was told the prime minister no longer had time for anything more than a speech. I politely declined and cancelled the event. In its place, I hosted a small group of people at my house who had signed up for a conversation on how we could work collectively to better conditions for Black Canadians.

I did eventually get a chance to speak with Trudeau on some of these issues. In April 2019, I and ten other Black business leaders met with the prime minister to talk about creating a

Black bank. One of the problems that plagues the Black community is a lack of access to capital. In April 2021, the Black Business and Professional Association released a report that revealed that 78.5 percent of Black female entrepreneurs had trouble accessing financing. The following month, a survey of 342 Black entrepreneurs commissioned by the African Canadian Senate Group and Senator Colin Deacon found that only 19 percent of respondents said they trusted banks to do what is right for them and for the Black community.

There are good reasons for their skepticism. Speaking to the CBC in the fall of 2020, Caroline Shenaz Hossein, an associate professor of business and society at York University, explained that Black entrepreneurs who try to secure funding through commercial banks commonly face culturally and racially insensitive interactions with bank employees, not to mention poor service. "It is just so perplexing the level of rudeness and bias that is occurring against people for simply wanting to get their projects funded," Hossein said. "It's kind of an interrogation of questions that really does make them feel badly or feel that the kinds of business they are doing are not worthy of financing."

Unsurprisingly, the difficulty Black folks face in securing bank loans for their businesses leads to all kinds of other stresses. Many end up using their hard-earned savings or even personal credit cards to get the ball rolling. Nearly half of the respondents to the African Canadian Senate Group survey said they were unable to pay themselves. Some business owners even hire white intermediaries to deal with financial institutions, both to avoid unpleasant interactions and to improve their shot at fair treatment. Black people face the same awful treatment and poor outcomes when pursuing mortgages, student loans, personal credit—basically any interaction an individual can have with a bank.

In 2006 I landed one of the biggest deals of my career to that point, the largest cash takeover deal in Canadian history, valued at $19 billion USD. My little fledgling firm won the job even though several large, bank-owned companies had pitched for it. When I was pretty sure we were going to get the business, I set up a meeting with my bank to prepare the way to work together and ensure that our work on the deal would go smoothly. This was a huge deal, and the bank had to be ready to issue very large payments to shareholders instantly (any hold on delivering the money would mean we'd have to pay interest on it while it was in our hands). My contact at the bank, who happened to be Black, brought his senior bosses to meet with me. I was treated so poorly by the bank's senior team that my contact called me after the meeting to apologize. They had peppered me with questions: "Why would they give this deal to you?" "Why wouldn't they not award it to our sister company in the same field as you?" "What's your capability to handle a deal this size?" "We are not sure if the bank would be interested in working with you on this deal."

When I landed the deal, I still needed a large bank behind me to pull it off, but I now knew those guys were not keen on working with me. So, I went to the chairman of Kingsdale Capital, Joseph Duggan, and told him about my treatment by the bank's senior people. I asked him if he would be willing to sit in a meeting with the bank as if he was the owner of Kingsdale, not me. He was a former investment banker and looked the part: a white man in his late fifties with grey hair.

We had the second meeting with the same group from the bank, and Joe led the conversation, highlighting his list of demands. I said absolutely nothing, and even though they'd met with me before about this exact same deal, no one seemed to find that surprising. I was young and Black. (I'm older and Black now, and I'm still rare on Bay Street.) The bank's senior executives asked Joe nothing about his capabilities, the size of his firm, why he was hired by his client—*nothing*. The bankers thanked him for giving them the opportunity to work with him, we shook hands and that was that. The senior banker who had given me the third degree in the initial meeting wore a fuchsia-coloured shirt to this one. To this day, I and my bank contact call him Mr. Fuchsia.

These are the reasons that we approached the government with the idea for a bank that understood Black culture and Black experience and would be able to treat Black people like human beings—something no existing bank in the country seemed capable of doing. We had lined up the funding ourselves, but we knew it would be really difficult to get a banking licence, especially since we were expecting a lot of resistance from major financial institutions, who would oppose us loaning money to Black people despite not doing it themselves. We met with then Finance Minister Bill Morneau first and then Trudeau, hoping to get them onside and willing to pave the way, making the bureaucratic processes not simply smoother but possible.

Both meetings were encouraging. We had great conversations that seemed to indicate that they were excited by the idea and willing to put some weight behind it. We followed up with a letter, putting the ask in writing. We're still waiting for a response.

Then I was approached at a Raptors game by Leisa Washington, a Black woman and founder and CEO of Camda Sports Foundation Canada. Washington represents NBA athletes. She asked if we could meet to discuss something she had in mind for the Black community in Canada. We got together on December 4, 2019, and she told me about what she termed a "Culture Meets Community" centre for Black Canadians. Her vision was for a beautiful facility that could run programming and host community events while also serving as a place to showcase Black excellence and celebrate the history of our community's contribution to Canada and the world. I thought it was a brilliant idea. I hadn't been able to make headway at the federal level; maybe a municipal government would prove to be a more willing partner.

I arranged a meeting with John Tory, the mayor of Toronto. When I told him we wanted to build a Black cultural centre in Toronto, at first he wouldn't even address the idea directly. Instead, he told me that the problem with the Black community was that everyone wanted something different. Over the years, he'd been approached by different Black groups that each had its own unique request. He said, "It makes it very difficult for me to make a decision."

It should go without saying that just because members of the Black community share experiences doesn't mean the community is monolithic. Why should it surprise anyone that people with a wide range of backgrounds and goals might ask for different things? Would white people only be granted one request? I bit my lip and offered a suggestion: "Mr. Mayor, how about you get all of us in one room, all the people who have communicated with you over the years. Bring us together and let's have a larger discussion about priorities and needs."

"You know, Wes, that's not a bad idea," he said.

It took several follow-ups, but eventually I got a note from the mayor's office to say he'd set up the meeting. It was held in a big conference room at City Hall on February 3, 2020. I recognized some of the people in attendance, but many were new faces to me. We mingled for a while, talking amongst ourselves, and then the mayor came in and gave an introductory speech. He did his bit about us not being able to agree on what we wanted and then said he was going to let us decide—without him in the room. His assistant would stay to hear where we netted out, and he would "work hard to find you that." Then he left the room.

It was a ridiculous setup. None of us believed that a single request would be sufficient to meet the community's needs, but neither were we prepared to walk away with nothing because we "couldn't agree." We talked about the fact that the mayor was essentially trying to pass the buck, ducking any decision or commitment while essentially saying, *It's your fault we can't do this*. We decided to take that away from him by focusing on a single request, stressing that making one unified request didn't mean we were closing the door on everything else the people in that room wanted to accomplish. Rather, what we asked for had to open doors for as many of the other ideas as possible. Ultimately, we decided that the cultural centre did that.

We didn't ask the city to build it for us. All we asked the city to contribute was a plot of land. I was the lead on the project, and I told the mayor's office that I would personally raise the money to cover the centre's construction, maintenance and operating expenses and soon I was able to secure a commitment of $1 million from philanthropist Seymour Schulich. I asked for land no developer wanted, something in a neighbourhood no one thought was "ready" for new condos. We'd take care of everything else. And we would encourage our corporate partners to invest not just in the building itself, but the whole neighbourhood. We would create a place for young people to direct their energy. They would find inspiration, instruction, diversion and fun, while the environment around them became a safer place, offering more and more opportunity.

Toronto has a long-running narrative around the plague of gun violence. It is a racially charged topic, with drugs and gangs constantly framed as a Black problem. But this issue isn't a Black problem; it's a people problem. Black kids aren't any more predisposed to violence than kids of any other race. Those who do get mixed up in bad situations—like my father feared I would—end up there because of a lack of alternatives.

That didn't happen to me, but I've witnessed it in my own family. In the early 1990s, shortly after Christine and I were married, I sponsored several of my relatives through the immigration process and brought them to Canada. Two of my brothers came: Ian, who'd split the porridge with me and Joan when my mother abandoned us, and Michael, the boy my mother had with my stepfather. Both of them got into selling drugs. I would lecture them every time we saw each other. I told them they had to play the long game like I was and work to build a career. I stressed that it would be difficult at the start, that it might be difficult the whole way through, but they would be more successful and have better lives in the future if they followed through. The problem was that it wasn't just difficult, it was impossible. Ian couldn't even find a job. He told me many times that it was just too hard to make ends meet here. After being arrested a few times, Michael was deported back to Jamaica. Ian wasn't that lucky.

In August 1995, I got a call from the police in Buffalo, New York, asking me to come there to identify a body. I drove down and saw my brother laid out on a table in a cold, grey morgue. He'd been found in a dumpster, beaten to death and wrapped in plastic. My phone number was written on a piece of paper in his pocket.

These are the types of outcomes we script for young people when we strip them of opportunities. If I was a young Black man in an underserved community and I didn't want to deal with racist people and a racist system designed to hold me in poverty, I'd have an alternative: I could turn to drugs and gangs. The best way to address the problems that spring from choosing crime and violence is to create other choices, actual opportunities, and hope for a different future. It's also important for youth to see successful Black people, to witness where hard work may lead.

Through the cultural centre, we were offering the city a way to do exactly that. All we asked for in return was a piece of land no one else wanted. I followed up several times and heard nothing. For all I know, the request is still sitting on the mayor's desk. I guess I was right to suspect that the mayor's argument about all Black people wanting different things and not being able to agree on anything was just a way to kick the can down the road.

19

BLACKNORTH

My phone lit up with a text from a friend: "Have you seen the video?"

It was the morning of May 26, 2020. Cellphone footage of the February murder of Ahmaud Arbery, an unarmed Black man who was chased down and shot to death by a white father and son while he was out jogging, had been circulating online since the beginning of the month. It was a horrifying video; I'd barely been able to watch it. "What video?" I wrote back. "I saw the one. Ahmaud Arbery. I saw that."

"No, no, no. There's another one," my friend answered. "Search 'George Floyd.'"

I think most Black people would tell you that 2020 marked a turning point for them. It was the year when, after four centuries of injustice and discrimination on this continent, after a lifetime of it for each of us individually, we finally said enough is enough.

I know I felt that way. There was just so much that piled up. From Arbery's death and the killing of Breonna Taylor by police as she slept in her own bed, to the death of Regis Korchinski-Paquet during a police wellness check in Toronto, to the Central Park confrontation that saw Amy Cooper, a white woman, try to weaponize the cops against a Black birdwatcher named Christian Cooper (no relation), it felt like there was a new heartbreaking and enraging story every week, every day. There was also the disproportionate impact of the COVID-19 pandemic (still ongoing at the time of this writing) on Black and racialized people, which saw Black folks unable to get equal access to medical care and dying at rates far beyond those seen in other communities. In other words, there were many things pushing over the edge. But at the same time, I think for each of us there *was* probably one thing. For me, it was the murder of George Floyd.

Floyd was approached by the police while he was parked on a Minneapolis street after he'd been accused of using a fake twenty dollar bill to buy cigarettes. He was unarmed. He told the officers he was scared, that he'd been shot by a cop before, that he'd recently lost his mother. He told them he was just recovering from COVID, that he was claustrophobic and had anxiety and didn't want to get in the back of a squad car. He eventually ended up handcuffed, face down on the ground with Officer Derek Chauvin kneeling on his throat. Floyd cried out that he couldn't breathe, that everything hurt. He cried out for his mother. Chauvin kept up the pressure on his neck as bystanders yelled that Floyd was being killed. Eventually, Floyd stopped moving and Chauvin continued to kneel on his neck. Another officer checked Floyd for a pulse and couldn't find one. Chauvin only got up after EMTs arrived on the scene. In total he knelt on Floyd's throat for nine minutes and twenty-nine seconds. Floyd was pronounced dead in hospital less than an hour later. But he was dead by the time he was placed in the ambulance.

This wasn't a new type of horror. There have been dozens of high-profile police killings of Black people in North America over the last decade alone, and hundreds that have gotten less attention. In 2014 another unarmed Black man, Eric Garner, died when a police officer put him in a chokehold during an arrest for selling loose cigarettes. Garner also told officers he couldn't breathe, and his death was also filmed.

I had never really sat with any of those earlier stories and videos, letting myself feel them the way I felt Floyd's murder. I would get upset when I saw them, but then life would demand something of me, and my focus would move elsewhere. I think, as they did for a lot of people, the lockdowns in the early months of the COVID-19 pandemic eliminated some of those distractions. I was still busy. I sit on the boards of SickKids Foundation, Pathways to Education and the Toronto International Film Festival, all of which were having crisis meetings. I was managing Kingsdale through COVID, as well as my two other companies, QM Environmental and Titan Supply. I was trying to save the hotel I own. And in February I'd been appointed to the Ontario government's Capital Markets Modernization Taskforce. But still, in what normally would have been the peak of proxy season in late May and early June, I had a little less on my plate. And I found that I was more willing to shift what was there to give myself time to process what I was feeling.

As I thought about the last moments of George Floyd's life, it struck me that there was nothing to keep the same thing from happening to me. No matter how successful I was, no matter how well I seemed to be navigating the system, there was always the possibility that I could suddenly find myself in a situation where everything that makes me who I am would be reduced to two words: Black male. George Floyd died at forty-six. He was five years younger than me. A sentence kept running through my head: *I am George Floyd.*

Like me, he knew the feeling of sitting between his mama's knees as she combed the knots from the back of his hair. He knew the safety and comfort of that moment, even if the comb caught and pulled now and again, the joy of feeling that care and attention directed at you. He knew the smell of a curling iron going through a Black woman's hair as she got ready for church on a Sunday morning, the routine and ritual it signalled. There was solidarity and kinship in these shared cultural touchstones. I was George Floyd.

And it wasn't just me. My friends were George Floyd. My brothers were George Floyd. My father was George Floyd. My sons were George Floyd. As long as we continued to live in a system that regularly stripped Black people of our individuality and humanity, everyone who looked like me could suffer the same fate. I realized then that the injustices—from smaller barriers in the workplace to being murdered in the street—would never go away on their own. People needed to fight them. *I* needed to fight them. What I was doing—which was waiting around on politicians— wasn't enough and it wasn't going anywhere. I needed to take a new approach.

I'd started with the politicians because they set policy and write laws, but also because it felt like a safer place for me to begin. Politics was not my world. Engaging politicians on these issues was, to my mind, a personal project I could keep separate from my professional life. But once I started working to engage with business leaders on these issues, I knew the border between personal and professional would be difficult to maintain. There is a long history of Black people being punished for speaking up about racism. More than five years after first taking a knee during the American national anthem before a pre-season game, Colin Kaepernick still didn't have a job in the National Football League. I didn't expect to be shunned, but it was natural to assume there would be professional consequences. But after George Floyd's death, I was more than ready to take action. My conscience demanded it.

That put me in an uncomfortable position. It is a central component of my faith that Jehovah's Witnesses are not to let themselves be pulled into worldly conflicts. Through elections, wars and social uprisings, we have refused to take any side but God's. Now I was appearing to take a side. I say "appearing to" because I don't think of myself as advocating for Black people *against* or *instead of* white people. What I'm fighting for isn't a side, but equality—something that benefits everyone. But to fight for equality, you have to advocate for the downtrodden and disadvantaged. That may not feel like taking a side to me, but it is certainly taking up a cause. In making this new commitment, I worried that I would damage or disrupt the commitment I'd already made to God.

As I considered pushing deeper into anti-racist activism, I spoke to elders in the faith. They told me what I already knew: what I was doing *was* in conflict. I wasn't yet at a point where I would be asked to leave, they said, but I had to be aware that this was a problem with only two possible resolutions. My faith gave me the most important and beautiful truth a person can discover, and a guide for how to live it every day. Anything that distracted from that path, or interfered with my ability to walk it, pulled me further from that truth and from God. Eventually, I would come to a place where I wouldn't be able to manage both—I would have to choose or the decision would be made for me. In the meantime, I would exist in a very uncomfortable condition, one of constant conflict between my faith and my conscience.

On June 3, 2020, *The Globe and Mail* published an op-ed I'd written on systemic anti-Black racism in Canada. In it, I shared that in the wake of Floyd's death, I started seeing him when I looked in the mirror and would think about all the ways violence is inflicted on Black people in our society. The article was a bit of a scary thing to release into the world. People had started sharing stories about their experiences with racial injustice in greater and greater numbers on social media, and protests had erupted first in Minneapolis and then in cities all over the world. But I hadn't yet seen any prominent Black business leaders join in the calls for change. It was uncomfortable to be among the first. I also couldn't shake all my doubts about whether I was the right person to speak up. I had faced discrimination but never what I thought of as Big Racism. I hadn't had people shouting the N-word at me. I'd never been denied access to proper health care because of the colour of my skin. I was, by every measure, a privileged person. *Should I cede the floor to people who have it worse than me?* I wondered.

Despite my doubts, I didn't mince words. "You may not be a racist. But the system is. That is why we have the term 'systemic racism,'" I wrote. "Each of us needs to take meaningful action to dismantle the system we inherited and apply an unparalleled effort to build a better one. We cannot allow complacency or inertia to rob us of this historic opportunity."

The day the piece ran, I started to get calls. On the other end of the phone were people I'd advised on deals, people I knew from my philanthropic work, people I'd worked against in deals—some of the most powerful executives in the country, reaching out to say, "Wes, I had no idea. What can I do to help?"

There were so many answers to that question. Many of these folks had the ability to substantially change the policies and operations of the biggest companies in Canada, affecting the working lives of hundreds of thousands of people. Yet they were telling me they'd never previously realized that systemic racism exists, and as a result they had done nothing meaningful to address it. Every possible solution, big and small, was an option that had yet to be tried. This was Hunter Harrison's fruit on the ground. I engaged every single person who called me after that article ran in a meaningful conversation. I asked them to look at themselves and their businesses, and I started pointing out all that fruit.

"Your board determines everything that happens in the company. Do you have any Black representation on the board?"

"The highest paid people in your organization are sitting around the C-suite table. How many of them are Black?"

"Only seven cents of every hundred dollars given to traditional charities in this country go to Black organizations. How much of the money your company donates goes to the Black community?"

"Every summer, your firm brings in a hundred or so summer students, right? How many of them are Black?"

"Last year your bank loaned billions to businesses. What percentage of them were Black-owned?"

These weren't accusations; I wasn't pointing a finger. When you go door-to-door as a Witness, you're bringing a truth people haven't felt in their own lives. It's your job to show it to them, to hold up a mirror and teach them to see themselves in a new way. This was the same process. I was putting a mirror in front of a white CEO, for example, someone who'd never experienced discrimination of any kind in his entire life, and I was pointing out some of what was reflecting back. And I was doing it in language he could understand.

"Look around your boardroom table," I'd say. "Are there any Black people there?"

"No."

"Do you ever ask yourself why that is?"

"Well, we use this headhunting firm and our policy is we only invite former CEOs of Fortune 500 companies to join our board."

"How many Black people are former CEOs of Fortune 500 companies in this country?"

A policy like that is a systemic barrier. It has nothing to do with a person's talent or capabilities. Instead, it requires them to have already been given a significant opportunity in their career to be eligible. White people are more likely to be given those chances, which then beget more chances. The formula works in reverse for everyone else. When I pointed out this or other systemic barriers in those early calls, the response was always the same: "I never thought about it that way before."

To me, that's a fair excuse. One of white supremacy's most devious defence mechanisms is its ability to disguise itself from white people. It's hard to see the effects of something that never directly impacts you. I get that. But the thing about that excuse is you can only use it one time. Once you know, you know. Now what are you going to do about it?

To their credit, the people who reached out did seem interested in taking tangible action, and that interest confirmed a suspicion of mine. When I'd first decided to go public with my thoughts, I was primarily motivated by how deeply George Floyd's death had affected me and my desire to try to make *something* positive out of the profound sadness I felt. But I'd made a calculation too. Even in the earliest days after the murder, I felt like there was a different energy in the air. The same pain and outrage had been felt and voiced in the Black community so many times before—after Atatiana Jefferson, D'Andre Campbell, Botham Jean, Dafonte Miller, Philando Castile, Freddie Gray, Tamir Rice, Michael Brown, Trayvon Martin, and on and on. But this time it seemed like the rest of the world felt that hurt too, like we as a larger society were finally ready to face the truth of systemic violence and discrimination against Black people and actually do something about it. The sense that now was the time to act—that we were living through a real and rare and possibly short-lived chance to rebuild the system—had been a key part of what pushed me to go public. The fire I heard on those phone calls proved to me that my sense of things had been correct. For the first time, it seemed like the perpetrators of these despicable acts against Black people were on the back heel. All eyes were on them, and at last it was making them uncomfortable.

As willing as I was to talk through these issues one-on-one, I knew my efforts couldn't end with writing an article and taking some phone calls. Backroom conversations about what needed to change to improve the lives of Black people were better than no conversations at all, but most major companies in Canada hadn't ever openly acknowledged that systemic racism exists. We needed real and lasting accountability, public-facing commitment to change, and it couldn't be all talk—we had to couple it to concrete plans.

There were already many committed individuals and organizations working to end anti-Black racism and doing fantastic work. But the challenge of dismantling and rebuilding the system was a massive one; the more people who set their minds to it, the more likely we were to find solutions. As I thought about the role I could play and the value I could bring to the fight, an idea occurred to me: I am an entrepreneur, not an activist. Why not apply a business approach?

Victor Dodig, the president and CEO of CIBC, had been the first person to call me after *The Globe and Mail* article ran. Victor had been a key voice in the push to get more women into board seats, and I spoke to him about the possibility of applying the same approach to racial barriers. I also received a call from Prem Watsa, the founder and CEO of Fairfax Financial Holdings, who said bluntly, "Wes, I came from India thirty years ago with nothing and built my wealth from the ground up. I knew Black people were treated differently, but until your article I didn't get it. What can I do to help?" Those conversations encouraged and inspired me. In mid-June, I created the Canadian Council of Business Leaders Against Anti-Black Systemic Racism. I asked Victor and Prem to co-chair the organization, which we also gave a second shorter, catchier name: the BlackNorth Initiative.

I imagined BlackNorth, rather than simply advocating for a cause, as an advisory firm, something like Kingsdale. Where Kingsdale offered expertise to help guide businesses through mergers and proxy fights, BlackNorth would help guide them in attacking and eliminating systemic barriers. It could also provide mentorship to Black-owned businesses, helping them scale up. Our first two steps were to announce that the inaugural BlackNorth Summit would take place that July, a gathering of business leaders for a series of discussions about systemic racism and potential solutions, and to have as many CEOs as possible sign a pledge stating that they would work collectively to dismantle systemic anti-Black racism, starting within their own organizations.

As more and more companies across Canada recognized the writing on the wall and scrambled to announce plans—or, at least, intentions—to address their internal lack of diversity, I felt it was important that the ones that signed on to work with BlackNorth didn't pass that responsibility down to their equity, diversity and inclusion leads or HR managers. Too often companies leave the work of addressing racism in the hands of people with no direct power to enact change. I wanted the efforts we got involved with to be led from the top, and I wanted commitments from people who wouldn't be able to excuse a lack of meaningful action by saying their hands were tied. The CEO had to be the one to sign the pledge, and we stipulated that only signatory companies could attend the summit.

The pledge, which is printed in full at the end of this book, says that any executive who signs is acknowledging the existence of systemic anti-Black racism and its crushing impact on Black Canadians. They are committing to search out and fully address any racial barriers within their company, and to be transparent in their process, sharing targets, successes, failures and best practices in the hopes of increasing the effectiveness of this work across corporate Canada. They are also agreeing to some measurable targets to be achieved by 2025: At least 5 percent of their student workforce will be Black. At least 3 percent of their corporate donations and sponsorships will go to organizations and initiatives in the Black community. And at least 3.5 percent of their executive and board roles will be held by Black leaders.

There was pushback from some companies. The most common argument was that the pledge shouldn't focus on the Black community and instead include minority groups across races, sexual orientations and genders. The pledge does include an acknowledgement of the need for diversity and equality of all kinds, not to mention the financial benefits of assembling diverse teams, but I argued hard for keeping its core focus. In the wake of George Floyd's death, it was the particular issue of racism and violence against Black people that had protesters taking to the streets in unprecedented numbers. There was focus to those actions because the discrimination faced by the Black community demanded that focus. It was the issue of the day, and we had every right to take aim at it. Our pledge, and our wider efforts, didn't preclude business leaders from tackling other forms of discrimination—we openly encouraged that. To argue that working to improve the lives of Black people meant you couldn't improve the lives of anyone else was, to my mind, ridiculous and wrong-headed. It was trying to pass the buck the way Mayor Tory had, by saying, *We can't do anything until you do the impossible and find a way for us to do everything all at once.*

By the start of the July summit, the pledge had 220 signatories, a number that included many of the biggest companies in Canada.

BlackNorth has only grown since that first summit. At the time of this writing, more than five hundred companies have signed the CEO Pledge. We formed sixteen different volunteer committees, each one tasked with finding approaches to eliminate systemic racism in a different sector of society, like health care or education. In late November 2021, under the guidance of our executive director, Dahabo Ahmed-Omer, we released the BlackNorth Initiative "Racial Equity Playbook," a detailed guide to help companies fulfill the commitments they've made to create opportunities for Black people and then push beyond them. (The playbook is available for free at blacknorth.ca.)

We have also expanded beyond the workplace. According to the United Way and Statistics Canada, median wealth for white families in Canada is ten times higher than for Black families. Lower wages and the lack of opportunities for advancement at work play huge roles in that disparity, and so does the difficulty Black people have in securing loans, particularly mortgages.

Home ownership is a key tool for building lasting wealth. When my father and stepmother were putting their kids through post-secondary school, they covered tuition costs by renegotiating the mortgage on their house. That one asset made access to higher education possible for my siblings, and there are countless other doors it can unlock. But that tool has only grown further out of reach for many Black families, especially with housing prices going through the roof.

So, in March 2021, we announced the creation of a $65-million Homeownership Bridge program with a goal of constructing two thousand homes across the country and issuing mortgages to Black and racialized families who might not otherwise be able to get them. We've also set plans in motion to build a Black Business Development Hub—an incubator and accelerator for Black entrepreneurs—and a version of the cultural centre I had pitched to the city of Toronto. We've also partnered with Kids Help Phone to begin development of RiseUp, a mental health support service for Black youth available twenty-four hours a day, 365 days a year, which will be the first of its kind in Canada.

These projects are only the beginning, and there is still so much to do, but they give me hope. The will to get them off the ground didn't exist prior to the summer of 2020, but look where we are already. Like a sprinter exploding from the blocks, each step builds momentum that carries us into the next.

I am living proof of what is possible when a person the system is designed to exclude finds a way past the barriers placed in front of them. In a single generation, I've taken my family from a zinc-roofed shack in The Barracks to a nice house in one of Toronto's wealthiest neighbourhoods, and I've gone from driving a shoe polish tin on a stick to a Ferrari 488 Spider. And my success has created value for more than just myself and my family: The businesses I either own outright or have personally financed employ over a thousand people and have played an instrumental role in some of the biggest deals in Canadian business history. My philanthropic work has touched thousands of lives, primarily those of children in Canada and the Caribbean. BlackNorth itself wouldn't exist without the opportunities given to me or made by me.

Imagine if we created an environment that supported and encouraged people like me instead of pushing us down. Imagine the positive impact that would have, the ideas that would come to life, the success and happiness that would be created. Imagine what it would mean for each subsequent generation.

The road map for achieving that goal exists. All we need is the will and the work ethic. There are people who will tell us it is impossible. Let them. It's nothing I haven't heard before.

THE BLACKNORTH
CEO PLEDGE

It is time for anti-Black systemic racism to end.

I, as the leader of my company, along with all CEO signatories, commit to implementing the following pledge. Where companies have already implemented one or several of the commitments, the undersigned commit to support other companies in doing the same.

We acknowledge the existence of anti-Black systemic racism and its impact on Canada's 1,198,540 Black citizens (or 3.5% of the population) and the need to create opportunities within our companies for Black people.

The persistent inequities across our country underscore our urgent, national need to address and alleviate racial, ethnic, and other tensions and to promote the elimination of anti-Black systemic racism wherever it exists. As leaders of some of Canada's largest corporations, we manage hundreds of thousands of employees and play a critical role in ensuring that inclusion is core to our workplace culture and that our businesses are representative of the communities we serve. Moreover, we know that true diversity is good for the economy; it improves corporate performance, drives growth, and enhances employee engagement.

Simply put, organizations with truly diverse teams perform better.

We recognize that diversity and inclusion are multifaceted issues and that we need to tackle these subjects holistically to better engage and support all underrepresented groups within the business community. To do this, we believe we also need to address honestly and head-on the concerns and needs of our diverse employees and increase equity for all, including, but not limited to, Black, Asian and other racialized communities in Canada, Indigenous peoples, members of the LGBTQ+ community, persons with disabilities, and women. Collectively as business leaders we agree that we must do more. For us, this means committing to seven goals we believe will move Canada toward ending anti-Black systemic racism and creating opportunities for underrepresented groups.

1. Working through the BlackNorth Initiative, we will increase our efforts to make our workplaces trusting places to have complex, and sometimes difficult, conversations about anti-Black systemic racism and ensure that no barriers exist to prevent Black employees from advancing within the company. We will create

and maintain an environment that fosters open dialogue, including listening forums where our people feel comfortable to gain greater awareness of each other's experiences and perspectives. By encouraging an ongoing dialogue and not tolerating any incongruence with these values of openness, we are building trust, encouraging compassion and open-mindedness, and reinforcing our commitment to a culture of inclusivity.

2. Working through the BlackNorth Initiative, we will implement or expand unconscious bias and anti-racism education. We all have unconscious biases—that is human nature. Unconscious bias education enables individuals to begin recognizing, acknowledging, and therefore minimizing any potential blind spots they might have. We will commit to rolling out and/or expanding education that addresses unconscious bias and anti-Black systemic racism within our companies and make non-proprietary unconscious bias education modules available to others free of charge.

3. We will share best—and unsuccessful—practices. We know that many companies are still developing programs and initiatives around true diversity and inclusion. We commit to helping them evolve and enhance their current diversity strategies and encourage them, in turn, to share their successes and challenges with others.

4. We will create and share strategic inclusion and diversity plans with our board of directors. We will establish at least one diversity leadership council and make efforts to ensure these groups include diverse representation, including senior Black leaders, within our organization. The diversity leadership council will work with the CEO, who will be accountable to our board of directors (or equivalent governing bodies) through the development and evaluation of concrete, strategic action plans to prioritize and drive accountability around diversity and inclusion, including as it relates to Black employees. We recognize that boards and CEOs play an important role in driving action together to cultivate inclusive cultures and talent.

5. **We will use our resources to work with members of the Black community through the BlackNorth Initiative.** Through the BlackNorth Initiative, we will ensure that Black communities across Canada are aware of opportunities of employment within our organization and that employment opportunities are set aside for Black people, including committing to specific hiring goals of at least 5% within our student workforce from the Black community. Through the BlackNorth Initiative, we will invest at least 3% of corporate donations and sponsorships to promote investment and create economic opportunities in the Black community, both by 2025. We also recognize the economic power of the company and the ability to influence broader change by encouraging diversity and the representation of Black people amongst our suppliers and those we choose to do business with.

6. **We will engage Canada's corporate governance framework.** The aim of the BlackNorth Initiative is to include both board Chairs and CEOs to foster inclusiveness for Black leaders at the

board level, as well as at senior management and executive levels. We are building a strong foundation of business leaders who are committed to meaningful, sustainable inclusion of Black people in business leadership. Our goal is to build a pipeline so there can be representation from the Black community on the Board of Directors and in our C-suite. In addition, as a numeric goal provides real impetus for change, we have made a goal of, at a minimum, 3.5% of executive and board roles based in Canada being held by Black leaders by 2025.

7. **We will create the conditions for success.** As in all business ventures, "what gets measured gets managed," so it's essential that we collect data on race and ethnicity, including from Black employees, to understand where we have gaps and when we are making progress. We will work through the BlackNorth Initiative to attract and retain talent from the Black community, and in partnership with our organization's governance committee, commit to developing and advancing Black people within our organizations to ensure a pipeline of talent as we build inclusive leadership teams that are representative of the communities we serve. We will set inclusive talent management goals and include them in senior executives' annual performance scorecards.

We also pledge to create accountability systems within our companies, share our goals internally and externally, track our progress, and share regular updates with each other to catalogue effective programs and measurement practices.

We recognize that these commitments are not the complete answer, but we believe they are important, concrete steps toward building more truly diverse and inclusive workplaces. We hope our list of signatories will grow, and we invite other CEOs across Canada to join us.

Let's come together to make good on the inherent promise that all of our people should be able to bring their best selves to work and unleash their full potential.

By working together toward true diversity and inclusion within our workplaces, industries, and broader business community, we can cultivate meaningful change for our society and end anti-Black systemic racism.

SIGNED:

_____

ACKNOWLEDGEMENTS

I never thought I would have a story to tell that would be worthy of a book. When you grow up in poverty, your main goal is to survive one day at a time not to dream about the future. I am extremely fortunate there are good people in this world—in fact, great people—who saw someone in need and leant a helping hand. After my mother abandoned me at the tender age of eighteen months, along with my four-year-old sister and my baby brother, and, again, after she threw me out of her house when I was thirteen, good people treated me with kindness and generosity. I cannot name all of those who helped me on this amazing journey here, but at the top of the list is my grandmother, Julia Vassell, to whose memory I dedicate this book. Even though she was already raising three of my mother's children and two of my cousins, as well as caring for an adult daughter with special needs, when she heard we had been abandoned, she did not hesitate to take us in. That was the day she became "Mama" to me.

Though I was raised on a plantation, I could see the hard work and wits of my grandmother every waking hour; as a result, we children didn't grow up with a plantation mentality. She made us believe that we were capable and deserving of much more. My grandmother taught me the definition of *tenacity* and instilled in me the tough work ethic that guides me to this day. She also taught me to walk through the world in *elephant skin*—not to let anything, not racism or any other kind of "ism," prevent me from achieving my objectives.

Writing this book also truly opened my eyes to the power of *unconditional love* in my life. I want to thank my supportive, beautiful wife, Christine, for being the rock that has grounded me for the past thirty years. I would not have the confidence to do what I do without her by my side. Without her, there would be no "King of Bay Street." Without her, there wouldn't be our beautiful children, whom I also want to thank: Darian, Brentyn, Keana, Skyla and Broghan. (Without you five, I would not know the definition of patience.)

Just as I took a chance on writing this book, I also want to thank those who took a chance on me. Glenn O'Farrell, who gave me my first break and was a great mentor; Laurel Savoy, who gave me the job in financial services that put me on this path; though we had our differences, Glenn Keeling, who took a chance on me at potentially great cost to his own career. Lancelot Dey, the "Black man" behind a desk at CIBC: when I approached him with my business plan to start Kingsdale, he loved it so much he convinced his bank to loan me the money I needed after the bank had already turned me down.

Finally, I need to thank Evan Rosser, who helped me write this book. At Random House Canada, my editor, Anne Collins, heard my story and immediately thought others needed to hear it too; and Sam Hiyate, my agent, convinced me to do this in the first place.

Finally, without my faith, I truly believe I would not be standing where I am today, and for that I thank Jehovah and my fellow Jehovah's Witnesses in the faith.

INDEX

Ackman, Bill, 229, 231–235, 237–238, 241
African Canadian Senate Group, 255
Ahmed-Omer, Dahabo, 275
Arbery, Ahmaud, 263, 264
Australia. *See under* deals, significant
Awake!, 133

Bargain Harolds, 97, 110
Barracks, The, 14, 15, 20, 38, 58, 244, 276
  grandmother in, 171–172
  grandparents' move to, 15
  hiding in, 38–40
  lack of opportunities in, 58
  living in, 21, 29, 30
  playing in, 27
  poverty in, 23, 28, 276
  stigma of, 14, 23, 30, 31, 244
Bay Street (Toronto's financial district), 111, 119, 143, 155, 157, 165, 201, 211, 250. *See also* King of Bay Street (nickname)
  prestigiousness of, 110, 112, 206–207
  racial discrimination on, 248, 257
Bible, 130, 131, 133, 136, 138, 142, 144, 145
Black Business and Professional Association, 255

BlackNorth Initiative, 2, 273, 275, 277, 279–284
  Black Business Development Hub, 276
  CEO Pledge, 2, 275, 279–284
  Homeownership Bridge, 276
  Racial Equity Playbook, 275
  RiseUp programme, 276
Brown, Michael, 271
Buffalo, USA, 261
Burns Security, 104, 105–106, 107, 110, 117
Business Wire, 182

Calgary, Canada, 237, 251
Camda Sports Foundation of Canada, 258
Campbell, D'Andre, 271
Canada. *See also* individual place names in
  adapting to life in, 2, 84–86, 94
  applying to law school in, 150, 153
  arriving in, 81–82, 92, 150, 246
  biggest companies in, 3, 230, 231, 275
  Black community's contributions to, 258
  business in, 152, 163–168, 191, 195, 211, 221, 222, 225, 236
  churchgoing in, 129

father bringing family to, 76, 99
father communicating from, 21,
    56, 74
father emigrating to, 9, 88
friends in, 97, 109
grandmother and, 171–173
life in, 89–90, 92, 96–97, 123
philanthropic work in, 276–277
preparing for life in, 77–80, 94
proxy solicitation industry in, 1,
    180, 187, 200, 205, 219, 233, 239,
    250 [see also Kingsdale
    Shareholder Services; Proxy
    Solicitation (company)]
school system in, 87
sponsoring relatives to, 260
systemic anti-Black racism in,
    117–118, 268–269, 272, 273–274,
    275, 280
Western, 236–237
Canada Newswire, 182
Canadian Council of Business
    Leaders Against Anti-Black
    Systemic Racism, 273
Canadian National Railway (CN),
    231, 236
Canadian Pacific Railway (CP).
    See under deals, significant
Canadian Society of Corporate
    Secretaries (CSCS), 152, 166, 183
CanWest Global Communications
    Corporation, 171, 250
first day at, 149–150
interview at, 119–122, 247
landing job at, 123–125
leaving, 155
working at, 153–154, 175
Capital Markets Modernization
    Taskforce, 265
Cassels Brock & Blackwell, 119

Castile, Philando, 271
CBC (Canadian Broadcasting
    Corporation), 2, 255
Chauvin, Derek, 264–265
Cheswick, Jamaica, 16
Chicago Bulls, 228
Chung, T.Y., 50–54, 68
Church of the Open Bible, 128
CIBC, 272
clients of, 166, 176
introduction to, 153–154
running AGMs for, 158–161
securing loan from, 206
starting at, 155, 181
working at, 165, 169–170, 177
Clarendon Parish, Jamaica, 50, 54, 68
Cleghorn, John, 229, 231–233, 238
Computershare, 218
Cooper, Amy, 264
Cooper, Christian, 264
COVID-19, 264–265
CRTC, 150

Deacon, Colin, 255
deals, significant
    Australian Energy v Canadian
        Energy (pseudonyms), 185,
        187–188, 190, 193, 195
    Bidco v Targetco (pseudonyms),
        195–200
    Canadian Pacific (CP) v Pershing
        Square, 229–241
    securing funding for, 256–257
    tech company (unnamed), 211–217,
        223
Dey, Lancelot, 206
Dodig, Victor, 272, 273
Dragon's Den, 2
Dubé, Richard, 116
Duggan, Joseph, 256–257

England, United Kingdom, 9, 74
Ernst & Young Entrepreneur of the
    Year, 243

Fairfax Financial Holdings, 272
Fairvest, aka Institutional
    Shareholder Services (ISS), 182
father. *See* Hall, Leonard (father)
Ferrari, 277
Financial Post, 219
Floyd, George, 263–265, 266, 267,
    268, 271, 274
Fortune 500, 176, 270

Garner, Eric, 265
George Brown College, 116
Georgeson, 187–190, 205, 207,
    208–209, 230, 234, 251. *See also*
    deals, significant
    big break at, 171
    Canadian headquarters, 175
    CEO (*see* Keeling, Glenn)
    in competition with, 211, 217–219,
        239
    new business model at, 188, 193
    New York office of, 167–169, 191,
        195–196, 200, 203
    resignation from, 201–203
    starting work at, 175–180, 227,
        250
    US operations of, 163–166
    working at, 183–186, 194
Globe and Mail, The, 268, 272
Golden Grove, Jamaica
    church in, 126
    father in, 82
    feeling at home in, 85
    grandmother's home in, 7, 10, 65, 171
    life in, 13–14
    market in, 20

moving on from, 58
playing in, 81
removed from, 31–32
returning to, 37–38, 41
school in, 47
Goodyear, 7, 8
Gordon, Lenford (stepfather), 36, 37,
    42, 43–45, 56, 57, 60, 129, 260
Governance Professionals of
    Canada. *See* Canadian Society
    of Corporate Secretaries
    (CSCS)
Graham family, 69–72, 79–80, 84,
    150, 235
Graham, Dave, 70, 71
grandmother. *See* Mama (grand-
    mother)
Gray, Freddie, 271
Green, Fred, 231–232

Hall, Bernice (stepmother), 77–78,
    88, 92, 96, 99, 100, 129, 131, 276
    about, 9–10, 73–74
    kindness of, 85
    meeting, 81–82
Hall, Brentyn (son), 168
Hall, Christine (wife), 2, 167–171,
    178, 201, 209, 226, 248, 260.
    See also Zoutman, Christine
Hall, Darian (son), 168, 212
Hall, Leonard (father), 113, 260, 266,
    276
    about, 9, 10, 60, 73–74
    brought to Canada by, 81–85, 150,
        246
    churchgoing with, 129–131
    correspondence with, 21–22, 56,
        72, 74–75, 77, 126
    Edna, sister of, 78
    grandmother's relationship with, 78

mother's relationship with, 7–10, 56
moving away from, 92–93
relationship with, 89–90, 93–94,
  96–97, 100, 123, 132
wife of (*see* Hall, Bernice
  (stepmother))
work and, 83–84, 85, 99, 106
Hall, Wes (cricket player), 9
Hamilton, Lewis, 26
Harrison, E. Hunter, 231, 234–37,
  240–241, 252, 269
Harvard, 187, 246
Hilal, Paul, 235, 237
Hilton Toronto, 234
Hossein, Caroline Shenaz, 255
Hurley's Restaurant, 95, 96, 97, 105
Hussen, Ahmed, 253

Institute of Chartered Secretaries
  and Administrators, 152

Jamaica, 14, 16, 27, 32, 78, 89, 90,
  92, 98, 129–130. *See also*
  individual place names in
accent from, 84, 86–87
attitudes against Jehovah's
  Witnesses in, 129
being foreign in, 79–80
born in, 1
churchgoing in, 128, 129
corporal punishment in, 36, 39
cricket in, 7, 8
cuisine of, 43, 69
cultural norms of, 38, 64, 65, 68, 91
elections in, 51
father bringing daughter from, 76
father leaving, 9, 73–74
friends from, 109
grandmother in, 172
houses in, 44

lack of opportunities in, 93
lack of privilege in, 117
living in, 81, 113
raised in, 123
school in, 85, 87
Jamaica Broadcasting Corporation
  (JBC), 25, 27
Jamaica Labour Party (JLP), 51, 54
Jean, Botham, 271
Jefferson, Atatiana, 271
Jehovah's Witness(es). *See also*
  Kingdom Hall
attitudes toward, 129–130, 143–144
baptism of, 137, 141
door-to-door work of, 139, 145,
  270
faith of, 133
introduction to, 135–137
Pioneer, 138
restrictions for, 253–254, 267
Jensen, Warren, 155–158
Jones, Evan, 14
Jordan, Michael, 228

Kaepernick, Colin, 267
Keeling, Glenn, 216, 224
first meeting with, 165–166, 167
job offer from, 168–170, 246
relationship with, 192, 194–195,
  200–203, 218–219
working with, 177–180, 181, 191,
  195–200
Kids Help Phone, 276
King of Bay Street (nickname), 207,
  244
Kingdom Hall, 129–132, 135, 226
Gerard congregation, 136
Markham congregation, 134
speaking at, 143
teachings at, 133, 146–147

Kingsdale Advisors. *See* Kingsdale
  Shareholder Services
Kingsdale Capital, 206–207, 256
  buy out from, 220
Kingsdale Shareholder Services, 220,
  227, 229, 234, 238–239, 241,
  246, 256, 265, 273. *See also*
  deals, significant
  biggest win of, 240
  CEO of, 146, 248
  first big deal of, 211–217
  founding of, 1, 97, 203
  growth of, 221–222
  starting up, 207–210, 223
  success of, 219, 243, 251
Kingston, Jamaica, 5, 13, 14, 20, 26, 78
  airport in, 81
  Half Way Tree, 32, 37
Korchinski-Paquet, Regis, 264

Lake Ontario, 140, 175
Lester B Pearson Collegiate
  Institute, 85
Liberal Party of Canada, 253
Life and Ministry School (formerly
  the Theocratic Ministry
  School), 142, 143, 145
Little Girl. *See* Hall, Bernice
  (stepmother)

Mama (grandmother)
  background of, 14–15
  character of, 11, 60–61, 83, 138, 173
  churchgoing of, 130
  cooking of, 20–22, 42
  Daphne, daughter of, 11, 17, 60
  death of, 171–173
  discipline by, 36
  Dorothy, daughter of (*see* Smith,
  Dorothy (mother))

faith of, 125, 127, 128
house of, 16–17, 26
husband of (*see* Smith, David
  (grandfather))
independence from, 75
influence of, 24, 60–61, 65–66,
  94, 132, 245
leaving home of, 31, 32
life with, 21, 22, 25–26, 29–30, 31,
  46, 56, 74, 126
love from, 21, 23, 31, 55, 58, 65
protected by, 29
raised by, 10, 11, 18, 24, 77–78,
  123, 126
returning to, 37–38
Winston, brother of, 15, 60
working life of, 1, 6, 18–19, 20, 28
Manley, Michael, 51
Maple Lodge Farms, 98, 101–103,
  105, 109
Markham, Ontario, 134, 141
Martin, Trayvon, 271
May Pen, Jamaica, 40
  arriving in, 36
  church in, 128
  friends from, 97, 109
  life with mother in, 35
  living in, 58, 65–66, 67–70
  mother's house in, 32, 33, 74
  mother's move to, 5, 7, 10
  Paisley Housing Scheme, 57, 63
  return to, 41
  running away from, 37–38
  school in, 47–48
  size of, 70
  violence in, 51
  working in, 50–51, 103
McCarthy, Ed, 136, 137
McCarthy, Judith, 137
Miller, Dafonte, 271

Miller, Larry H., 228
Minneapolis, USA, 264, 268
Montreal, Canada, 231–232, 251
Morant Bay, Jamaica, 7, 14, 32, 37
Morneau, Bill, 257
mother. *See* Smith, Dorothy
  (mother)

National Football League, 267
New York City, USA, 78, 167–168,
  191, 195–196, 200, 203
  Wall Street, 110
Newmarket, Canada, 201
Norton Rose Fulbright, 225

O'Farrell, Glenn, 170–171
  description of, 121–122
  interview with, 122–124
  mentorship of, 153, 246
Olasker, Patricia, 229
Ontario, Canada, 87, 89, 243, 265.
  See also individual place
  names in
Order of Canada, 231
Osborne Store, Jamaica, 67

Papa. *See* Smith, David (grandfather)
Pasparakis, Orestes, 225
Pathways to Education, 265
Patrick (friend), 109–110, 170, 246
People's National Party (PNP), 51–52
Pershing Square Capital
  Management. *See under* deals,
  significant
PMO (Prime Minister's Office), 254
Port Antonio, Jamaica, 14
proxy solicitation. *See also* deals,
  significant
  about, 137, 159–160, 163, 164, 175,
  181

Blair v Enfield, 224–225
  changes in, 222–223
  competition in, 205, 209, 218
  granddaddy of (*see* Shanks, Roy)
  nascent industry of, 166, 180, 250
  promoting, 181–184, 190
  reinventing, 187, 205–206
  starting out in, 178
  success in, 200, 219, 221, 228, 251
Proxy Solicitation (company), 163,
  164, 185

QM Environmental, 265

racial discrimination, 2–3, 106–107,
  117–119, 120–121, 143–144, 191,
  248–250, 251–252, 260–261,
  267–269. *See also* BlackNorth
  Initiative
Rice, Tamir, 271
Roger (friend), 109
Rolodex, 176, 180, 208
Ross, John, 163–164, 205
Royal Bank of Canada, 231
Ryerson University's Diversity
  Institute, 251

Salt Lake City, USA, 228
San Francisco, USA, 166–167, 169
Savoy, Laurel, 154–155
Schulich, Seymour, 260
Seaga, Edward, 51
Securities Act, 115
Shanks, Roy, 181, 182, 194–195
siblings
  Antonella (half-sister), 76
  Barbara (half-sister), 10
  Carlton (stepbrother), 36, 49,
  51–54, 57, 60
  Chanel (half-sister), 84

Hillary (stepsister), 36, 42, 44, 46, 50, 54–57, 128–129, 131
Ian (half-brother), 5, 6, 10, 11, 260–261
Joan (half-sister), 5, 6, 11, 260
Marcia (half-sister), 74, 85, 88, 92, 94, 141
churchgoing of, 132, 135
influence of, 133–134, 136
Michael (half-brother), 36, 42, 50, 84, 86–87, 260–261
Natalie (half-sister), 36, 42, 50
SickKids Foundation, 265
Smith, David (grandfather), 15–18, 60, 125
Smith, Dorothy (mother), 260
abandonment by, 5–6, 10, 35
abuse by, 35–39, 41–48, 57–60, 90–91, 113–114, 126, 245
root causes of, 55–56
ambitions of, 7, 56
description of, 6, 30
escaping from, 54, 61, 92
father's relationship with, 8–10, 56, 74–75
fear of, 52, 80
friends of, 51
moving in with, 30–33
name change of, 35–36
Oscar, friend of, 65–66
religion of, 128
thrown out by, 63, 90
visits from, 29–30
Winnifred, sister of, 55
Smith, Yvonne. See Smith, Dorothy (mother)
Soliman, Walied, 225
St. Elizabeth, Jamaica, 14, 15
St. Lucia, 55
St. Thomas, Jamaica, 37

accent of, 86
The Barracks (see Barracks, The)
born in, 1
capital of, 32
colourism in, 15
father's celebrity in, 7
father's return to, 10
living in, 9
mother's fear of returning to, 40
playing in, 27
poverty in, 13, 14
superstition in, 26
stepfather. See Gordon, Lenford (stepfather)
stepmother. See Hall, Bernice (stepmother)
Steve (friend), 98, 109
Steve's mom, 98, 100 – 103
Stikeman Elliott, 119, 123
Christmas party at, 134
colleague(s) at, 121, 122, 124, 149, 151
culture of, 112, 114–115
girlfriend at, 133, 134–135
hired at, 110–111
microaggressions and racial discrimination at, 117, 118, 187, 247, 250
tuition costs paid by, 116, 170
working at, 116–117, 125, 138
Stockton, John, 228
Suncor, 231
Supreme Court, 224–225
System for Electronic Document Analysis and Retrieval (SEDAR), 183

Taylor, Breonna, 264
Titan Supply, 265
Tony (friend), 109

Toronto, 110, 137, 144, 168, 195, 220, 233, 251, 264, 276
  arriving in, 85
  Brampton, 98
  Commerce Court West, 111
  downtown, 134, 206
  east side, 136
  father moving to, 9, 74
  financial district (*see* Bay Street (Toronto's financial district))
  gun violence narrative in, 260
  Hupfield Trail, 83
  King Street West, 175
  Labatt Avenue, 104
  Malvern, 82, 89, 97, 109
  Marigold Avenue, 168
  mayor of, 258
  North York, 96, 98
  Regent Park, 104–105, 144
  Scarborough, 82, 89, 98, 103, 104
  TD Bank Tower, 218
  TD North Tower, 175
Toronto International Film Festival, 265
Toronto Pearson International Airport, 82
Toronto Raptors, 258
Toronto Star, 97
Toronto Stock Exchange, 221
Tory, John, 258–259, 275
Trudeau, Justin, 253–254, 257
Turpin, Melvin, 228
Tyson, Mike, 167

United Bakery, 50, 53, 68, 69, 85, 113, 235
United Kingdom, 57, 79. *See also* individual place names in
United States, 57, 79, 163, 164, 180, 223, 233, 239. *See also* individual place names in
Upjohn, 103, 105
Utah Jazz, 228

Vancouver, Canada, 251
Vassell, Julia (grandmother). *See* Mama (grandmother)

Walkerton, Canada, 137
Washington, Leisa, 258
Watchtower, The, 133
Watsa, Prem, 272–273
West Indian cricket, 8, 9, 88–89
Winchester, Jamaica, 5, 7, 10, 65, 73

York University, 255
Yukon, Canada, 225

Zoutman, Andy, 136–137
Zoutman, Christine. *See also* Hall, Christine (wife)
  first date with, 140
  introduction to, 137–138
  marriage to, 141
  working with, 139, 141, 144
Zoutman, Susan, 137

WES HALL, as the executive chairman and founder of Kingsdale Advisors, is one of North America's most influential power-brokers and Canada's preeminent leader in shareholder advisory services, playing pivotal roles on multi-million and billion-dollar transactions for Air Canada, Xstrata, Citigroup, Tim Horton's, PetroCanada and many others. Hall is also the owner of QM Environmental, a leading national environmental and industrial services provider with over 450 employees, among other businesses. An instructor at the Rotman School of Management at the University of Toronto, he teaches Black Entrepreneurship & Leadership, a first-of-its-kind course in North America; he is the founder of the anti-Black racism initiative, BlackNorth; and is one of the investors on the hit series *Dragon's Den*.